Ritual, Performance, Media

By drawing on insights from ritual analysis to explore the diversification of performance contexts and audiences *Ritual, Performance, Media* furthers our understanding of social action.

Anthropology is the study of society, but as this book demonstrates, it is individual inventiveness which makes society a process of dynamic inter-action between creativity and convention. Whether performing in a London theatre, invoking spirits in Nigeria or Papua, being a ballerina in Stockholm or a Conchero dancer in Mexico, going on pilgrimage to Walsingham or facing a bull in Cordoba, reviewing a film from Macedonia in Los Angeles or judging a disco dance competition at the National Eisteddfod in Wales, human beings perform their roles in accordance with the context while creatively devising ways of extending their engagement with the situation, actively constructing the world in which they live for personal satisfaction and social advantage.

Ritual, Performance, Media provides a fascinating range of case studies about human behaviour in relation to contexts in which reality is more than that of everyday routines. It will provide essential reading for all students of social and cultural anthropology, cultural studies and performance and media studies.

Felicia Hughes-Freeland is Lecturer in Social Anthropology at the University of Wales Swansea.

ASA Monographs 35

Titles available:

Ritual, Performance, Media

Edited by Felicia Hughes-Freeland

London and New York

First published 1998
by Routledge
11 New Fetter Lane, London EC4P 4EE

Simultaneously published in the USA and Canada
by Routledge
29 West 35th Street, New York, NY 10001

Typeset in Times by
Ponting–Green Publishing Services, Chesham,
Buckinghamshire
Printed and bound in Great Britain by
Biddles Ltd, Guildford and King's Lynn

British Library Cataloguing in Publication Data
A catalogue record for this book is available from the
British Library

Library of Congress Cataloging in Publication Data
Ritual, performance, media / edited by Felicia
    Hughes-Freeland.
        p.   cm. – (ASA monographs; 35)
    Based on papers first presented at the ASA Conference,
held at the University of Wales, Swansea, in Mar. 1996.
    Includes bibliographical references and index.
    1. Rites and ceremonies–Congresses.   2. Performing arts–
Congresses.   3. Mass media–Congresses.
I. Hughes-Freeland, Felicia, 1954–   II. Association of
Social Anthropologists of the Commonwealth. Conference
(1996: University of Wales Swansea)   III. Series: A.S.A.
monographs; 35.
GN473.R593   1998
306.4–dc21   97–12264
CIP

ISBN   0–415–16337–4 (hbk)
ISBN   0–415–16338–2 (pbk)

Contents

Figures

Contributors

Keith Brown is Lecturer in Social Anthropology at the University of Wales Lampeter.

Simon Coleman is Lecturer in Social Anthropology at the University of Durham.

Charlotte Aull Davies is Lecturer in Sociology and Anthropology at the University of Wales Swansea.

John Elsner is Lecturer in Classical and Early Christian Art at the Courtauld Institute.

Charles Gore is an artist and researcher, and part-time Lecturer in Social Anthropology at the City Literary Institute and Hammersmith and Fulham Adult Education Centre.

Kirsten Hastrup is Professor of Social Anthropology at the University of Copenhagen.

Eric Hirsch is Lecturer in Social Anthropology at Brunel University.

Felicia Hughes-Freeland is Lecturer in Social Anthropology at the University of Wales Swansea.

Sarah Pink is Lecturer in Sociology and Cultural Studies at the University of Derby.

Nigel Rapport is Professor of Anthropological and Philosophical Studies at the University of St Andrews.

Susanna Rostas is Research Associate in Social Anthropology at the University of Cambridge, and part-time Lecturer at the University of Cambridge and Goldsmiths' College, University of London.

Edward L. Schieffelin is Lecturer in Social Anthropology at University College, London.

Helena Wulff is Lecturer in Social Anthropology at the University of Stockholm.

Preface and acknowledgements

The contributors to this volume first presented their work at the ASA conference on 'Ritual, Performance, Media' at the University of Wales Swansea in March 1996. The object of the conference was to explore what – if anything – developments in the fields of performance and media studies can contribute to anthropological approaches to ritual, in the broadest possible sense. I here take the opportunity to extend my warm thanks to *all* the participants, including those whose papers are not included in this book. Mario Aguilar, Peter Collins, Sandra Bell, Andrée Grau, Mark Hobart, Sue Jennings and Jon Mitchell all made valuable contributions to the conference, and it is to be hoped that their papers will soon appear in other publications. Nor can this book represent other ways in which the resonances of the topic were explored. The proceedings were enlivened by Sue Jennings's solo performance as Elizabeth Garrett Anderson, the first female physician and surgeon, in *My Dear Emily*, and by the writer Michael Eaton, who gave a talk, 'From Hauka to Hollywood', about Jean Rouch's film *Les Maîtres Fous* (*The Mad Masters*) to elucidate the ritual form of the dominant contemporary cinematic narrative.

It is appropriate here to express formally my thanks to the valiant team of discussants who helped us organize our thoughts about a wide range of papers: Jane Cowan, Nigel Rapport, Jean La Fontaine, Marie Gillespie, Ronnie Frankenberg, Nickie Charles, Tamara Kohn and Kirsten Hastrup.

I also extend my warmest thanks to local organizers of the conference, Dr Charlotte Davies and Dr Margaret Kenna, from the Department of Sociology and Anthropology, University of Wales Swansea, who, having prepared for at least one year before the event, proceeded to carry out with unfailing patience and generosity the increasing burden of chores as the event grew closer, and continued to deal with all manner of unimaginable episodes and requests during the conference. Everyone present appreciated the way in which they conjured up an unforgettable event which did more than justice to commemorate a hat trick of celebrations: the 50th anniversary of the founding of the ASA in 1946, the 75th anniversary of the founding of the University of Wales Swansea in 1921, and, by happenstance, the 95th birthday of our Life President, Sir Raymond Firth. Far from these august commemorations sinking under the weight of their own historicity, I am pleased to say that energy prevailed over pomp. A gratifying number of delegates, including the professoriat, made as impressive a display in an evening of Welsh folk dancing as in their intellectual pursuits – a fact made still more impressive by the mental agility required to cope with having to be a 'lady' or 'gentleman' in dizzying alternation due to the exigencies of the caller. The liveliness of our meeting was enhanced by the presence of postgraduate students and local undergraduate helpers. I am also very gratified that the contributors to the conference and to this volume include some of the youngest professional anthropologists in the field as well as those who are already familiar.

I am also grateful to the Department of Sociology and Anthropology at Swansea for providing enormous assistance.

My thanks go to Mats Bäcker for the use of the photograph of the Royal Swedish Ballet in Chapter 5, and to Tim Davies for the photograph of his work in Chapter 7. All other photographs are provided by the individual authors.

We are grateful to the following for the verse extracts appearing in this volume: Everyman's Library for permission to quote from *The Complete English Works of George Herbert* (1995), edited by A.P. Slater, published by Everyman Press; Meic Stephens for permission to quote from *Harri Webb: Collected Poems* (1995), edited by M. Stephens, published by Gomer; Gerallt Lloyd Owen for permission to quote from *Cerddi' r Cywilydd* (1972), by G.L. Owen and *Dafydd Iwan* (1981), by D. Iwan, both published by Gwasg Gwynedd.

Finally, thanks to Heather Gibson for her delicate direction in the theatre of deadlines.

Felicia Hughes-Freeland
Swansea, February 1997

Introduction

Felicia Hughes-Freeland

This volume considers anthropological approaches to ritual in relation to theoretical developments in social and cultural analysis. What the analyst considers as ritual is frequently those aspects of social life and social action which appear bizarre and exotic in relation to what she or he is used to. Anthropological approaches to ritual have, in their various ways, tempted us to distance our topic from our own experience. As Milner (1956) demonstrated in his solemn disquisition on the bizarre body rituals of the Nacirema – their annual visits to holy mouth-men, monthly baking of the head in small ovens by the women and daily scraping and lacerating of the skin by the men – it is anthropology which constructs the exotic view of, in this case, North American concerns with dental hygiene, a well-set hairdo, and a clean, close shave.

It is to correct residual tendencies to exoticize certain behaviours that this book brings ritual into a relationship with two frames of reference: first, to the analysis of actual theatres and performances, and second, to social reality as mediated by technologies, such as television or film.

A CAVEAT

This book is not 'about' ritual, and its contributors do not have any interest in defining it in essential terms. Rather, the area is explored relationally to performance and/or media, and in some cases dispensed with after a cursory mention. Our object here is to find ways of thinking and writing about varieties of social practices and situations. The contributors reject the need for definitional strategies and employ ritual heuristically and contingently, as an odd-job word or a semi-descriptive term which is subordinate to the larger category of 'situated social practice ... constituted and framed in relation to [its] own historical trajectories as well as to other traditions of social practice' (Gore, this volume).[1]

To anyone who might invoke Goody's influential scepticism (1977) and suggest that anthropology books about ritual are marginal to our present concerns with consumption and identity, I would respond with the exhortations of subaltern anthropologists (Rosaldo 1989, Tsing 1993) who specify margins and border-crossings as the proper objects of our current concerns. To place ritual in a relation with performance and media is to address the effects of the rapidly changing intellectual geographies we inhabit. It is time to recognize that what has made anthropology distinctive is becoming part of a range of disciplines, and we need to consider the implications of this for our practices now and in the future. The analysis of ritual has long been 'good to reflect with', and it is time to take stock. The proliferation of analytical styles and approaches presents anthropology with a problem of identifying its boundaries.[2] We can now buy 'textbooks' and 'readers' on interculturalism, a key concept in performance studies. Meanwhile, anthropologists continue to pursue cross-cultural agendas and maintain that it is time to work from similarities and not just cultural differences – and yet seem unaware that others are running off with the ideas we have been slowly nurturing and developing over the years.

One object of this book, then, is to restore the anthropological tone to debates in other, newer disciplines – cultural, performance and media studies – so as to forestall possible trivializations of theory and practice which have been maturing for over a century. The title of this book refers to three different orders of conceptualization, and is deliberate in its attempt to initiate resonance between the loose and unequal adjacencies of its terms. This unsteady adjacency invites reflections on how ritual imbues social action and makes it more than the everyday. Ritual generally refers to human experience and perception in forms which are complicated by the imagination, making reality more complex and unnatural than more mundane instrumental spheres of human experience assume. Ritual in these terms is part of distinct situations. The questions posed by the contributors to this volume are therefore questions about how anthropologists and social actors frame reality, and what the relationship is between the ordinary and the non-ordinary in terms of social action.

RITUAL, PERFORMANCE, MEDIA: THE CONNECTIONS

Turner's influential work on ritual attempted to explain human behaviour in more animated terms than (most) functionalist accounts had tended to do.[3] His solution was to attribute to ritual the potential to release humans from the structure of their quotidian life into a creative and liberating 'anti-structure', or 'communitas' (1969). This approach has been challenged recurrently by claims that ritual's function is restrictive and produces conformity (Bloch 1974), or that 'communitas' is pervaded by political differences and competing interests (Sallnow 1981). It is a shame that the energetic qualities of Turner's model of social process have been undermined by a dichotomization between 'art' and 'life', particularly in view of

Tambiah's (1985 [1981]) parallel model, which gives ritual the potential to engage with the political as well as the cosmological (or imaginative) dimensions of social experience – what Tambiah calls 'indexicality'.[4] I have frequently been reminded of Tambiah's emphasis on duality and contingency in ritual efficacy while preparing this book, which, as will become evident, locks horns with dualities over and over, including those in Turner's model.

The uses of performance analogies and dramaturgical metaphors to give expression to the structures and processes of human behaviour in the social sciences are numerous, and this book refers frequently to 'frontstage', 'backstage' (Goffman 1959, 1974) and 'social dramas' (Turner 1974). These analogies have been criticized for exaggerating problems which arise in the relations between the thinking theorist and acting object in ritual analysis (Bell 1992: 39), for allowing the symbolic to dominate the functional, and for resolving the question of *what* is being communicated in a performance model by resorting deterministically to a prior *text*, or a given structure of meaning (1992: 53).[5] In this book, however, there is no invocation of Geertz's (1973) interpretation of the Balinese cockfight as western tragedy. Instead, the contributors renounce the performance-as-text model (see Schiffelin, this volume). Indeed, Bell's definition of ritualization as 'a way of acting that is designed and orchestrated to distinguish and privilege what is being done in comparison to other, usually more quotidian, activities' (1992: 74) applies equally well to performance if it is not understood as the replication of a given script or text (Coleman and Elsner, this volume). It is the techniques and technologies of the self/selves (to build on Mauss's 'techniques of the body' (1973)), rather than the model of the text, which is a key concept in this book.

The move from performance analogies to actual performance contexts in themselves is partly associated with Turner, who restored his metaphor of social drama to the stage as he embarked on an exploration of theatre as a form of social life (1982, 1992 [1987]). This approach has been highly influential outside social science departments, both in the USA (Schechner 1985, 1993, Schechner and Appel 1990) and Europe (Barba 1995, Barba and Savarese 1991). Schechner develops Turner's evolutionary model of performance to complement his practical theatrical experimentation in order to identify the biological and neurological as well as the social bases of performance as ritualized action (in Turner 1992 [1987]: 7–20; also Schechner 1993: 228–9).[6] The ongoing relevance of humanity's capacity for ritual – 'a kind of performative behaviour' (Schechner 1986: 353) – and the means to make it manifest and give it a place in the emergent world resides in the commonality of ritual and theatre: 'The future of ritual is the continued encounter between imagination and memory translated into doable acts of the body' (Schechner 1993: 263).

Intercultural performance is also explored practically and theoretically by Eugenio Barba, a theatre director whose experiences as an Italian immigrant in Norway (1995: 4) produced the reflexivity which prompted him to explore and theorize about different traditions of embodiment and action. It is Barba's translocal experience, not a training in anthropology, which galvanizes his work. Despite the collaboration of his Odin Teatret with anthropologist Kirsten Hastrup in the play *Talabot* (Hastrup 1992, 1995: 123–45), Barba is specific about his project of 'theatre anthropology':

> Theatre Anthropology is not concerned with applying the paradigms of cultural anthropology to theatre and dance. It is not the study of the performative phenomena in those cultures which are traditionally studied by anthropologists. Nor should Theatre Anthropology be confused with the anthropology of performance . . . [it] refers to a new field of investigation, the study of the pre-expressive behaviour of the human being in an organized performance situation.
>
> (Barba 1995: 10)[7]

The work of performance practitioners such as Schechner and Barba to bring together performers (with or without anthropological interests) from different societies and traditions, into a single frame for comparative analysis and practice, leaves unanswered many questions about the validity of their assumptions about the generality of human behaviour. Some of these questions are taken up in this book, though not necessarily in Schechner and Barba's terms of reference. The ASA constituency as yet remains to be persuaded of the fruitfulness of this field of study: Kirsten Hastrup alone draws on theatre anthropology.[8] Meanwhile there is a growing body of anthropological literature on specific performance situations, with or without reference to interculturalism and theatre anthropology (for example, the monographs by Keeler 1987, Fabian 1990, Kuipers 1990 and Kersenboom 1995, which includes an interactive compact disk; and edited collections such as Ajmer and Boholm 1994, Kim and Hoppál 1995).[9] There is clearly ample scope for anthropologists to respond to the positive results of experimental theatre, and to develop their own distinctive approaches to situate theatre in the field of social analysis.

The invitation to consider the relationship between ritual and media (and performance) met with a certain amount of suspicion, but the contributors who engaged with this relationship have made important steps in this potentially rich field of enquiry. While media practices have tended to be analysed with reference to consumption, an approach recently applied also to religious activity (Starrett 1995: 65), there have been a number of other approaches which remain underexplored (Spitulnik 1993).[10] For instance, Crain (1992) was among the first to explore the effects of media practices on ritual events, arguing that the mass media, tourist agencies and municipal authorities transformed the El Rocio pilgrimage in Spain from a ritual to a spectacle. Building on precedents such as Crain's, the contributors to this book give strong signs that performative approaches may usefully conjoin with insights derived from exploring the interface of ritual and media. For example, Hughes-Freeland (1991b) analyses the interaction of media with traditional ideas of legitimacy to effect the transformation of a crown prince into a man fit to be king in Java, and more recently, how Balinese people think about the difference between live and broadcast theatre (Hughes-Freeland 1997b). Another precedent is Little's (1995) application of 'ritual' and Tambiah's important concept of indexicality (1985 [1981]; see above) to an analysis of the dislocation and relocation by the media of the Rio Earth Summit. In this book, media practices are analysed in terms of agency, in some cases with reference to performance.

This book, then, refers to a body of work which has extended the sense of ritual from the sacred to the secular (Cohen 1974, Moore and Myerhoff 1977, Handelman 1990, Boissevain 1992, Chaney 1993, Parkin, *et al.* 1996).[11] The chapters examine ritual in a diversity of situations – theatre in western Europe, Christian pilgrimage in England, initiation rites in Nigeria, vigils and dances in Mexico, ballet in western Europe, bullfighting in Spain, the Welsh National Eisteddfod, cinema in Macedonia and the USA, time-share operations in England, healing seances and dances in Papua, and television viewing habits in England – with reference to a number of questions. How does performance help us to understand the relation between creativity and constraint in ritual? What do analyses of performance and media contribute to our theoretical approach to ritual action? What theoretical implications are there for anthropology in the diversification of performance contexts and audiences, such as television and cinema?

The contributors respond to these questions in varying combinations, and the book is structured to provide a contingent framework based on their resonances with each other. Hastrup makes an opening case for why anthropologists should pay more attention to western theatre. Coleman and Elsner, Gore and Rostas consider the relationship between the 'ritual process' and performance in religious rituals, while Wulff, Pink and Davies analyse secular performances and spectacles. The theme of media, already introduced by Gore and tackled more extensively by Pink and Davies, occupies centre stage in Brown's discussion of how reception varies between audiences. Rapport and Schieffelin return us to performance in a theoretical mode, and Hirsch's reflections on the effects of performance in a media context and a ritual context close the book with a convergence of its three strands.

THEMES

As each contributor does more than justice to his or her particular case, I can do little more here than provide an overview to highlight for the reader some of the convergences and divergences which run through the chapters. These themes concern agency and intentionality in ritual and performance; creativity and constraint; the participatory nature of spectatorship; and the implications of different framings of relationships between reality and illusion to evaluate the performance model.

Agency and intentionality in ritual (and) performance

Intentionality and deliberateness have been identified as a crucial component of performance: 'A performance is not necessarily more meaningful than other events in one's life, but it is more deliberately so; a performance is, among other things, a deliberate effort to represent, to say something about something' (Peacock 1990: 208). A recent argument claims that ritual(ization) produces distinctive forms of action resulting from a disengagement from purpose which transforms the intentionality of action: 'In this transformed situation the intentions and thoughts of the actor make no difference to the *identity* of the act performed . . . the actors both are, and are not, the authors of their acts' (Humphrey and Laidlaw 1994: 5). These authors consider 'the analogy of theatrical performance' extraneous to their discussion:

> We shall give no consideration . . . to that substantial body of literature which, following the later writings of Victor Turner, subsumes the study of ritual into that of emotionally affecting performance . . . our purpose will be to point out the uniqueness of ritual, not to suggest that ritual is a genre of performance.
>
> (Humphrey and Laidlaw 1994: 81 n.1)

The contributors to this book disagree with the formulation that ritual is a 'genre of performance' and subsumed by it, and instead argue that performance in part constitutes ritual practices and ritualization. Rostas (this volume), for example, claims that ritual events cannot be explained without a model of intentionality or 'performativity'. The relationship between ritualization and performativity is variable and oscillatory, and the model can account for variations and transformations of forms of practice: Mexica dancers, rejecting the Catholic spirituality of the Concheros, dance projectively for an external audience, their intentionality sharpened into a deliberately political focus.

This duality of ritual action resonates with the characterization of the (theatrical) actor as 'double agent' to demonstrate how theatre can elucidate general anthropological problems of action and motivation (Hastrup, this volume). Double agency addresses the 'never-ending reflexivity' of the split consciousness of the western actor, having to be and not be oneself, an embodied state of immanence and openness, expressed in the theatre anthropology concept of 'dilation': an actor is not only a cognitive being, but a motivated, decided and dilated body (Hastrup 1995: 77–98).

The effectiveness of acting, however, is not based on the separation of an actor's individuated intention. The actor can move an audience because of a field of associations with her or his actions which refer to shared understanding, a field of relations with reference to acknowledged forms of skill or artistry. Artistry is a dispersed quality which imbues the space of the theatre with resonance beyond the intention, single or double, of the actor. This resonance in theatre is efficacious in a magical sense in the same way as a Trobriand canoe-board object dazzles because of the magical ideas associated with it (Gell 1992: 46).

This account suggests a process of feedback which works as long as there is a matching between the skill and the expectation. If this breaks down, there is no art and no persuasiveness. Aesthetic power realized in the world is contingent, which raises questions about the conditions which bear on such contingency (see Schieffelin, this volume).[12] What Hastrup's argument here suggests is that even in the controlled, delimited space of the theatre, acting is interactive, its efficacy dispersed among all those present; a point which will concern us again below.

Creativity and constraint

Contingency and convention in diverse forms are preconditions for creativity and variable practices may emerge in ritual(ized) situations, be they invented ritual events such as the Walsingham pilgrimage (Coleman and Elsner, this volume) or the Welsh National Eisteddfod (Davies, this volume), or traditional ones (Rostas and Gore, both this volume).[13] These contributors argue for the importance of expressive diversity in the forms of action in these different contexts rather than fixed and regular patterns over time. Individual participants may experience a ritual differently on different occasions (Coleman and Elsner), or the acceptable constituent parts of a spectacle may change over time (Davies), or between groups (Rostas) or between cases: for example, possessed men and women at spirit shrines in Benin City, Nigeria, strategize and innovate in moves and gestures (Gore).

Such performative diversity, however, is not unfettered agency but creativity contingent on a structure or a field of preconditions which constitutes a set of references: a liturgical script, an idea of the best outcome, such as the Concheros' scheme of 'Union, Conformity, Conquest' (Rostas), the shared understanding of what is a traditional performance in an Eisteddfod (Davies), or the different framing conventions of western ballet (Wulff, this volume). Without such preconditions to act against or play with, creativity would not emerge: for the pilgrims, both serious and ironic performance 'actually require the presence of canonical forms as symbols and actions against which to define themselves' (Coleman and Elsner, this volume). Or, as Gore notes (this volume), spirits only have shrines if they are demonstrated to be legitimate. The creativity of the priests and their clienteles is framed by the context of the spiritual legitimacy of the deities, a constraint that 'provides the dynamic for innovation and individuation within urban contemporary shrine configurations, and provides a framing in which individuals develop the conventions of the various traditions of ideas and practices configured within it'. Even outside the field of ritual performance events, in a Goffmanesque scheme of performance in the micro-situation of an encounter with a time-share salesman, it is claimed that the language-game performances which produce selves are themselves overdetermined (Rapport, this volume). If 'the social is at base personal', the personal is constituted by structures – in this case in language – which make behaviour, action or performance possible.[14]

These contributions, then, suggest that the dichotomization of structure and anti-structure breaks down in a performative approach to behaviour in ritual(ized) situations (of diverse scales and formulations). The effect of this is perhaps to re-present the ritual process as a form of practice, in which agency, creativity, structure and constraint become simultaneous, rather than distinguished in time and space, whether real or metaphorical.

Spectatorship as participation

It is evident that the forms of constraint and determination discussed by contributors are dispersed across the field of performance. This is also the case if we turn to the way contributors responded to the question of audiences, and the significance of the diversification of audience contexts. In cultural studies, the audience has been a focal problem (Morley 1992, Ang 1996), but anthropologists have taken issue with the invention of a unitary audience and an ethnocentric view of human action as consumption, proposing instead that local perceptions and categories should be used to analyse responses to media (Hobart n.d.; also Hughes-Freeland 1992). However, the discussions in this book suggest that agency is not attributed to one group at the cost of another who are cast as audience, either in live events (be they ritual or spectacle) or in situations where television or cinema broadcast events. Agency does not reside in a specific group of performers who are separate from an audience of passive spectators.

In the case of actual events, if we focus on the formal ceremonial aspect of a public spectacle, an audience may be primarily observers in formal ceremonies; but in the surrounding activities and informal performances that make up a spectacle, the category of audience is not distinguishable from that of participant: 'the audience is part of the spectacle, is itself spectacle, and its ways of participating – audience performances – may reconstruct the nature and meaning of the spectacle itself' (Davies, this volume). The Welsh National Eisteddfod is a spectacle which is given definition by its media representations, which legitimize not only traditional performances but also innovations, thereby producing performances indicative of a variety of Welshnesses.

In the case of media, there is no clear division into active performers and passive spectators. Even the apparent delimitation of signification in a film, for example, as compared to the wide field of interests which are available to participants at an event, does not limit audiences to one kind of experience or interpretation. In his exploration of the readings produced by viewings of a film made by a Macedonian-born director (with an international crew), shot on locations in Macedonia, Brown (this volume) considers the different responses to the film by Macedonians and non-Macedonians (in this case, Americans). To do this, he gives primacy not to the text, but to the agency of the 'audiences'. This agency is highlighted, he explains, 'because the goal is to illustrate that the impact of media texts cannot be understood without paying attention to the distinctive and persisting differences between modes of imagining that an audience may undertake'.

The theme of participatory spectatorship is taken up by all the chapters which tackle the media. Gore explores the way in which real-time video documentation has become a new option for engaging in status play in shrine rituals in Benin City, Nigeria. Sarah Pink argues that the televisation of bullfights in Spain has enhanced the possibility for women to enter the top ranks of the sport, while at the same time fragmenting the ritual structure of traditional 'live' bullfights,[15] producing a transformed cultural commodity which is consumed at home, but not by passive spectators: this is constitutive consumption, itself a kind of performance which undermines the separation upon which commoditization and consumption are founded (see also Hirsch, this volume). As Pink notes (this volume), 'The media performance should not necessarily be compared *negatively* to the live event as non-ritual . . . It is a dynamic event, subjected to a variety of public gazes and developing in relation to discourses created in the societies on which it depends for its audiences and performers.'

Media thus produce alternative frames which militate against fixity, reification and essentialization. Realities and roles become constituted by the situations we find ourselves in, by our variable agency. This is not merely easy and flexible, however: the acceptability of different forms of reception or agentive response became contentious when some of the ASA audience was moved to laughter by the druidical costumes of the Eisteddfod rituals, which presented an anomalous case of 'the other' at home. The criticism this evoked also demonstrates how swiftly a group can also check itself and put limits on its behaviour.

Questions of scale and standardization are taken at a different level in Hirsch's comparison of the outcomes of performance in two different situations: a middle-class family's discourses on viewing television in London, and those of the Fuyuge of Papua New Guinea's *gab* ritual. Rejecting presuppositions of universal personhood, Hirsch argues that culturally based forms of identity construction are demonstrated in particular, local instances of media and ritual practice, in relation to processes of bounding and unboundedness which themselves vary over time and place.

Hirsch criticizes cultural studies for using ethnography in an impoverished way, but finds it helpful to draw on media studies to show how general cultural patterns can be arrived at by including media behaviour in our ethnographic work. The overall object should be to understand behaviour, not consumption. Rather than locating media and ritual in a neo-evolutionist perspective (Friedman 1994), he shows how particular practices reveal particular forms of local identity which are predicated on cultural ideas of selfhood, as indeed are Papuan responses to television (cf. Kuhlick and Willson 1994). Far from reifying cultural difference, Hirsch's model tackles the relations between media, ritual, performance and sociality to reveal the common ground between different situations.

This final chapter, then, explores an assumption which lurks in the performative approach to ritual, which is this: if, as the performative approach to ritual claims, ritual really *does* something other than mystify, what does 'really' mean here? Hirsch's answer is that performance, in ritual and other contexts, produces persons, either in a bounded sense or in a process of unboundedness, depending on circumstances, just as Rapport (this volume) argues that Goffman-like performance produces action and selves.

The contributors thus consider the commonalities between ritual, performance and media. Such an exploration is important. What media studies bring to our understanding is another way of thinking about the problems of formulating explanatory models for diverse and increasingly dispersed forms of social action. It is also the case that questions concerning the nature of media's impact on 'real' life (Seiter *et al.* 1989) are similar in form to those which have concerned those interested in ritualization and the patterning of empowerment and constraint. If the degrees of technological intervention differ between media events and live ones, this is not an intervention which negates the agency of the viewers or audiences. The diversity of experiences within a fixed site in media becomes subject to the variables of time and space: the media event is decontextualised, disconnected, diffused, re-diffused, and raises questions about methodological procedures for understanding it. The conclusions of the contributors here suggest that ethnographic procedures remain appropriate and adequate to the task.

The place of the imaginary and the virtual in the spheres of ritual and performance are also crucial to the sphere of media and are suggestive for the framing of social analysis. Despite some contributors' reservations about the generality of framing, as it is a representational strategy which is not universal, I conclude this survey of the book's themes with some comments about how frames of reference which the consideration of ritual, performance and media elicits can contribute to ways of identifying orders of reality.

Reality and illusion: a question of frames

Ritual, performance and media all raise questions about the framing of reality, the forms of participation within an event or experience, the limits of representation, and questions of scale.[16] All three are in some sense virtual realities, mediated by technologies, be they magical or mechanical, in contradistinction to sensate, everyday reality (a provisional phrasing, perhaps, given the depth of Goffman's penetration by ritual into the everyday).

Before considering briefly what each chapter is about, it is pertinent to consider two reservations about the performance model discussed by Fabian: first, the desirability of demarcating it from a sociological theory of action instead of making a conflation; and secondly, its inherent problems of ethnocentrism: 'Performance . . . should not be projected onto the societies whose images of theatricality we study in order to contrast them with our own, which we see as engaged in serious business' (Fabian 1990: 14).

Fabian points here to the danger of conflating an ethnocentric performance model with a general model of action, resulting in an invented, relativized world where no categories can be sustained, and all sense of scale is lost. Whether or not theatre is 'serious', this touches on a fundamental problem of social analysis, which Schechner also approaches when discussing performative models in symbolic interactionism. He proposes a distinction between two classes of performance: 'those where the participants and spectators know a performance is going on, and those where there is ignorance or doubt regarding whether or not a performance is occurring' (Schechner 1986: 367–8). This is helpful, but it raises awkward questions about different kinds of tacit knowledge and styles of judgement. For example, in one British folk model, behaviour is praised for being naturalistic, and performance which deviates from being a sincere expression of one's true inner self – 'not being yourself' – is viewed with suspicion. This 'being natural' is a mark of effective socialization, and defines what we find acceptable or not. We are attracted by ritualized behaviour because it challenges our socialized expectations of 'normal' behaviour. These British (middle-class English) evaluations are cross-cut by an oppositional moral scheme, with performance being healthy while media (the broadcast or visual technologies at least) are bad for you (see the Simon family's attitudes in Hirsch, this volume). However, my experiences of anthropological research and film-making in Java, where socialization puts a positive value on performing everyday life, have sensitized me to the highly relative forms of naturalness in indigenous concepts of behaviour, and this has implications for where performance is situated. In attempting to analyse what makes documentary film a genre which contrasts with fiction film, Nichols uses the phrase 'virtual performance' to describe action which 'has the power and effect of actual performance without being one . . . [it] presents the logic of actual performance without signs of conscious awareness that this presentation is an act' (1991: 122). Such is the action of people caught by the documentary-constructing camera. The documentary/fiction distinction may not represent a universal generic opposition (Hughes-Freeland 1992), but it helps articulate arguments about issues of reality and its representationality (see Brown, this volume).

So, to return to Fabian: yes, to research ethnographies of the theatre is to the good, but rather than simply rejecting the promulgation of dramaturgical metaphors, we need to consider the implications of asserting naturalistic models of action which themselves might be as ethnocentric as dramaturgical ones.

These issues are represented in this book in the following terms. The contributors distinguish ritual from theatrical performance, though not necessarily ritual from performance. Ritual is seen primarily as 'a context marker, possibly meaningless in itself while something else is meaningless without it . . . By contrast, theatre provides its own context: the frame is part of the event. There is no meaning to theatre outside its own structure' (Hastrup, this volume). However, ritual and theatre converge in a relation of theatre as life, albeit carefully contextualized to in western theatre. For Hastrup, 'The main point of departure, however, is not theatre as *art* as much as it is theatre as *life*. As Peter Brook has it: "theatre has no categories, it is about life. This is the only starting point and there is nothing else truly fundamental. Theatre is life."' Coleman and Elsner's discussion of pilgrimage as a series of performances of ironic or serious play (Bruner 1984, Peacock 1990) is approached through an evocation of Brook's (1968) 'Holy Theatre', thereby breaking down boundaries between drama, formalization and 'real life'. In this case, however, the theatrical analogy draws on *actor* models, not *analyst* ones: to quote the young man 'very involved in the Church of England' on what goes on at Walsingham:

> It's very theatrical. . . . There is in it something quite self-conscious. . . . I can't take it too seriously. . . . It's two-dimensional in the way that camp is often two-dimensional. . . . It's in good bad taste. . . . You know, you can enjoy it and enter into it, but you never need take it too seriously. But I do know that people do take it seriously.
>
> (Coleman and Elsner, this volume)

Ritual has also been compared to theatre because it is between reality and imagination and involves a suspension of disbelief in actuality, or authenticity (Myerhoff 1990). Ritual as play or as performance deals not just with the world of facts, but with the world of possibilities: it is 'a fusion of the dreamed-of and lived-in orders of reality' (Geertz 1966: 28). The 'virtual art of theatre consists in showing what is not, and as such it functions as society's spiritual "double"' (Hastrup, on Artaud, this volume). Wulff uses Myerhoff's framing of 'let's pretend' to explore ballet by recognizing the frames by which it is constituted – and their fragility – and to examine the different perspectives which constitute ballet. If we take into account dancers, critics and different kinds of audience members' dancing/appreciation, we discover there is no single unified object, no singular, regular, authentic and meaningful reality out there. However, whereas Myerhoff considers gestural reality and the belief which is concentrated in the gesture as being the heart of transformations, and not personal experience and consciousness, Wulff (this volume) argues that ballet makes possible a personal 'transcendence', which has an impact on the real world and causes those who experience these conversion-like transformations to change their behaviour or their life courses. The discussion of transcendence in Conchero dancing comes closer to that described by Myerhoff (see Rostas, this volume).

The work of Goffman and Bauman is invoked by those who use the performative model to break down boundaries between ritual and everyday life. For Rapport, survival rather than transcendence is the best that can be gained, as the performativity of everyday life surprises unsuspecting citizens on unpredictable stages, as recounted in his own attempt to perform in a time-share set-up, which all but fails when confronted with the practised skills of the salesperson. Rapport's experience at the hands of a time-share salesman shows that such an interaction was as much a performance by both parties concerned as any more public and formalized cultural performance, and as salient. The ethnography of micro-situations is as telling as that of rituals in an event-based paradigm. Rapport's experience is different from that of participating at a performance. For all the poetics of his narrative re-presentation, however, Rapport's performance is hardly theatre as 'poetry in the mode of action' (Hastrup, on Langer, this volume).

We have not yet reached the point where a typology of action constructed around distinctions within the category of performance might be made, and for now we remain reliant on using frames. However, a number of contributors refer to the issues identified by Fabian and indicate an alternative solution to his questions about category limits and ethnocentrism.

Schieffelin's work has been crucial in elaborating the instrumental role of performativity in ritual (1976, 1985). His chapter takes a hard look at the current uses of performance, and argues that sociological models of performance (Goffman 1959, 1967, Bauman 1986) draw on western dramaturgical concepts, at the heart of which lies the notion of illusion. It is illusion which has characterized western theatre since Aristotle, and which gives power to Goffman's models of rational manipulation: the model of action as sleight of hand and trickery here is not the magic *ex nihilo* action described by Hastrup, but a case of the fake, the unreal, the simulacrum. The concept of 'performance' is thus weighted down with western, dichotomous presuppositions ('deceit/authenticity', 'activity/passivity', etc.) and must be released from this burden if it is to fulfil its potential to help us understand the important project, which for Schieffelin is the 'social construction of reality'. Schieffelin thus agrees with Fabian about the dangers of ethnocentrism, but not perhaps with the view that performance should be kept distinct from more general theories of action. As he writes: 'without living human bodily expressivity, conversation and social presence, there would be no culture and no society . . . performativity is not only endemic to human being-in-the-world but fundamental to the process of constructing a human reality' (Schieffelin, this volume).

Schieffelin is not alone in having reservations about western stage-acting as a model for social action in general. Gore argues that there is a measure of conformity among priestly performance at shrines and a standardization against which the deviant, the illicit and the fake may be identified – whereas fakery is not a moral problem in the theatre. Another difference noted by Pink is that theatricality in a bullring, prototype of our modern theatres, differs from staged drama because there is real danger as human encounters bull: this is where the risk of theatre, discussed by Wulff (this volume), intensifies into the danger of sport. Danger in bullfighting is at the heart of the performance, whereas, as Wulff's chapter reminds us, staged performance may be dangerous, but that is not (normally) part of the intention. Accidents occur when performance frames break down, resulting in a botched show unless expertly managed. Suspense is a dramatic feature, but dangers vary.[17] Whether ritual, spectacle, or fragmented and commoditized on television, bullfighting is about the relationship between the fighter and the bull's horns, unequivocally embodied. The artistry derives from that simple juxtaposition; it is a context of very high risk.

The most powerful arguments for the place of ritual performance in a model of being-in-the-world have been developed with reference to rituals of healing, such as the Kaluli seances, although Schieffelin's account of the Gisalo exchange also demonstrates that the emotion produced in performance is *real*, and dangerous. It is noticeable that ritual and performance have converged most persuasively in the analysis of ritual and performance in an emphasis on curative rites (Kapferer 1991, Laderman 1991, Roseman 1991, Suryani and Jensen 1993). These works indicate that it might be useful to consider whether or not there is an instrumentality in the performance of healing rituals which serves as a criterion by which to distinguish the commoditized and commercial spaces of popular entertainment or high art from another kind of activity, Aristotelian transferrals of the metaphor of catharsis from the medical to the theatrical notwithstanding. It is one thing for a patient suffering from demonic illness to laugh at 3 a.m. in Sri Lanka, and quite another to laugh at Jo Brand or Ben Elton in your local theatre or on television.[18] Laughter may 'make you feel better', but without it, in the first case, you would remain ill, and in the second – well, what? – normal, perhaps, or less relaxed. There are arguments to be made for a continuum between healing and entertainment. For now, we can simply say that the effects of ritual in the world vary, as do those of theatrical performances.

It might appear that the book leaves us with an unresolved problem about the value of western performance models to anthropological analysis. However, the relationship between performance and pre-existent references both converges and diverges in the discussion of theatricality and performance. In a criticism of textual models, Schieffelin noted that 'performance does not construct a symbolic reality in the manner of presenting an argument, description or commentary. Rather, it does so by socially constructing a situation in which participants experience symbolic meanings as part of the process of what they are actually doing' (1985: 709). It might seem that Kaluli healing seances and western theatre are polar opposites in how performance might be understood to operate. However, despite the existence of a script in (most) western theatre, Hastrup makes a case for acting as a bringing into being out of nothing, an act which is magical, and which is made efficacious by the interaction with the audience: creativity is in the space between the actors and the audience. So Schieffelin's argument about the incompleteness of symbolic materials in the message allows us to understand western acting as an interactive process. The two authors make a case for performances in both Papuan healing seances and western theatre centring on the *emergent nature of creative significance*, on a process which is performed, not 'pre-formed' (Hirsch, this volume). A ritual is not a text with a pre-established structure of meanings, but something which emerges as participants bring together bits and pieces of knowledge in the performance: it creates reality and selves experientially. What validates the performance is that it is made real by the audience. Performance, then, whether in the context of ritual or theatre, despite all framing and formality, in these analyses remains fundamentally risky and interactive (Schieffelin, this volume). Again, as in the case of where to draw the line between healing and entertainment, this varies in degree and scale. There remains work to be done on how the danger of the bullfight compares and contrasts with that of the Kaluli seance or a performance of *Hamlet* or *Talabot*.

The contributors therefore propose that human performance, whether discussed in terms of agency, of intentionality, of the production of the self, or of the production of action, cannot be explained anthropologically without reference to the specific context which frames the action and/or performances. The agency of situations is one which is constituted by a range of participants. The focus on performance allows us to understand situations interactively, not in terms of communication models, but in terms of participatory ones. To assist at a performance, to bear witness, to sanction: these are active roles which militate against the notion of the audience as passive recipient of a clear communication (Hughes-Freeland 1991a). While not entirely resolving the problems raised by Fabian, these remarks suggest first that anthropologists arrive at an understanding of their own categories with reference to different models (in this case the Melanesian one), and second that such convergences will help to develop the next stage in the debate about the relationship of the various expressions of imagination to other forms of life.

THE CHAPTERS

Kirsten Hastrup's chapter forms part of her attempt 'to reintroduce theatre into general anthropology, and to investigate the power of acting'. She argues that the anthropological engagement with performance studies and theatre anthropology will enhance our understanding of reflexivity in social action in the broadest sense. Starting with theatre director Peter Brook's concept of theatre as life not art, she traces the development of western theatre, and argues that while it is distinct from ritual, as 'Holy Theatre' it has features in common with ritual process: the theatre is a site of passage, its stage a sacred, liminal space, but theatre acting can help us understand action and motivation in broader terms: 'In so far as we see theatrical performances as telescoped social performances, or as concentrated life, this qualification of agency applies equally to both theatre and life in general.' Such performance is 'the process by which "newness" enters the world', and 'moves' the audience in the manner of magic. Actors are the means to this movement; every actor is a double agent, who acts within two 'motivational' spaces: 'the space of training and performative mastery and the space of the character', becoming and being at the same time the one 'who practises the site and makes a passage possible for others by way of vicarious experience'.

Where Hastrup's subject is theatre, Simon Coleman and John Elsner's is pilgrimage as theatre. Agreeing with Eade and Sallnow's (1991) view of pilgrimage as being constituted by multiple discourses, they take issue with this multiplicity being possible because of an absence: 'the "religious void" is in fact full. It is full in the way that the "empty space" of a theatre is full – crowded with material props, holy objects and reminiscences of other holy sites'. Christian pilgrimages to Walsingham in Norfolk include elements of 'ritualized "browsing"' and 'ironic play' which interact performatively with given liturgical structures, reconstituting and transforming them. These performances 'simultaneously genuflect towards conventional ritual forms and yet subvert those forms in the very act of genuflection. In the process, the boundaries of ritual action are shifted and expanded.' Ritual is a strategic deployment of symbolic resources, not a form of coercion acting on the pilgrims, offering more scope for misreading than theatre. Also unlike theatre, this 'Christian theme park' is not simply a liminoid space. Instead, pilgrims locate themselves with reference to the wider liturgical frame, but in two different modes of ritual performance: 'canonical enactment' is serious, reverential, liminal; 'ironic play' is camp, ludic, liminoid. The authors are struck by the fact that the pilgrims who take a more subversive, ludic, ironic approach to their pilgrimage appear more conventional than those who perform in a serious liturgical mode: 'ironic pilgrims – somewhat ironically – seem almost more conventional as pilgrims given their Chaucerian stress on secular fun combined with spiritual devotions'. They conclude that pilgrim-age is a mixed genre which breaks down boundaries between drama, liturgy and 'real life', acts as a 'pressure cooker' for human relationships, and provides general insights into the practices of modernity of which it forms a part.

A critical evaluation of the ritual process in relation to a broader context of action is also the subject Charles Gore's analysis of initiations at urban shrines in Benin City, Nigeria, but his performative approach draws on the conceptual framework of agency, locality, strategy and skill as developed in the history of art to consider the relationship of creativity to convention and legitimacy. Each shrine is owned by a priest (*ohen*) who uses his or her relationship with the spirit world to effect results in the physical world. The *ohen*'s clientele worship at the shrine by means of song, dance and music. The *ohen* is possessed by the deities she or he has a relationship with, and possession occurs among the members of the congregation, whether initiated or not. Behaviour at these shrines is variable according to the deity and the knowledge of the *ohen*. The initiation rituals fit the Van Gennep/Turner model to a certain extent, but the model is then shown to overobjectify ritual and ignore variation arising from strategies in local contexts. Gore demonstrates that possession and dance are not liminal but, as in the case of the performances by pilgrims at Walsingham, are creatively construed within the framing of the conventional. 'Local agents creatively construct and constitute these events, in relation to the various traditions of ideas and practices articulated both within the urban shrine configurations and outside them.' What an initiate can learn depends on the resources available to him or her: 'it is the localized strategies of individuals over time that constitute urban shrine configurations.' The chapter concludes with a discussion of how recent innovations, such as disco dancing and, more importantly, videoing and televising initiations, are being integrated into the practices, and becoming part of the status game.

Susanna Rostas evaluates ritual process in an analysis of dance performances by the Concheros of Mexico. Ritualization and performativity highlight differences in action. Ritualization is non-intentional and constrained whereas performativity is what 'gives an enactment its zest': it is intentional and creative, 'meaning to mean'. The events described consist of a nocturnal vigil and circle dancing, and although the vigil tends to be ritualized and the dance to be performative, there is an oscillation between the two: 'an analysis of the activities of the Concheros makes it difficult to differentiate ritual from performance'.

The Concheros speak of ritual as 'work', 'sacrifice' and 'union'. If the vigil is effective, it produces the 'conformity' which allows for the dancing to represent a spirituality which the Concheros call 'conquest'. The relationship between ritualization and performativity is thus transformable, and expresses two different aspects of action which may come together to produce 'transcendence'; it is not a fixed processual sequence. This transcendence is not equivalent to Turner's group 'communitas'; it is 'a state or space rather than a process and is communal rather than individual; thus ritualization can be seen as a tendency towards "communitas", but is not "communitas" itself'. Rather, it is personal experience, and closer to what Turner called 'flow'. There is also a case in which performativity is not controlled by ritualization. Mexica dancers deliberately reject the Catholic identifications of Conchero dancing and promote a pre-Colombian identity. Performance and ritual part company as the Mexica perform what is classed as 'puro show'.

Dance is also the subject of Helena Wulff's chapter, but ballet is dance in a theatrical context, analysed not as a spectacle or a ritual but as art. Drawing on Bateson, Goffman and Bauman, she adopts Myerhoff's (1990) suggestion of 'let's pretend' as a key to understanding the framing of reality. Ballet is constituted as a practice by diverse frames of reference. The irreconcilable perspectives of critics, balletomanes and dancers suggest that there can be no one frame. Furthermore, within the different camps of *doing ballet* and *watching ballet*' there are diversified experiences. Audiences watch dancers with different levels of knowledge and commitment, in particular the critics, who write not for dancers but for another audience. Dancers say that 'critics don't know anything about ballet'. From the dancers' point of view, ballet art is a practice constituted by three different levels: 'frame maintenance, audience awareness and acting'. Ballet is risky, and frames sometimes slip. Frontstage and backstage are different worlds, which are separated. Choreographic innovators like William Forsythe even play with frames within the 'doing ballet' context, and break down the boundaries between rehearsal and performance.

Ballet performances are not rituals as processes which resolve social crisis in the manner of, for example, the Notting Hill carnival, but they do involve transformations – for the dancers, in the liminal spaces in the wings, offstage, into the character; for the audience as an intense personal experience, close to conversion, which may result in a child deciding to become a dancer, or an adult to become a balletomane. Despite the delimited space of its embodied enactment, ballet is neither an event nor a phenomenon that can be known as an objective fact. It exists as overlapping experiences and actions constituted by different interests and experiences.

The chapter by Sarah Pink considers bullfighting in relation to the social construction of gender identity. As a form of commercial spectacle, bullfighting might initially seem to be sport rather than art, but there is as powerful a performance aesthetic in bullfighting as in ballet, though the order of risk differs between the two. Pink shows that media representations of the Spanish bullfight have influenced its practice by providing a niche for female bullfighters. Drawing on her research in Cordoba, she challenges anthropological interpretations of the bullfight as 'ritual sacrifice' or as being 'copulatory' in imagery. The televisation of bullfights, which are watched at home or in bars, has made it possible for female bullfighters such as Cristina Sánchez to have a role because of the altered nature of the mediated event.

But the performance is embodied action: 'Women bullfighters act roles *in* not *with* their bodies.' It differs from theatre because in bullfighting, the danger is real, not evoked.

In answer to the question 'do women pervert the ritual bullfight or do they create a different ritual?', she shows how live bullfights have a masculinist ethos or *ambiente*, but televised ones invite a different response and constitute different representations. However, although the ritual structures of the traditional bullfight are fragmented by the televised body and the television gaze, the result 'is less a "ritual hybrid" . . . than a televised interweaving of media and ritual agendas'. The media bullfight thus contributes to the production of culture and, if anything, enhances the cultural significance of bullfighting.

The relationship of ritual, spectacle and the media is also the subject of Charlotte Aull Davies's analysis of the Welsh National Eisteddfod, in which she challenges the comparison of public spectacle and ritual. Unlike the Durkheimian view of it as a community-generating event, ritual in plural societies is expressive of conflict and a desire for cultural change, and it usually involves outsiders. It is the varied nature of the audience/participants that makes these characteristics more salient to spectacle, which 'is affected by the nature of the audience, both the actual crowds who watch and those who are imagined to be observing'.

Taking issue with a recent discussion of Welshness, Davies draws on direct observation and media representations of performances in recent Eisteddfods to show these events as contestations of essential identity. Situating these events in the contexts of Welsh nationalism and cultural politics, Eisteddfodds comprise different and conflicting performances and forms of identification – as in the case of the Welsh parent who, despite his being a Welsh speaker and an active campaigner for Welsh-medium education, did not identify at all with 'the things' of the Eisteddfod, describing it as 'the Welsh form of self-torture'. The Eisteddfod may express conflict – over the consumption of alcohol on the Eisteddfod field, for example. It also expresses a desire for change – raves as well as recitations are now part of the event. Television, while appearing to support traditional performances, has served to legitimize alternative events. It has become a site of contesting meanings which may change over time. However, there is a commonality, if not 'communitas', in allowing a variety of performances to qualify as spectacle. 'This combination of continuity in form and fluidity in content', Davies concludes, 'provides the basis for the claim of spectacle to express collective identity.'

Where Davies concentrates on intracultural constructions, Keith Brown considers problems of reception theory in media studies and interpretation across '-scapes' (Appadurai, in Brown, this volume), with reference to a cinematic case of cultural representation. How, he asks, can a film 'contribute to understanding the relationship between representation and realism in the context of national culture'? The chapter explores the 'different modes of interaction' between different audiences and the cinematic image, to relocate the creation of its meaning at the point of its reception. 'Frames of belief' shape responses to *Before the Rain*, a film directed by a Macedonian which was released in the USA in 1995 and nominated for an Academy Award for the 'best foreign-language film' category. As such it is an interesting example of a translocal product, reflected also in its main character being a successful photo-journalist returning from the west.

Newspaper film criticism provides the data for understanding how the film has been construed by non-Macedonian audiences in the USA and by Macedonian ones. For outsiders, responses to the film are framed in the context of 'the horror of the Balkans': the film is 'about' Macedonia: location is mistaken for actuality. Brown notes that the outsiders' view is doubly ironic, in view of Macedonia's exclusion from severe ethnic conflict, and the fact that the film landscape was created – by building roads and making constructions editorially. The distant audience view the film as a spectacle of Macedonia, whereas for Macedonian audiences the film is about the main character, not the place. Like Davies, Brown questions the generality of the media text beyond certain limits, and affirms the significance of locality, despite the 'thinly spread' global technologies which make the representation and its distribution possible.

The undermining of the determination of reality which in Brown's chapter is caused by gaps in technology is discussed in Nigel Rapport's chapter. Where Brown took the audience away from the ritual context, Rapport takes the actor into a social interaction which would not normally be considered as either theatre or ritual. His chapter is a reflexive redescription of his own participation in the sharp end of a time-share operation, described as 'the ritual of modernity', to argue that performance is 'the activity of individual consciousness'. Rapport presents two sets of theory – 'agreeing terms' and 'disagreeing conclusions', drawing on Bauman, Goffman, Simmel, Garfinkel, Steiner and Foucault, among others – to frame the narrative of his experience as an unwitting performer in a ritual of consumption, in a language-game with a time-share salesman. The nature of this Simmelian exchange as ritual(ized) performance is microscopically analysed in terms of discourse, choice and knowledge, but raises questions about globalization and modernity. Like many other contributors, Rapport argues for a primacy of agency over structure: 'It is through narrational performance that we maintain conscious selves; through the performance of narratives, we continue to write and rewrite the story of our selves.' Ritual cannot be framed as an essential form or genre of event. Performance is personal, a form of personalized exchange; what emerges is a narrative, with the potential to subvert routine. However, routines, like technologies, have gaps: if there is a metatheoretical position it is inscribed in the individual 'who stands beyond discourse', but, para- doxically, presence is no guarantee of authenticity: language games are overdetermined, or one might say that to be called an actor or agent is already to have been set on a specified route.

The next chapter is a critical appraisal of performance by an important proponent of the performative approach to ritual, which 'deals with actions more than text'. Here Buck Schieffelin considers the 'enormous power and potential ... of the notion of "performance" in our discipline'; it is a prerequisite for culture and society. However, refining his case for a phenomenological foundation to anthropological theorizing about practices, he warns of the dangers of exporting local concepts. For example, Goffman's (1967) and Bauman's (1986) 'performance' models in social science focus respectively on the *structure* of events and *performativity* as an aspect of action, but both 'draw their inspiration and conceptual terminology from the western notions of theatrical performance'. However, if social acts as practices in Bourdieu's (1977) sense are 'structured or "regulated" improvisations' or 'the strategic articulation of practice', then performance 'embodies the *expressive dimension*' of that practice. In the final analysis, the western theatrical tradition sees performance as 'performative manipulation', 'a simulacrum' – virtual reality, not true 'being-in-the-world'.

Illusion may be 'endemic' to performative models in the social sciences, but there is an alternative model which is interactive, contingent, risky, and productive of real effects. The seance healing and the Gisalo ritual of the Kaluli of Papua New Guinea demonstrate a different relation between audience and performers, in which the audience responds not conventionally but with real emotion: the effects of performance here on the audience are real, not illusory. What is privileged in the Kaluli model is the 'actual psychological and social effects of the poetic act over its purely aesthetic and representational qualities, and the process of social reciprocation over (what we would call) the suspension of disbelief'. The focus on performance in anthropology therefore should move away from the representation of reality to the social construction of reality, 'the imaginative creation of a human world'. Schieffelin thus claims that 'the concepts "performance"/"performativity" have the potential to open a considerable domain for anthropological exploration of the way that cultures actively construct their realities'.

Hirsch too draws on the Melanesian model of performance, but in a very different approach to the issue. He brings together core ideas from media and cultural studies and anthropology to evaluate the use of ethnography in the different disciplines. He proceeds by comparing certain outcomes of performances – 'the ways in which a person or persons appear efficacious in specific cultural contexts of "audienceship"' – in two contexts: the way in which the Simon family of north London regard television, and the way in which the Fuyuge of Papua New Guinea regard the *gab*, a ritual which shares a number of features with Gisalo (see above).

Hirsch models these two outcomes in the north London case and in the Papuan one. He characterizes the western example as 'the culture of the

exhibition', a concept predicated on the production of standardized units –
this culture is thus constituted by a separation of persons and objects,
producing commodities and persons-as-individuals. As the Simons engage
with media technologies such as their video recorder, they create their
individuality by unbounding the imposed standardization, and assert their
own agency. If this 'performative self-creation' asserts their visibility as
implicated in the 'culture of the exhibition', they none the less work against
the way this culture normally commoditizes media by imposing a separation
between spectator and audience. They become agents through the process of
unbounding such standardized units, making them more distinctly 'persons'.
The comparison between London and Papua does not result in essentialized
differences. Fuyuge sociality is more explicitly pervasive in its relationality,
with a model of persons as dividuals rather than individuals. The Fuyuge do
not have a representational approach to the world, but they do work at
creating themselves as units which have particular sorts of visibility. This
visibility, however, is distinguished from the culture of the exhibition by the
fact that it is is not predicated on separability. Despite attempts by colonialists
and missionaries to impose standardization, the disjunction between object
and person which is the core of the 'culture-of-the-exhibition' model did not
replace the Melanesian one, which is predicated on the recurrent transformation of unbounded entities into bounded units of specific scale and form.
Hirsch thus demonstrates that performance enables us to see social processes
in disparate contexts without having to make essential, fixed distinctions.

This argument is used to reject the view presented by Ang (1996) that
globalization and technology mark the end of the ethnographic context as
local. Hirsch argues that media studies reify and overprivilege the role of
media, and need to take on anthropology's broader conception of ethnography. Media studies need to understand more clearly local contexts of
cultural performance and patterns of cohesion and separation, and to understand how television becomes systematized and collated within particular
performative local contexts. In other words, a more comprehensive ethnographic approach, as is used by anthropologists, is required.

CONCLUSIONS/WORK POINTS

One conclusion of this book is that anthropology has more to offer performance, media and cultural studies than it needs to borrow from them, and is
not at risk of being taken over by them. None the less, insights about the
varieties of practised behaviour in diverse situations are to be generated by
the meeting of these different approaches.

Other general themes emerge. The re-evaluation of the ritual process by
means of performance produces an emphasis on agency and creativity, which
does not preclude structural constraint. Instead of a process which moves
from one to the other in time and space, creativity and constraint are

simultaneous, co-present, and co-dependent in performative practices embodied in different forms of participation.

With respect to representational issues, there is a theoretical tendency towards discussing situated social practices from perspectives which preclude objectivism. However, in so far as contingency plays an important role in these models, it is possible to invoke a metalanguage on a contingent basis, in an 'odd-job' manner, in order to make a representational articulation of those situated social practices possible. Once again, we are brought back to the impossibility of comparability, and its necessity. While many of us prefer to start from indigenous categories, such ethnographic particularism none the less relies on prior formulations which we may not be aware of. It is by becoming aware of these that we can build bridges between our ethnography and our readers, even if we prefer to burn those bridges down once we have carried our readers into the specific situation we wish to explore.

The arguments here also lead to a consideration of the nature of reality: where do we draw the line between real and unreal experience? Where do we situate the life of the imagination in the analysis of social action? By examining ritual through the frames of performance and media, we can reconsider core questions in anthropology, to reflect on the way we arrive at our insights into the analysis and framing of social action, and to reaffirm the value of close-grained ethnography which comes from participant observation. While translocal connections are theoretically possible, in the same way that choices in our everyday lives are theoretically possible, ethnography is able to specify the scales, standards and orders of magnitude of the way in which connection and connectability work in practice in the world in which we live, as experienced, as imagined and as perceived, at the very least.

NOTES

1 This responds to Mark Hobart's criticism, made in the ASA conference that gave rise to this book, that Turner's theoretical move from ritual to theatre remains in the sphere of analyst's categories which produce circular arguments. Instead we should follow Fabian's warnings against 'the dangers of misplaced concreteness that always loom when scientific discourse makes use of concepts that come along carrying a heavy load of cultural connotations' (Fabian 1990: 13–14), and focus on situated social acts, keeping account of 'the contingencies of the actual, social, and political contexts' (Fabian 1990: 14) in which an ethnography is produced. There is of course, a metalanguage at work even in these formulations; see my concluding comments.

2 Although at the 1996 meeting of the Group for Debates in Anthropological Theory in Manchester, the motion 'Cultural studies will be the death of anthropology' was defeated by 31 to 20, discipline boundaries are changing as British higher education is being redefined.

3 Bateson's (1958) innovative work, first published in 1936, remains an important exception.

4 For an excellent example of a discussion focusing on the contingency of ritual form and effects, see Lincoln's (1989) reappraisal of Gluckman's analysis of the Swazi Ncwala ritual.

5 These problems have been well rehearsed in Holy and Stuchlik (1983: 35–44).

6 Although Turner's focus on performance has been lauded as 'a humanization of anthropology and . . . a way of reintroducing an element of fun into its teaching' (Fabian 1990: 10), this neo-evolutionism, also evident in his work on pilgrimage, is deemed a source of 'consternation' (1990: 17).

7 'The pre-expressive base constitutes the elementary level of organization of the theatre' and is concerned with 'the network of fictions and "magic ifs" which deal with the physical forces that move the body' (Barba 1995: 9; see further Barba and Savarese 1991: 186–294).

8 During the ASA conference mentioned in n. 1, only Andrée Grau presented a case for performer-anthropologists.

9 There are also very useful non-anthropological books on theatre of interest to regional specialists, such as van Erven's (1992) work on political theatre in a number of Asian societies.

10 Fiske and Hartley's discussion of television viewing as social ritual (1978: 83–9) resonates with the theme of this book, but is limited by the textual nature of its analysis.

11 Peacock's pioneering attempt to analyse Javanese theatrical performance in terms of ritual (1968) is referred to by contributors only in its appearance in a later essay (1990).

12 For a previous set of approaches to creativity, see Lavie et al. (1993).

13 For a discussion of when Javanese dance constitutes art and when it does not, see Hughes-Freeland (1997c).

14 Implicit in Rapport's chapter is a response to Bourdieu's attack on Goffman, in which he accuses him of having 'a Berkleian vision of the social world, reducing it to a theatre in which being is never more than perceived being, a mental representation of a theatre performance [représentation]' (1986 [1979]: 253, also 579 n. 32).

15 Pink challenges Parkin's (1992) argument that spatial orientation is crucial to ritual by her analysis of live and televised bullfights.

16 Nichols's discussion of magnitude in the varying forms of representation of fiction film and documentary film is relevant for developing the general problems addressed in this book (1991: 230–3).

17 It is often the case in a transforming situation that a dance group may use the possibility of trance to give an otherwise mundane performance an intensity evident in the sharpened interest of the onlookers, all caught up in the question 'Will they go over the edge, out of control?'. On Javanese views about trance and performance, see Hughes-Freeland (1997a).

18 Kapferer (1991) demonstrates how in exorcistic healing rituals in Sri Lanka performative elements such as music, dance, trance, drama, and comedy work by making a symbolic reordering of pre-existent classificatory ideas and re-establishing the relationships between the patient and audience and the world which have been destroyed by demonic illness. Comedy restores the patient to

health by enabling him or her to share in the audience's laughter and to see the
demon not as a terrifying subjective form, but as essentially absurd and comical.

REFERENCES

Ajmer, Göran and Boholm, Åsa (eds) (1994) *Images and Enactments: Possible Worlds
in Dramatic Performances*, Gothenburg: Institute for Advanced Studies in Social
Anthropology.

Ang, Ien (1996) *Living Room Wars: Rethinking Media Audiences for a Postmodern
World*, London: Routledge.

Barba, Eugenio (1995) *The Paper Canoe: A Guide to Theatre Anthropology*, London:
Routledge.

Barba, Eugenio and Savarese, Nicola (eds) (1991) *The Secret Art of the Performer:
A Dictionary of Theatre Anthropology*, London: Routledge.

Bateson, Gregory (1958 [1936]) *Naven*, second edition, Stanford: Stanford University
Press.

Bauman, Richard (1986) *Story, Performance, Event*, Cambridge: Cambridge University Press.

Bell, Catherine (1992) *Ritual Theory, Ritual Practice*, Oxford: Oxford University
Press.

Bloch, Maurice (1974) 'Symbol, song, dance and features of articulation: is religion
an extreme form of traditional authority?', *European Journal of Sociology*, 15:
55–81.

Boissevain, Jeremy (ed.) (1992) *Revitalizing European Rituals*, London: Routledge.

Bourdieu, Pierre (1977) *Outline of a Theory of Practice*, Cambridge: Cambridge
University Press.

—— (1986 [1979]) *Distinction: A Social Critique of the Judgement of Taste*, London
and New York: Routledge and Kegan Paul.

Brook, Peter (1968) *The Empty Space*, Harmondsworth: Penguin.

Bruner, Edward M. (ed.) (1984) *Text, Play and Story*, Washington DC: American
Ethnological Society.

Chaney, David (1993) *Fictions of Collective Life: Public Drama in Late Modern
Culture*, London: Routledge.

Cohen, Abner (1974) *Two Dimensional Man*, London: Routledge and Kegan Paul.

Crain, M. (1992) 'Pilgrims, "yuppies", and media men: the transformation of an
Andalusian pilgrimage', in J. Boissevain (ed.) *Revitalizing European Rituals*,
London: Routledge.

Eade, John and Sallnow, Michael (eds) (1991) *Contesting the Sacred: The Anthropology of Christian Pilgrimage*, London: Routledge.

Erven, Eugène van (1992) *The Playful Revolution: Theatre and Liberation in Asia*,
Bloomington and Indianapolis: Indiana University Press.

Fabian, Johannes (1990) *Power and Performance: Ethnographic Explorations
through Proverbial Wisdom and Theater in Shaba, Zaire*, Madison: University of
Wisconsin Press.

Fiske, John and Hartley, John (1978) *Reading Television*, London: Methuen.

Friedman, Jonathan (1994) *Cultural Identity and Global Process*, London: Sage.

Geertz, Clifford (1966) 'Religion as a culture system', in M. Banton (ed.) *Anthropological Approaches to the Study of Religion*, ASA monograph 3, London: Tavistock
Press.

—— (1973) 'The Balinese cockfight', in *The Interpretation of Cultures*, New York:
Basic Books.

Gell, Alfred (1992) 'The technology of enchantment and the enchantment of technology', in Jeremy Coote and Anthony Shelton (eds) *Anthropology, Art, Aesthetics*, Oxford: Clarendon Press.

Goffman, Erving (1959) *The Presentation of Self in Everyday Life*, Garden City NY: Doubleday Anchor.

—— (1967) *Interaction Ritual*, New York: Doubleday Anchor.

—— (1974) *Frame Analysis*, New York: Harper and Row.

Goody, Jack (1977) 'Against "ritual": loosely structured thoughts on a loosely defined topic', in S.F. Moore and B. Myerhoff (eds) *Secular Ritual*, Assen, The Netherlands: Van Gorcum.

Handelman, Don (1990) *Models and Mirrors: Towards an Anthropology of Public Events*, Cambridge: Cambridge University Press.

Hastrup, Kirsten (1992) 'Out of anthropology: the anthropologist as an object of dramatic representation', *Cultural Anthropology*, 7: 327–45.

—— (1995) *A Passage to Anthropology: Between Experience and Theory*, London: Routledge.

Hobart, Mark (n.d.) 'Consuming passions? Overinterpreting television-viewing in Bali', unpublished paper to the Australian Research Council Project Workshop on Modernity in Bali, Wollongong, 10–11 July 1995.

Holy, Ladislav and Stuchlik, Milan (1983) *Actions, Norms and Representations: Foundations of Anthropological Inquiry*, Cambridge: Cambridge University Press.

Hughes-Freeland (1991a) 'Classification and communication in Javanese palace performance', *Visual Anthropology*, 4: 342–66.

—— (1991b) 'A throne for the people: observations on the *Jumenengen* of Sultan Hamengku Buwono X', *Indonesia*, 51: 129–52.

—— (1992) 'Representation by the other: Indonesian cultural documentation', in P.I. Crawford and D. Turton (eds) *Film as Ethnography*, Manchester: Manchester University Press.

—— (1997a) 'Consciousness in performance: a Javanese theory', *Social Anthropology*, 5 (1): 55–68.

—— (1997b) 'Balinese on television: representation and response', in M. Banks and H. Morphy (eds) *Rethinking Visual Anthropology*, Yale: Yale University Press.

—— (1997c) 'Art and politics: from Javanese court dance to Indonesian art', *Journal of the Royal Anthropological Institute*, 3 (3).

Humphrey, Caroline and Laidlaw, James (1994) *The Archetypal Actions of Ritual*, Oxford: Clarendon Press.

Kapferer, Bruce (1991) *A Celebration of Demons*, second edition, Oxford: Berg, Princeton NJ: Smithsonian Institution Press.

Keeler, Ward (1987) *Javanese Shadow Plays, Javanese Selves*, Princeton NJ: Princeton University Press.

Kersenboom, Saskia (1995) *Word, Sound, Image: The Life of the Tamil Text*, Oxford: Berg.

Kim, Tae-gon, and Hoppál, Mihály (1995) *Shamanism in Performing Arts*, Budapest: Akadémiai Kiadó.

Kuhlick, Don and Willson, Margaret (1994) 'Rambo's wife saves the day: subjugating the gaze and subverting the narratives in a Papua New Guinea swamp', *Visual Anthropology Review*, 10 (2): 1–13.

Kuipers, Joel C. (1990) *Power in Performance*, Philadelphia: University of Pennsylvania Press.

Laderman, Carol (1991) *Taming the Winds of Desire: Psychology, Medicine and Aesthetics in Malay Shamanistic Performances*, Berkeley CA: University of California Press.

Lavie, Smadar, Narayan, Kirin and Rosaldo, Renato (eds) (1993) *Creativity/Anthropology*, Ithaca NY: Cornell University Press.

Lincoln, Bruce (1989) *Discourse and the Construction of Society: Comparative Studies of Myth, Ritual, and Classification*, New York: Oxford University Press.

Little, Paul E. (1995) 'Ritual, power and ethnography at the Rio Earth Summit', *Critique of Anthropology*, 15 (3): 265–88.

Mauss, Marcel (1973) 'Techniques of the body', *Economy and Society*, 2 (1): 70–88.

Milner, Horace (1956) 'Body ritual among the Nacirema', *American Anthropologist*, 58 (3): 503–7.

Moore, Sally F. and Myerhoff, Barbara (eds) (1977) *Secular Ritual*, Assen, The Netherlands: Van Gorcum.

Morley, David (1992) *Television, Audiences and Cultural Studies*, London: Routledge.

Myerhoff, Barbara (1990) 'Ritual performance is ludic', in R. Schechner and W. Appel (eds) *By Means of Performance: Intercultural Studies of Theatre and Ritual*, Cambridge: Cambridge University Press.

Nichols, Bill (1991) *Representing Reality: Issues and Concepts in Ethnography*, Bloomington and Indianapolis: Indiana University Press.

Parkin, David (1992) 'Ritual as spatial direction and bodily division', in D. de Coppet (ed.) *Understanding Rituals*, London and New York: Routledge.

Parkin, David, Caplan, Lionel and Fisher, Humphrey (eds) (1996) *The Politics of Cultural Performance*, Oxford: Berghahn.

Peacock, James L. (1968) *Rites of Modernisation: Symbolic and Social Aspects of Indonesian Proletarian Drama*, Chicago and London: University of Chicago Press.

—— (1990) 'Ethnographic notes on sacred and profane performance', in R. Schechner and W. Appel (eds) *By Means of Performance: Intercultural Studies of Theatre and Ritual*, Cambridge: Cambridge University Press.

Rosaldo, Renato (1989) *Culture and Truth*, London: Routledge.

Roseman, Marina (1991) *Healing Sounds from the Malaysian Rainforest: Temiar Music and Medicine*, Berkeley CA, University of California Press.

Sallnow, M. (1981) 'Communitas reconsidered: the sociology of Andean pilgrimage', *Man*, n.s., 16: 163–82.

Schechner, Richard (1985) *Between Theater and Anthropology*, Philadelphia: University of Pennsylvania Press.

—— (1986) 'Magnitudes of performance', in V.W. Turner and E.M Bruner (eds) *The Anthropology of Experience*, Urbana and Chicago: University of Illinois Press.

—— (1993) *The Future of Ritual: Writings on Culture and Performance*, London: Routledge.

—— and Appel, Willa (eds) (1990) *By Means of Performance: Intercultural Studies of Theatre and Ritual*, Cambridge: Cambridge University Press.

Schieffelin, Edward L. (1976) *The Sorrow of the Lonely and the Burning of the Dancers*, New York: St Martin's Press.

—— (1985) 'Performance and the cultural construction of reality', *American Ethnologist*, 12 (4): 707–24.

Seiter, Ellen, Borchers, Hans, Kreutzer, Gabrielle and Warth, Eva-Maria (1989) *Remote Control: Television, Audiences and Cultural Power*, London and New York: Routledge.

Spitulnik, Debra (1983) 'Anthropology and mass media', *Annual Review of Anthropology*, 22: 293–315.

Starrett, Gregory (1995) 'The political economy of religious commodities in Cairo', *American Anthropologist*, 97 (1): 51–68.

Suryani, Luh Ketut and Jensen, Gordon (1993) *Trance and Possession in Bali*, Kuala Lumpur: Oxford University Press.

Tambiah, S.J. (1985 [1981]) 'A performative approach to ritual', in *Culture, Thought and Social Action: An Anthropological Perspective*, Cambridge MA: Harvard University Press.

Tsing, Anna L. (1993) *In the Realm of the Diamond Queen: Marginality in an Out-of-the-Way-Place*, Princeton NJ: Princeton University Press.

Turner, Victor W. (1969) *The Ritual Process: Structure and Anti-Structure*, Ithaca NY: Cornell University Press.

—— (1974) *Dramas, Fields and Metaphors: Symbolic Action in Human Society*, Ithaca NY and London: Cornell University Press.

—— (1982) *From Ritual to Theatre: The Human Seriousness of Play*, New York: PAJ Publications.

—— (1992 [1987]) *The Anthropology of Performance*, New York: PAJ Publications.

Chapter 1

Theatre as a site of passage
Some reflections on the magic of acting

Kirsten Hastrup

> We must believe in a sense of life renewed by the theater, a sense of life in which man fearlessly makes himself master of what does not yet exist, and brings it into being.
>
> (Artaud 1958: 13)

In 1968, that year of revolt and of imagination, Peter Brook launched an attack on the 'deadly theatre' (Brook 1968). Deadliness had settled most comfortably within the European textual tradition, notably the Shakespearean, which made the audience smile out of recognition and confirmation rather than from the experience of surprise. Deadliness, however, is not attached to a particular genre; it may occur anywhere, according to Brook. This chapter seeks to explore its opposite, the living theatre, theatre that moves.[1] My concern is related to a more general interest in retracing the process by which 'newness' enters the world, and thus in identifying a point of agency that truly matters (cf. Hastrup forthcoming). Thus my emphasis is more on the historical potential of theatre than on its 'meaning'. Although my argument is quite literally 'staged', it is still squarely within recent epistemological concerns in general anthropology (cf. Hastrup 1995a).

In anthropology, we have talked at length about social dramas or cultural performances, and many studies have been carried out with the explicit aim of studying the spectacular qualities of social life (e.g. Cohen 1981, Geertz 1980, Turner 1974). Far fewer studies have been devoted to theatre and spectacle *per se* (cf. Beeman 1993: 370), which is all the more strange since theatricality seems to have been at the roots of the overwhelming interest in ritual, for instance. If there is any tradition of 'theatre anthropology', then this originates in the world of theatre studies (e.g. Barba and Savarese 1991, Hastrup 1996a, Watson 1993). In many ways this field is (deliberately) at odds with social or cultural anthropology, seeking to decontextualize the art of acting, historically and culturally, and aiming at an understanding of the universal, 'natural' dimensions of performers' work. However, with its clear focus on the secret art of the performer, transculturally, theatre anthropology in Barba's sense provides a singularly apt comparative perspective for the renewed attempt within social anthropology to come to grips with theatre as a moving force in the world.

This chapter should be seen as an attempt to reintroduce theatre into general anthropology, and to investigate the power of acting. My perspective is not that of the audience, or that of the passing anthropological observer, but that of the players. The 'native point of view' in this context is embedded in the world of European theatre, from where we get a new perspective on the world beyond the stage. The implicit point is that 'the playful' is an integral part of social experience and cultural reproduction, not something existing outside it (cf. Turner 1982, Bruner 1984), much like 'the painful' on the less pleasant side of life (Hastrup 1993). Cultural reproduction in this sense points not to stability but to a domain of implicit motivation.

Theatre belongs to the domain of art. This domain is notoriously difficult to talk about without either subscribing to the cult of self-perpetuating admiration or reducing it to craft (cf. Geertz 1983: 94–5, Bourdieu 1996). Craft or technique is, of course, an integral part of art's peculiar power of enchantment (Gell 1992), yet there is something more than that, which defies our words and locks our tongues. To talk in a scholarly way about art we need a kind of 'methodological philistinism', akin to the methodological atheism needed when studying religious forms elsewhere: 'Methodological philistinism consists of taking an attitude of resolute indifference towards the aesthetic value of works of art – the aesthetic value that they have, either indigenously or from the standpoint of universal aestheticism' (Gell 1992: 42). Theatre being one art form among others, this point should be kept in mind during my argument on the power inherent in the players' investment of themselves in a process of becoming what they are not.

The main point of departure, however, is not theatre as *art* as much as theatre as *life*. As Peter Brook has it: 'theatre has no categories, it is about life. This is the only starting point and there is nothing else truly fundamental. Theatre is life' (Brook 1993: 8). Evidently, it differs from everyday life, or there would be no point in making theatre; but the difference is one of condensation. Theatre is a concentrate of action, which is what makes it so (potentially) powerful. This view of theatre goes back to Aristotle, who defines tragedy as an imitation of action, or literally as a mimesis of praxis, and claims that it represents 'an action which is complete, and of a certain magnitude' (Halliwell 1987: 39). This 'magnitude' is what makes theatre:

> indeed tragedy would be irrelevant otherwise. It is true, actions in tragedy are usually larger than actions in life: they have more complications and weightier consequences, and involve individuals of higher rank. But that they are large is what makes them worth putting on the stage. It does not make them different in kind.
>
> (Bittner 1992: 98)

The magnitude of action must be transformed to life by the actor. In a general depiction of the actor's craft, Colley Cibber (1671–1757) compares the actor Thomas Betterton to the painter Vandyke and the playwright Shakespeare himself:

> The most that a Vandyke can arrive at, is to make his portraits of great persons seem to *think*; a Shakespeare goes farther yet, and tells you what his pictures thought; a Betterton steps beyond them both, and calls them from the grave, to breathe, and be themselves again, in feature, speech, and motion.
>
> (Cibber, in *Actors*: 105)[2]

It is Betterton and his like that are at the centre of my attention here. Betterton (1635–1710) was a player of Shakespeare, and among his most famous roles was that of Hamlet. In what follows, Hamlet will be a more or less constant companion on my tour towards a greater understanding of the art of acting. Deadliness is not necessarily *his* attribute, even if mortality is. Other companions will join the tour at various points in the interest of bringing us closer to the power of acting which seems to cut across time and space – – if still based within the European tradition. It is the source of that power which we are setting out to ensnare, in the general interest of investigating social agency.

PLACE: THE LIMINALITY OF THE STAGE

In anthropology it has often been stressed that theatre has developed from ritual, and that both are in some sense an answer to people's need for 'communitas' and spectacle (e.g. Turner 1982, Schechner 1988). In this section I shall circle around the possible relationship between theatre and ritual, with a view not to origins but to history and structural parallels. First a brief note on history.

It seems well established that Greek theatre developed in connection with Dionysian festivals as part of the performance culture of Athens, and evolved into a highly specialized entertainment, involving dancers, a chorus, and a composer who played the lead, and who eventually evolved into one among the other actors, while the playwright withdrew from the stage (Green 1994, Ley 1991, Rehm 1992). Dramas were produced and masks were constructed to suit the cities' desire for play at times of almost carnivalesque 'communitas'. Whether actually evolved from ritual or not, theatre in ancient Greece was not an everyday performance. It was a regular feature of the Hellenistic world, however, and as such it probably spilled over into the Roman realm via plays enacted on wooden stages in Greek outposts in southern Italy (Beacham 1995: 7ff). In classical Rome, the first stages were temporary wooden constructs, much like the ones depicted on Greek vases. It was not until 55 BC that the first of those monumental stone theatres that have been left for posterity was constructed in Pompey, seating some 17,500 spectators (Beacham 1995: 56). This theatre staged power and prestige, but it also featured a ritual component in that a small temple was built at the top.

Roman theatre dwindled with the fall of the Roman Empire, and what was left was wandering groups of players of a motley breed. Theatricality was transferred to the church. It has been suggested that (early) modern European theatre grew out of the Christian rite celebrating the Lord's supper, and with it the entire passion (Harris 1992: 3–4). The staging of Christianity and the implied moral dimension were to influence later Elizabethan drama heavily, if again by way of small troupes of itinerant players (Harris 1992: 166). Greek, Roman or medieval, it appears that the stages set for public drama were always set apart from the space of everyday life, and heavily laden with religious or ritual connotation. In between, itinerant players made imagination reign in the streets.

The paradigmatic form of modern western theatre, deriving from the Renaissance, also took place on a well-bounded stage. If we concentrate briefly on Elizabethan England, we notice how, in the world of Shakespeare and his contemporaries, a new sense of theatre was created, along with a manifest orchestration of the city as inherently theatrical (Smith *et al.* 1995). A new sense of rites and sites was promoted, and among the innovations were proper theatres, where none had been before. They were erected in the London Liberties, side by side with leper hospitals, in 'a site of passage' (Mullaney 1991: 17; see also Mullaney 1988). The Liberties were social margins, a space of freedom *and* restraint. Inside the city walls, ritual and spectacle were organized around the figures of central authority and were emblems of cultural coherence, not unlike the spectacles of the Balinese 'theatre state' analysed by Geertz (1980), and of ancient Rome. By contrast, the 'figures we encounter outside the city walls are liminal ones, and the dramaturgy of the margins was a liminal breed of cultural performance, a performance of the threshold, by which the horizon of community was made visible, the limits of definition, containment, and control made manifest' (Mullaney 1991: 22). Thus an ambivalent space between inside and outside turned the dualism into a tertiary construct. And this was the place where the stage was set for Elizabethan drama, when it was not played at court. Among the theatres raised in this space was Shakespeare's theatre, the Globe.

What is happening here is part of a larger development, gradually setting artists free from their patrons and benefactors; it is a process of autonomization of artistic and intellectual work, eventually placing these in a rather restricted field of cultural production (Bourdieu 1993: 113–14). The restrictedness of the field is what eventually was to produce the cult of *Art*. At the time of the Globe, around 1600, the artists were still partly at the mercy of royal or other interest, yet they also had their own space. In this autonomous space, 'freedom' of course was dependent upon market and other factors, and certainly Shakespeare's theatre was also about balancing the books, and making profits (Thomson 1992). With the putting up of regular stages in theatres of the threshold, the artistry of acting became a different kind of profession. The process of canonizing the play could take off, just as Bourdieu has described it for art in general, leading to an increasing degree of consecration (Bourdieu 1993: 123). This process presupposes a distinctive field, a theatre firmly bounded off from the everyday.

Before Shakespeare, England had itinerant comedians and troupes of players, and elsewhere in Europe there were other, related forms of performance in market places, on streets and in churches. But theatre now emerged at the verge of modernity, witnessing a transformation of 'spectacular society' to a 'society of spectacle' (Chaney 1993). Ritualized dramatization of social life was gradually replaced by institutionalized reflexivity on stage. Whether or not this is an absolute before and after modernity as Chaney implies, with Elizabethan theatre professional acting was disrupted from social drama in general. Today, in the postmodernist era, this process may be reversing yet again, making of the street a new and powerful stage (cf. Schechner 1993).

The means to do this was to allot to it a liminal space. And it is this liminality which provides us with the first clue to theatre in general as a site of passage, structurally related to ritual, and in its own way englobing the world. This last point has received notable attention by Frances Yates, whose work points to a possible link between classical philosophy and Shakespearean cosmology in which the idea of the globe was all-pervasive:

> The Globe Theatre was a magical theatre, a cosmic theatre, a religious theatre, an actors' theatre, designed to give fullest support to the voices and gestures of the players as they enacted the drama of the life of man within the Theatre of the World. These meanings might not have been apparent to all, but they would have been known to the initiated. His theatre would have been for Shakespeare the pattern of the universe, the idea of the Macrocosm, the world stage on which the Microcosm acted his parts. All the world's a stage.
>
> (Yates 1987 [1969]: 189)

This is a not too distant echo of the classical view in anthropology of ritual as a condensed symbol of the social. If Yates's words are the real clue to the (now recreated) Globe theatre in the (long-lost) London Liberties, being at one and the same time liminal and inclusive, then they may also provide our cue for the next section.

SPACE: THE ALCHEMY OF ACTING

Space is a practised place (Certeau 1984: 117); if the stage makes up the *place* of theatre, it is for the players to create a proper social *space* through their practising of the place. What kind of space results from the actors' practising of the liminal space, and what is the power inherent in this space? Artaud points to a mysterious identity between the principle of alchemy and the principle of theatre: both of them are virtual arts and do not carry their end within themselves (Artaud 1958: 48). The virtual art of theatre consists in showing what is not, and as such it functions as society's spiritual 'double'. This again connects to ritual and to a magic space beyond the ordinary. Peter Brook takes us further into this space with his notion of the 'Holy Theatre'.

The Holy Theatre could as well be called the Theatre-of-the-Invisible-Made-Visible (Brook 1968: 47ff). It is not just the dream of a romantic and meaningful theatre when the idea of play was closer to its sacred origins, even though this dream is constantly refurbished by the cult of *art*, and the longing for a better, nicer and more just world. 'Even if theatre had in its origins rituals that made the invisible incarnate, we must not forget that apart from certain Oriental theatres these rituals have been either lost or remain in seedy decay' (Brook 1968: 50). The Holy Theatre, rather, should be seen as a vehicle for establishing contact with a sacred invisibility. Brook also refers to the surrealist dramatist and poet Artaud, for whom the Holy Theatre was a blazing centre of intoxication and infection, like the plague. Theatre becomes magic in this perspective; not in the form of a bourgeois laudatory metaphor but in a reality of making the invisible visible through the submission of the natural laws to one's will. With Marcel Mauss, we may say that 'magic is the domain of pure production, *ex nihilo*. With words and gestures it does what techniques achieve by labour' (Mauss 1972: 141). The parallel between acting and magic is immediate, and is further substantiated by Lévi-Strauss's claim that magic consists in a 'naturalization des actes humaines' ('naturalization of human actions': cf. Lévi-Strauss 1962: 292–3). From the perspective of the theatre director this is further underscored:

> The actor's expressivity derives – almost *in spite of himself* – from his actions, from the use of his physical presence. The principles guiding him in these actions make up the pre-expressive bases of expressivity.
>
> It is our actions which, *in spite of us*, make us expressive. It is not the *wish to express* which determines one's actions; the wish to express does not decide what is to be done. It is the *wish to do* which decides what one expresses.
>
> (Barba 1986: 134)

The actor's wish to do links up once again with alchemy. If 'holy', then the holiness of theatre has little to do with creed; for Grotowski, it is explicitly secular. He says that just as a great sinner can become a saint according to theological doctrine, so the actor's wretchedness can be transformed into a kind of holiness:

> If the actor, by setting himself a challenge publicly challenges others, and

through excess, profanation and outrageous sacrilege reveals himself by casting off his everyday mask, he makes it possible for the spectator to undertake a similar process of self-penetration. If he does not exhibit his body, but annihilates it, burns it, frees it from every resistance to any psychic impulse, then he does not sell his body but sacrifices it. He repeats the atonement: he is close to holiness.

(Grotowski 1975: 34)

This sacrifice is what invokes a sacred space of acting. It is not to be mistaken for the barbaric art of which Bertolt Brecht spoke in his critique of a theatre that refused to become a theatre for the age of science and remained a relic of a long bygone past:

Shakespeare's great solitary figures, bearing on their breast the star of their fate, carry through with irresistible force their futile and deadly outbursts; they prepare their own downfall; life, not death, becomes obscene as they collapse; the catastrophe is beyond criticism. Human sacrifices all around! Barbaric delights! We know that the barbarians have their art. Let us create another.

(Brecht 1990: 189)

This is a sacrifice of characters in the interest of the story; what Grotowski speaks of is the actor's self-sacrifice in the interest of making the invisible visible. It is *the act* that makes the actor holy, not the text or the story. The act can be painful, as related by Ben Kingsley playing Othello: 'Here in my secret play is where Othello and I feel such a crushing inexpressible pain that we [*sic!*] attempt to leave the arena' (Kingsley, in *Players 2*: 173).[3] The wording is revealing.

Actor Torgeir Wethal (a member of Odin Teatret, Denmark) makes us see that the holiness is not necessarily painful, but can also be related to the wholeness of the situation, a wholeness that is not unrelated to Kingsley's use of the pronoun 'we' for Othello and himself: 'I have continued working on every production until I feel I have complete control of the whole space. Maybe it's my imagination, but I feel I reach a complete wholeness with what I am doing, almost a kind of invulnerability. It's a strange feeling' (Wethal, cited in Christoffersen 1993: 179). Anyone recalling Lévi-Strauss's account of Quesalid will recognize the magic truth in the implicit proposition that 'grand acting' precedes the moving of the audience. Quesalid entered into apprenticeship with a great shaman in order to unveil the true nature of his magic bluff. In spite of himself, and although he had indeed uncovered the apparent fake, he became a great shaman himself.

Quesalid n'est pas devenu un grand sorcier parce qu'il guérissait ses malades, il guérissait ses malades parce qu'il était devenu un grand sorcier.

(Lévi-Strauss 1958: 198)

> Quesalid did not become a great shaman because he cured his patients, he cured his patients because he had become a great shaman.
>
> (ed.'s trans.)

Quesalid's mastery was one of technique; this was the stuff of his wish *to do*. With Barba's words in mind, we may say that whatever Quesalid wished to express, it was outdone by his wish to do. His craft and his art were one. While not independent of a spectator or an audience, 'the power of art objects stems from the technical processes they objectively embody: the *technology of enchantment* is founded on the *enchantment of technology*' (Gell 1992: 44).

Ritual may be seen as primarily a context marker, possibly meaningless in itself while something else is meaningless without it (Ardener 1992). By contrast, theatre provides its own context: the frame is part of the event. There is no meaning to theatre outside its own structure; there may evidently be consequences and interpretations that will affect people, individually or collectively, but theatre as such works at the threshold of established meanings. Thus there are questions that cannot be posed to theatre. Listen to actor Michael Pennington, once again on Hamlet:

> There are matters in the part that I have never in any case been happy to discuss, such as Hamlet's 'madness', which seems to me undiscussable outside the terms of performance. Whether Hamlet is 'mad', whatever that is, depends very much on how mad the spectator or the actor happen to be. Sometimes it is the theatre's job to pass on a riddle, not to solve it.
>
> (Pennington, in *Players 1*: 127)

The riddle is passed on not by way of interpretation but by way of enchanted technique. Such is the message from Philip Franks, playing Hamlet for the Royal Shakespeare Company in 1987, and relating his first encounter with the director, Roger Michell:

> When I first met Roger to discuss the play we both found that large questions of definition and interpretation were not of much use. We skirted around the usual ones – what is the play saying? Who is Hamlet? Is his madness real or feigned? – and discarded them, with relief, in favour of a detailed and organic approach, a mining of the text and discussion of particular relationships. Thereafter, we hardly ever talked about 'interpretation', only about the choices available within a scene, a speech, a line or a word.
>
> (Franks, in *Players 3*: 191)

What is expressed here is not solely a view of interpretation having of necessity to give way to more practical concerns, but also an echo of the fact that meaning cannot be a fixed relation between sentences and objective reality, as objectivism would have it. 'Grasping a meaning is an *event* of

understanding' (Johnson 1987: 175); it is a dynamic, interactive and fundamentally imaginative process relating to previous experiences and embodied
knowledge. Meaning is always for someone situated in a particular social
space, and the criteria of relevance rest on and reveal our whole system of
values (Putnam 1981: 202).

The true subject of the work of art is the artistry not the artist (Bourdieu
1993: 118); it is the artistry, the actor's technique or 'technology of
enchantment', which is the source of power inherent in acting. But the artistry
of acting implies that the actor knows how to make a character which
somehow resonates with the audience's system of values. The artist always
works with his or her audience's capacities (Geertz 1983: 118). In the
following we shall explore this further through a discussion of the particular
artistry inherent in acting.

THE ACTOR: A DOUBLE AGENT

Having identified theatre as a site of passage, and the stage as a sacred space,
we must now turn to the actor as the one who practises the site and makes a
passage possible for others by way of vicarious experience (cf. Hastrup
1996b). The ancient Greek word for actor was *hypokrites*, which allegedly
meant 'answerer' originally; and apparently the original actor was the
composer, who answered the chorus on stage (Ley 1991: 26). His scene was
set, if not in a liminal place then at least in the liminal time of the Dionysian
festivals, when he would add a dimension to the society's self-understanding
by re-enacting the cosmological, and – increasingly – the social order. The
great tragedies became a fixed part of society's remembering itself (cf.
Connerton 1989).

Shakespeare's theatre, the Globe, provided us with the clue to the liminality
of the stage, and Shakespeare's plays now provide us with the clue to the dual
nature of the actor, foreshadowed by the *hypokrites*. *Hamlet* in particular is
a play about acting; quite apart from the play within the play, there is an
unusual tendency to expose its characters as actors (Thomson 1992: 135).
Generally, the Elizabethans were familiar with the idea of the world as a
theatre, and with much of the metaphorical imagery associated with it; the
metaphors had not yet lost touch with reality, so when people crossed the
Thames to attend to the Globe's world they knew that the actors were men
and vice versa (Thomson 1992: 119–20). John Webster (d. 1634) wrote on
'The Excellent Actor':

> Whatever is commendable in a grave orator, is most exquisitely perfect in
> him; for by as full and significant action of the body, he charms our
> attention: sit in a full theatre, and you will think you see so many lines
> drawn from the circumferences of so many ears, while the actor is the
> center . . . By his action he fortifies moral precepts with example; for what

we see him personate, we think truly done before us ... All men have
been of his occupation: and indeed, what he does feignedly that do others
essentially: this day one plays a monarch, the next a private person. Here
one acts a tyrant, on the morrow an exile.

(Webster, in *Actors*: 88–9)

For the actors, the stage was their real playground. Metaphors subsided as
life was restored on stage. Here the player became the centre of a real world
of his own making. All human agents are moving centres of attention to the
world, but what is eminently characteristic of the players' world is their
explicit reflexivity. If all agents are capable of self-observation and cor-
rection, and this is part of what makes them human, actors must be constantly
engaged in this process on their road towards a character. It is this never-
ending reflexivity, and their combination in the actor-cum-character on stage,
which suggest that we see players as 'double agents'.

Double agents reside in single persons, whom we are likely to see as
indivisible subjects in the west. This, of course, is a particular model of the
individual, and one which the players may actually challenge. From their
experience perhaps the self *is* 'dividual'. However, their vision of the world
is embodied and forms one centre of attention. We may read our contemporary South African playwright, Athol Fugard, as paradigmatic in this
respect when he says: 'the only truly safe place I have ever known in this
world, in this life I have lived, [is] at the centre of a story as its teller'
(Fugard 1992: 76).

The centre of the universe created by the actor is within herself or himself,
and it resembles what T.S. Eliot called 'the still point of the turning world'.
Stillness in this sense coincides with a sensation of a sacred place. Listen for
instance to director Peter Brook:

> The presence of an actor, what it is that gives quality to his listening and
> looking, is something rather mysterious, but not entirely so. It is not totally
> beyond his conscious and voluntary capacities. He can find this presence
> in a certain silence within himself. What one could call 'sacred theatre',
> the theatre in which the invisible appears, takes root in this silence, from
> which all sorts of known and unknown gestures can arise.
>
> (Brook 1993: 76)

Echoing this from the player's point of view, Odin actress Iben Nagel
Rasmussen says about her training: 'When I am training I am in a kind of
meditation, even though I may be working very quickly and reacting. I have
a kind of inner stillness but I am nevertheless thinking and on the lookout for
new physical possibilities' (cited in Christoffersen 1993: 105). What we
encounter here is a kind of 'concentric dualism' of being in the player's work.
There is an echo of this in another Odin actress, Roberta Carreri, when she
relates an extraordinary experience of hers in her early years of training. She

tells how something special was happening, when she discovered that she could 'turn on the switch' and be completely present during a rehearsal situation, 'be in the "now", in the action and burning in it'. She continues: 'It felt unbelievable because I did not know where the switch was, just that it had been turned on. It was a little like having jumped from one part of the brain to the other. Like jumping into another form of reality, one that is even more real, more real than your average daily reality' (Carreri, cited in Christoffersen 1993: 156). The Odin Teatret works in the vein of Grotowski, who spoke of the actors being 'penetrated' by themselves. For Peter Brook this has transformed into an 'act of possession'. In both cases there is something 'extra' to the actor which changes her or him. Barba has made a firm distinction between the daily and the extra-daily technique of the actor; it is the latter which accounts for the *life* of the character (Barba 1995: 16). It is not a matter simply of bodily mastery, like that of an acrobat, but of a dilation of energy – whether by penetration, possession or something else. Whatever the name chosen, the sensation of a doubled reality is by no means exclusive to that particular vein of theatre. Playing Hamlet, John Gielgud remembers:

> In rehearsing Hamlet I found it at first impossible to characterize. I could not 'imagine' the part, and live in it, forgetting myself in the words and adventures of the character . . . It was not until I stood before an audience that I seemed to find the breadth and voice which enabled me suddenly to shake off my self-consciousness and live the part in my imagination, while I executed the technical difficulties with another part of my consciousness at the same time.
>
> (Gielgud 1987 [1939]: 105)

This is an articulate double agency which inadvertently gets a troubled expression in Frances Baker's reminiscences of playing Ophelia in *Hamlet* (1984) with Roger Rees as Hamlet: 'As the scene proceeds and Hamlet becomes even more violent towards her, Roger clasped my face, spitting out all his accusations against women directly at her, implying that women, and particularly herself, are the direct cause of his troubled mind' (Baker, in *Players 2*: 143). The switch between third and first person for Ophelia is matched by a switch between 'Hamlet' and 'Roger' for her adversary. Without undue psychological speculation we may at least suggest that this switch is significant.

We are familiar with shifting pronouns in anthropology, and with the anthropologist finding her or his first person 'I' transformed into a third person 'she or he' in the field, where she or he is objectified by others (Hastrup 1987). Both Baker's 'Ophelia and me' and Kingsley's 'Othello and I' echo this, and it seems that in general the double agent evolves into a third person, acting on his or her own behalf, as it were.

This is exemplified by Michael Pennington, who, after having told about the extremely obliging nature of the part of Hamlet, tells how during the process of preparation, 'my imagination contracted and the play seemed to burst out of our confining thought'. As the rehearsal process moves on, so his confinement shifts from that of his own thoughts to the space left for Hamlet within the world of the play:

> I was beginning to taste the famous isolation of the part, feeling the emotional tides of a man adrift from the behaviour, the humour, the very language of his neighbours: a disorientation that in some equivalent way was beginning to separate me from colleagues and friends.
>
> (Pennington, in *Players 1*: 125)

The speaking 'I' is a third person, built from the split between the actor and the character. It is a person dilated by the energy inherent in the actor's shift to the extra-daily mode of acting. The alchemy of living theatre starts here. In the words of Richard Schechner, all effective performances share a double negation: 'Olivier is not Hamlet, but also he is not not Hamlet. . . . Performer training focuses its techniques not on making one person into another but on permitting the performer to act in between identities; in this sense performing is a paradigm of liminality' (Schechner 1985: 123). Between identities, the performer acts as a double agent.

Double agency makes it possible to work on 'becoming' and 'being' at the same time. The power of acting stems from the becoming rather than the being, as we are told by Gell about art in general: it is the magic by which a particular object is construed as having come into the world that dazzles us, not just the physical object (Gell 1992: 46). Again, the true subject of the work of art, or its efficacy in moving people, is the artistry not the artist.

This displaces agency from the actor to the actor-cum-character on stage. The result is a double agent, able to act convincingly and consistently within two motivational spaces: the space of training and performative mastery and the space of the character. It is as if the peculiar quality of the stage as a site of passage has been internalized and reflected within the actor. As agents, actors are doubly 'habituated'; if a habitus is embodied history, so deeply internalized that it is forgotten as history (Bourdieu 1990: 56), the actor must work on the basis of two of them. One is his bodily training, in which technical knowledge becomes incorporated to such a degree that it becomes second nature (cf. Hastrup 1995b); the other is the internalization the moral universe of the character and acting as deeply encultured by that universe.

Agency always takes shape within a moral horizon (Taylor 1985), and this applies no less to double agency. The actor works within two such horizons: the ethos of acting and the ethos of the character. The former motivates professionalism, the latter legitimates the passions of the character. That this is not a new insight is testified to by John Webster's remark above on the actor fortifying moral precepts with example, and even more explicitly by

Thomas Betterton, an actor who was as concerned with the qualifications of a player as are modern theoreticians in the field:

To know these different characters of established heroes the actor need only be acquainted with the poets, who write of them; if the poet who introduces them into his play has not sufficiently distinguished them. But to know the different compositions of the manners, and the passions springing from those manners, he ought to have an insight into moral philosophy, for they produce various appearances in the looks and actions, according to their various mixtures.

(Betterton, in *Actors*: 100)

So the prime companions of actors are poets and moral philosophers. One could also say that if, as Susanne Langer has suggested (cf. Geertz 1983: 29), theatre is poetry in the mode of action, then these actions are as much motivated by a moral horizon as they are inspired by the words. We cannot reduce human agency to mechanistic principles (cf. Taylor 1985). No more can acting, as an instance of agency, be reduced to common principles or natural laws. It always takes place in a particular space and within a particular corporeal field.[4]

Within this field, the agent is deeply motivated and often already 'decided' (Hastrup 1995a: 77ff). The decided body belongs to the domain of experience, not words, and the artistry of the actor partly consists in reproducing that experience (Barba 1995: 33). That is where the conviction of the art is anchored. Decisions, whether new or already 'made', are made with reference to 'strong evaluations', which form the background of our understanding of ourselves as persons (Taylor 1985: 3). Neutrality in decision making is an illusion; facts, including the facts of acts, are imbued with value (Putnam 1981: 127ff). The procedural rationality implied by objectivism rests on an ideal of disengagement, that can no longer be sustained in general (Taylor 1985: 6), and certainly not in the magic space of acting.

CURTAIN

With these last remarks on agency we are getting close to a much more general problem in anthropology than the one of reclaiming theatre as a field of study. If theatre works by way of creating 'possible' experiences, it moves its audience by demonstrating the secret world beyond the visible. The site of passage thus transferred to the spectators, they may claim a new, 'third' world for themselves. This may be the source of unprecedented empowerment.

Acting implies a kind of agency that is of necessity governed by a sense of worth; there is no human motivation without an implicit morality. The quintessential feature of human agency is the power to evaluate and rank desires and satisfactions (Taylor 1985: 17), not simply the power to act upon desires and redress sensations of pain. People respond rather than react; a sense of responsibility is part and parcel of agency.

In so far as we see theatrical performances as telescoped social performances, or as concentrated life, this qualification of agency applies equally to both theatre and life in general. Theatre provides a social drama of heightened vitality because it 'condenses' the agents' energy, not because it transforms it. Agents, whether actors on stage or in life, must be seen as self-interpreting and reflexive humans, whose motivation is governed as much by implicit moral evaluations as by disengaged minds. Motivation informs the hidden dance and transforms embodied energy into action. This is what dilates the performer's presence and potentiates him or her.

In theatre, of course, the motivation must become visible; the hidden dance must be consciously explored. Or, if you wish, motivation and intention must conflate. Just as poetry explores the language parallax to the highest degree and effect (Friedrich 1986), so theatre must explore what I would like to call the 'performative parallax' to its most radical conclusion. It is in the power of poetry and of performance to point to a world that is 'like' the one we know, yet also removed from it and placed in a parallel space. In poetry as well as dramatical performance, the practitioners deliberately enter the dynamic zone of poetic or performative indeterminacy; that is, a zone where the emotions and motives of the agents are significantly beyond the scope of exhaustive verbal description and accurate prediction (Friedrich 1986: 2). Just as poetry may have its master tropes, so theatre may have its key expressions. In both cases, the limits – of language or of ordinary bodily action – are explored and altered. This is true creativity – a creativity that reveals.

It should be recalled that this particular kind of creativity is sited in the artistry rather than in the artist; there are differences in dramatic talent, of course, but the main difference lies in the mastery of the actor's technique. This is what moves people – not by providing answers but by redirecting their own enquiries. It is for theatre as for the spirit seance studied by Schieffelin:

> the performance is gripping not because of the vivid display of symbolic materials but because the symbolic material is incomplete. Reality and conviction reside not in the spirit's message but in the tension produced when something important seems clear, while, in fact, it is still ambiguous. It is the experience of inconclusiveness and imbalance that gives people little choice but to make their own move of creative imagination if they are to make sense of what is happening.
>
> (Schieffelin 1993: 292; cf. Schieffelin, this volume)

The creative potential in theatre resides in the space between the actors and the audience, even if the artistry belongs to the actor. It is artistry which makes the audience see the possible world – beyond the obvious.

'By means of such genres as theatre . . . performances are presented

which probe a community's weaknesses, call its leaders to account, desacral-
ize its most cherished values and beliefs, portray its characteristic conflicts
and suggest remedies for them, and generally take stock of its current
situation in the known "world"' (Turner 1982: 11). In other words, just as
poetry constructs a voice out of the voices that surround it (Geertz 1983: 117),
so acting constructs an action out of those actions that surround it.

In the general theatre of self, agency is likewise centred in a corporeal field
in which meaning is always emergent or inscribed, never given or prescribed.
The parallactic potential is always latent in performance, because the subtext
of all performance is nothing but the unprecedented act itself. There is no pre-
text for action outside the doubly decided performer. The actor learns the
words, but the character acts. The power of persuasion resides in this double
agent. In the void between the two, a surplus history is created. Therein lies
the magic of acting.

NOTES

1 This chapter contains some preliminary reflections on theatre and creativity. They
   are preliminary in the sense that I am just beginning to invest research interest in
   the field (see also Hastrup 1992, 1994, 1996a, 1996b, forthcoming). It is more of
   an invitation to shared reflection, then, than it is a presentation of results. For the
   printed version I am grateful to the participants of the ASA conference mentioned
   in the preface, and not least to the convenor and editor, Felicia Hughes-Freeland,
   for constructive comments.
2 All references to *Actors* are to the volume edited by Cole and Chinoy, *Actors on
   Acting* (1970).
3 References to *Players* are to the series of *Players of Shakespeare*, volumes 1–3,
   edited by Philip Brockbank (1989, volume 1), and Russel Jackson and Robert
   Smallwood (1988, 1993, volumes 2 and 3).
4 The notion of 'corporeal field' is owed to Hanks, and denotes that larger space
   with which every individual is inextricably linked by way of the physical, sensing
   and moving body (Hanks 1990: 92ff). Thus it implies that the body is acknowledged as the locus of agency.

REFERENCES

Ardener, Edwin (1992) 'Ritual og socialt rum', *Stofskifte*, 25: 23–8.
Artaud, Antonin (1958) *The Theater and its Double*, New York: Grove Weidenfeld.
Barba, Eugenio (1986) *Beyond the Floating Islands*, New York: PAJ Publications.
—— (1995) *The Paper Canoe: A Guide to Theatre Anthropology*, London: Routledge.
Barba, Eugenio and Savarese, Nicola (eds) (1991) *The Secret Art of the Performer:
   A Dictionary of Theatre Anthropology*, London: Routledge.
Beacham, Richard C. (1995) *Roman Theatre and its Audience*, London: Routledge.
Beeman, William O. (1993) 'The anthropology of theater and spectacle', *Annual
   Review of Anthropology*, 22: 369–93.
Bittner, Rüdiger (1992) 'One action', in Amélie Oksenberg Rorty (ed.) *Essays on
   Aristotle's Poetics*, Princeton NJ: Princeton University Press.
Bourdieu, Pierre (1990) *The Logic of Practice*, Cambridge: Polity Press.

—— (1993) *The Field of Cultural Production*, Cambridge: Polity Press.

—— (1996) *The Rules of Art*, Cambridge: Polity Press.

Brecht, Bertolt (1990) *Brecht on Theatre: The Development of an Aesthetic*, ed. and trans. John Willet, London: Methuen.

Brockbank, Philip (1989) *Players of Shakespeare 1: Essays in Shakespearean Performance by Twelve Players with the Royal Shakespeare Company*, Cambridge: Cambridge University Press.

Brook, Peter (1968) *The Empty Space*, Harmondsworth: Penguin.

—— (1993) *There Are No Secrets: Thoughts on Acting and Theatre*, London: Methuen.

Bruner, Edward M. (ed.) (1984) *Text, Play and Story*, Washington DC: American Ethnological Society.

Certeau, Michel de (1984) *The Practice of Everyday Life*, Berkeley CA: University of California Press.

Chaney, David (1993) *Fictions of Collective Life: Public Drama in Late Modern Culture*, London: Routledge.

Christoffersen, Erik Exe (1993) *The Actor's Way*, London: Routledge.

Cohen, Abner (1981) *The Politics of Elite Culture: Explorations in the Dramaturgy of Power in a Modern African Society*, Berkeley CA: University of California Press.

Cole, Toby and Chinoy, Helen Krich (eds) (1970) *Actors on Acting: The Theories, Techniques, and Practices of the World's Great Actors, Told in their Own Words*, New York: Crown.

Connerton, Paul (1989) *How Societies Remember*, Cambridge: Cambridge University Press.

Friedrich, Paul (1986) *The Language Parallax: Linguistic Relativism and Poetic Indeterminacy*, Austin TX: University of Texas Press.

Fugard, Athol (1992) 'The arts and society', postscript to *Playland*, Johannesburg: Witswatersrand University Press.

Geertz, Clifford (1980) *Negara: The Theatre State in Nineteenth-Century Bali*, Princeton NJ: Princeton University Press.

—— (1983) 'Art as a cultural system', in *Local Knowledge*, London: Basic Books.

Gell, Alfred (1992) 'The technology of enchantment and the enchantment of technology', in Jeremy Coote and Anthony Shelton (eds) *Anthropology, Art, Aesthetics*, Oxford: Clarendon Press.

Gielgud, John (1987 [1939]) *Early Stages*, London: Hodder and Stoughton.

Green, J.R. (1994) *Theatre in Ancient Greek Society*, London: Routledge.

Grotowski, Jerzy (1975) *Towards a Poor Theatre*, London: Methuen.

Halliwell, Stephen (1987) *The Poetics of Aristotle: Translation and Commentary*, London: Duckworth.

Hanks, William (1990) *Referential Practice, Language and Lived Space among the Maya*, Chicago: University of Chicago Press.

Harris, John Wesley (1992) *Medieval Theatre in Context: An Introduction*, London: Routledge.

Hastrup, Kirsten (1987) 'Fieldwork among friends', in Anthony Jackson (ed.) *Anthropology at Home*, London: Routledge.

—— (1992) 'Out of anthropology: The anthropologist as an object of dramatic representation', *Cultural Anthropology*, 7: 327–45.

—— (1993) 'Hunger and the hardness of facts', *Man*, 28: 727–39.

—— (1994) 'Anthropological knowledge incorporated: discussion', in Kirsten Hastrup and Peter Hervik (eds) *Social Experience and Anthropological Knowledge*, London: Routledge.

—— (1995a) *A Passage to Anthropology: Between Experience and Theory*, London: Routledge.

——(1995b) 'Incorporated knowledge', in Thomas Leabhart (ed.) *Incorprated Knowledge: The Mime Journal*, 1995: 2–9.

—— (ed.) (1996a) *The Performers' Village: Times, Theories and Techniques at ISTA*, Copenhagen: Drama.

—— (1996b) 'Theatrum mundi: the making of theatre and history', in Kirsten Hastrup (ed.) *The Performers' Village: Times, Theories and Techniques at ISTA*, Copenhagen: Drama.

—— (forthcoming) 'Othello's dance: cultural creativity and human agency', in John Liep (ed.) *Locating Cultural Creativity.*

Jackson, Russel and Smallwood, Robert (eds) (1988) *Players of Shakespeare 2: Further Essays on Shakespearean Performance by Players with the Royal Shakespeare Company*, Cambridge: Cambridge University Press.

—— (1993) *Players of Shakespeare 3: Further Essays on Shakespearean Performance by Players with the Royal Shakespeare Company*, Cambridge: Cambridge University Press.

Johnson, Mark (1987) *The Body in the Mind*, Chicago: University of Chicago Press.

Lévi-Strauss, Claude (1958) *Anthropologie Structurale*, Paris: Plon.

—— (1962) *La Pensée sauvage*, Paris: Plon.

Ley, Graham (1991) *Ancient Greek Theater*, Chicago: University of Chicago Press.

Mauss, Marcel (1972) *A General Theory of Magic*, London: Routledge and Kegan Paul.

Mullaney, Steven (1988) *The Place of the Stage: License, Play, and Power in Renaissance England*, Chicago: University of Chicago Press.

—— (1991) 'Civic rites, city sites: the place of the stage', in David Scott Kastan and Peter Stallybrass (eds) *Staging the Renaissance. Reinterpretations of Elizabethan and Jacobean Drama*, London: Routledge.

Putnam, Hilary (1981) *Reason, Truth, and History*, Cambridge: Cambridge University Press.

Rehm, Rush (1992) *Greek Tragic Theatre*, London: Routledge.

Schechner, Richard (1985) *Between Theater and Anthropology*, Philadelphia: University of Pennsylvania Press.

—— (1988) *Performance Theory*, London: Routledge.

—— (1993) *The Future of Ritual: Writings on Culture and Performance*, London: Routledge.

Schieffelin, Edward L. (1993) 'Performance and the cultural construction of reality', in Smadar Lavie, Kirin Narayan and Renato Rosaldo (eds) *Creativity/ Anthropology*, Ithaca NY: Cornell University Press.

Smith, David L., Strier, Richard and Bevington, David (eds) (1995) *The Theatrical City: Culture, Theatre and Politics in London 1576–1649*, Cambridge: Cambridge University Press.

Taylor, Charles (1985) *Human Agency and Language*, Cambridge: Cambridge University Press.

Thomson, Peter (1992) *Shakespeare's Theatre*, London: Routledge.

Turner, Victor (1974) *Dramas, Fields and Metaphors: Symbolic Action in Human Society*, Ithaca NY and London: Cornell University Press.

—— (1982) *From Ritual to Theatre: The Human Seriousness of Play*, New York: PAJ Publications.

Watson, Ian (1993) *Towards a Third Theatre: Eugenio Barba and the Odin Teatret*, London: Routledge.

Yates, Frances A. (1987 [1969]) *Theatre of the World*, London: Routledge and Kegan Paul.

Chapter 2

Performing pilgrimage
Walsingham and the ritual construction of irony
Simon Coleman and John Elsner

INTRODUCTION: PILGRIMAGE AS PERFORMANCE

> Walsingham is like a huge icon. It's almost like a Christian theme park, in
> which we set out the wares and then allow people to make of it what they
> will. And I think there's something about that which is very therapeutic:
> that they'll make the stations of the cross; they'll just come and sit in the
> shrine; they'll sit in the gardens; they'll go and light candles; they'll sit in
> the Holy House and just look at the image; they'll go for a walk up to the
> parish church; they'll go and visit the Orthodox chapel or they'll go and
> buy things in the shops to take home. All of that I think is very, very
> significant, because it's the best kind of spiritual direction, which actually
> allows a pilgrim to find his or her own way in what God offers. . . .
> And I think we just make available these resources, and people use them
> as they find best.

These are the words, spoken in an interview, of a priest at the Anglican shrine
of Walsingham, north Norfolk. They indicate some of the elements he
considers key to the performance of a successful pilgrimage: the sense, for
instance, that a pilgrim must find a spiritual direction not only on the way to
a sacred shrine, but also within the environs of the sacred space; the
conviction, as well, that ritualized 'browsing', far from representing an
heretical evasion of fixed liturgical structures, will have divinely sanctioned
and therapeutic – even performative – effects.

Such attitudes might initially seem surprising because they come from a
source hardly known for its encouragement of liturgical innovation. The
Anglican shrine at Walsingham has the reputation within ecclesiastical
circles of being a defender of old-style, High-Church principles, indicated as
much by its continuation of unashamedly 'smells and bells' styles of ritual
as by its apparently firm opposition to the ordination of women. In this chapter,
however, we wish to argue that the priest has nevertheless identified an
important aspect of much contemporary pilgrimage to Walsingham. We
propose to examine the relationship between carrying out pilgrimage rituals
and the cultivation of creativity in performance by exploring the ways in

which many visitors to the site use Christian tradition and liturgy less as sources of fixed legitimacy than as flexible symbolic means or resources through which to ritualize social relations.

Some pilgrimages to both the Anglican and the Roman Catholic shrines at Walsingham can be described as 'official' and 'controlled' in the sense that they involve organized journeys, usually arranged by a given parish, to the sacred sites of a single religious tradition. Many visitors, however (including some who come on supposedly collectively co-ordinated pilgrimages), act as self-conscious spiritual bricoleurs, constructing their own paths through the numerous sacred foci of the village. The shrines of both main religious groups in the village encode implicit narrative versions of the Walsingham tradition in their spaces and liturgies, yet such narratives can be subverted by pilgrims as they cut and paste their way through the village, experimenting with a variety of religious genres without necessarily endorsing any single one of them. In practice, Walsingham – or rather 'the Walsingham experience' – offers a continuum of ritualized performances: at one end lies the potential for full and deliberate submission to liturgical order; at the other a self-conscious cultivation of pilgrimage as innovation is evident, in which ritual improvisation is invested with a form of sacramental irony.

We contend that the power of many of the more innovative examples of pilgrimage we examine lies in the self-aware transformation of traditional liturgy into performances that simultaneously genuflect towards conventional ritual forms and yet subvert those forms in the very act of genuflection. In the process, the boundaries of ritual action are shifted and expanded. People may create sacralized performances incorporating the pubs, gift-, souvenir- and tea-shops and even the nearby seaside in their pilgrimages, or draw canonical texts and liturgy into dialogue with personal, often overtly secular images and practices taken from everyday life, the imagination, literature, films and theatre. In these instances, ritual is not merely submitted to determination by history and evaluation by participants through being performed (cf. Schieffelin 1995); it is actively accommodated to personal preferences before it is even staged.

Walsingham therefore acts as a physical 'medium' for pilgrimage, offering various spaces for the enactment of rituals. However, as a holy site the village is not so much a single place as a roughly defined set of activities broadly contained within a permeable temporal and spatial frame. Such activities involve shifting fields of social relations that can move over periods of hours or days around sometimes interlocking, sometimes separate arenas of action. During a pilgrimage, a person can experience a number of sites or liturgies with varying combinations of friends, partners or kin, and then return in future years to repeat a similar process.

In some of the following, then, we shall move far from the view of ritual constructing a coercive formality that links particular events into a pre-existing order (cf. Bloch 1974). Where pilgrims become authors or self-conscious orchestrators of their own pilgrimages, the degree to which they are forced into submission by established liturgical orders is greatly reduced. The pilgrimages described here raise complex issues regarding the relationship between constraint and creativity (cf. Hastrup and Gore, both this volume). While pilgrimage is turned into a kind of 'play' in many cases, casual tourists as well as pilgrims may also come to see themselves as engaging in activities that transcend purely self-indulgent leisure. Furthermore, even improvised performances are not usually created *de novo*, since they are defined by simultaneously echoing and altering conventional forms.

It should be clear by now that we view the performance of ritual as involving much more than the mere replication of a given liturgical script. Rather, in the case of Walsingham it can frequently be seen as a strategic deployment of symbolic resources. Performance in this sense comes close to Bell's definition of the process of ritualization as 'a way of acting that is designed and orchestrated to distinguish and privilege what is being done in comparison to other, usually more quotidian, activities' (1992: 74). The virtue of this definition is that it does not presume to specify universal, necessary features of sacred or secular activity, but rather stresses the idea of differentiating – by whatever means – one form of action or behaviour from another. Adapting Bell's notion of ritualization, one can argue that ritual performances carried out by pilgrims act semiotically to create a sense of 'difference' in relation to whatever other actions they wish to invoke and transcend. Many parishes do not come to Walsingham in order to engage in novel forms of ritual *per se*. Instead, their pilgrimage enables them to carry out their normal forms of worship in a particularly authoritative context. To celebrate Mass or carry out the stations of the cross at a national shrine – and moreover one where unknown others are seen to be doing the same –therefore gives such actions a significance they would not have in a local church. Their ritual action as pilgrims is defined not merely in relation to everyday life, but also in comparison to other ritual in a more 'workaday' context. For others, the playful 'misuse' of conventional liturgical forms is a form of ritualization of ritual, in the sense that it is an active transformation of Anglo-Catholic or Roman Catholic liturgy, a metacommentary on religious orthodoxy that signals association with, but also distance from, such orthodoxy.

WALSINGHAM AS A GENRE OF PILGRIMAGE

Our characterization of ritual performance at Walsingham has implications for analyses of pilgrimage as a whole. Broadly Durkheimian perspectives see the phenomenon as a ritual means of integrating disparate sections of society (e.g. Wolf 1958). Others have characterized pilgrimages as legitimating oppressive ideologies (e.g. Gross 1971). The Turners (1978) famously proposed that pilgrimage provides a ritual means of reversing conventional social structures, not least through the generation of states of 'communitas', though critics have viewed their work as expressing more of a religious ideal than a sociological reality (e.g. Sallnow 1981, Coleman and Elsner 1995). Recently, Eade and Sallnow (1991) have attempted to distance themselves from the alleged determinism of Durkheimian, Marxist or Turnerian analyses. Their thesis is that a deconstruction of the fetishized notion of an autonomously powerful holy place is necessary. Rather, pilgrimage should be seen as involving:

> an arena for competing religious and secular discourses, for both the official co-optation and non-official recovery of religious meanings, for conflict between orthodoxies, sects, and confessional groups, for drives towards consensus and communitas, and for counter-movements towards separateness and division.
>
> (Eade and Sallnow 1991: 2)

Eade and Sallnow's position is a powerful one, avoiding the dangers of essentializing pilgrimage and its constituent elements. However, we contend that they do not give sufficient weight to the infinitely modulated nuances in performing pilgrimage which are evident in many of the ritual forms we discuss. For Eade and Sallnow, apparent holiness lies in the emptiness of shrines, with the latters' universalism 'ultimately constituted not by a unification of discourses but rather by the capacity of a cult to entertain and respond to a plurality' (1991: 15). We agree on the issue of multiple discourses, but would stress that in another, important sense, the 'religious void' is in fact full. It is full in the way that the 'empty space' of a theatre is full – crowded with material props, holy objects and reminiscences of other holy sites; crowded with pilgrims who may even be reaffirming the sanctity of the site not least through performances of ritual.

Walsingham, then, can be understood as an 'empty space' in the theatrical sense proposed by Peter Brook (1968) (cf. Hastrup, this volume). The sacred site is a particular kind of dramatic arena in which an overdetermination of material resources is offered to pilgrims, providing props with which to enact their own play – whether this means wholesale participation in the range of 'official' activities on offer, ironic reflection on such activities, or private rituals whose value is defined by their personal significance to the actors. The sanctity of Walsingham as England's prime Marian shrine lies in the constant interaction of its complex topography and rich material culture with different scripts endlessly performed by different groups of pilgrims.[1]

The idea that a sacred site like Walsingham may effectively be a stage, well equipped for certain kinds of performance which its pilgrims come to enact, resonates with recent discussions of the museum in western culture. Carol Duncan argues (1995: 7–20) that art museums are sites imbued with sanctity through their architectural forms, their shrine-like displays and the elevated levels of aesthetic contemplation many visitors expect to attain there. They are thus liminal spaces in which visitors indulge in particular forms of ritual which involve both watching the 'play' of objects put on by the curators and constructing their own performances of interpretation, in which: 'people continually "misread" or scramble or resist the museum's cues to some extent; or they actively invent, consciously or unconsciously, their own programs according to all the historical or psychological accidents of who they are' (1995: 13).

Where the pilgrimage site is more radical than both museum and theatre is in its provision of a much more active space for 'misreading'. While misunderstandings of and resistance to an official or established narrative in the theatre or the museum tend to lie in the area of the interpretation of a series of givens (a play's script or a museum display), in Walsingham the potential for such resistance is actively encouraged in the spaces provided for personal pilgrimages. What the official liturgies and topography of the site provide – apart from an establishment script for those who want it – is precisely a series of cues to be missed, a great number of props to be played with, a formal structure of ritual to be ironized.

SETTING THE SCENE: WALSINGHAM AS A STAGE

The stage

Little Walsingham, a small and picturesque village in Norfolk, is an extra-ordinarily rich venue for the interactive and processional theatre of pilgrim-age. At the heart (both of the village and of the pilgrimage, physically and conceptually) lies an absent centre: the ruins of a medieval Augustinian priory destroyed in the Reformation in 1538. This ruin, set in the grounds of a privately owned minor stately home, is open to tourists.[2] It is also the probable site of the original 'Holy House' of Walsingham, built according to legend in Anglo-Saxon times in response to a vision of the Virgin granted to an aristocratic woman named Richeldis. The structure was supposed to represent, in accordance with the wishes of the Virgin, an exact copy of the house Jesus occupied in Nazareth, and as a result Walsingham is sometimes called 'England's Nazareth'. In the sixteenth century, the Holy House and its medieval statue of the Virgin formed a principal target of iconoclasts.

Directly to the north of the priory ruins is the Anglican shrine, a privately owned and administered centre of Anglo-Catholicism which moved there in 1931 from the parish church. The shrine is not only the spiritual centre of Anglo-Catholic pilgrimage to Walsingham, it is also its functional heart, offering hospices, dining facilities and a social centre for pilgrims. Its church is built over what appears to be a Saxon well, the only monument in Walsingham to date back to the legendary period of Richeldis and her vision.[3] However, the *pièce de résistance* is a rebuilt Holy House placed within the

Figure 2.1 Procession with the Host through the grounds of the Anglican shrine, adjacent to the church containing the Holy House

church, whose fabric is in part composed of stones gathered from monasteries destroyed in the Reformation (see Figure 2.1). This building houses the Anglican replica of the statue of Our Lady of Walsingham.

Beside the Roman Catholic parish church on the south side of the village is a hospice and pilgrim bureau. These organizations provide accommodation, food and a social centre for visitors whose pilgrimage focuses not on the village but on the Slipper Chapel and Chapel of Reconciliation at the Roman Catholic shrine, situated about a mile outside the village to the south. The Slipper Chapel is a fourteenth-century building which was once (probably) a stopping-off point for medieval pilgrims to Walsingham, but is now owned by the Roman Catholics and houses their replica of the medieval statue of Our Lady.

Between the shrines, in particular along the High Street and around the Village Pump, are ranged a string of souvenir shops, pubs and tea-rooms. These offer a treasure trove of sacred knick-knacks: Virgins that glow in the dark, icons and statues, postcards with religious themes and other souvenirs. The shops help to orchestrate a spatial dynamics in which they indicate that the 'truly' holy spots – the shrines, the ruins – are yet to be approached. They provide acceptable spaces of apparent secularity within the process of modern Walsingham pilgrimage, as opposed to other kinds of secular space like the housing estate to the north-west of the village which is divorced from the pilgrimage complex and which provides a mostly invisible backdrop to the conventional staging of ritual performance.

The sets and props

Some material 'props' upon which pilgrims' performances can focus are familiar features of Christian ritual – such as the stations of the cross available at both shrines. Others are more unusual or at least flamboyant by the standards of English worship. These include the many offertories, relics, sacred objects and votives which clutter the space of the Anglican church. The two polychrome replica statues of Our Lady of Walsingham kept in the Slipper Chapel and in the Holy House clearly mark the most conventionally sacred spots of their respective settings. Before these images, both imitations of an original, medieval image, and housed in buildings with the maximum of medieval resonance, pilgrims often pray in private as well as celebrating Mass.

Both shrines also offer visitors numerous other opportunities to engage physically with the site. The Slipper Chapel and the Holy House encourage pilgrims to light candles, and both include areas to collect holy water to take home or drink on the spot. The places are to be interacted with and not merely viewed, even if the visitor's knowledge, commitment and/or liturgical competence are somewhat limited. Thus, below is a piece of dialogue overheard by one of the authors in the village museum. Two tourists question a guide, apparently regarding Anglican and Roman Catholic sites as undiffer-entiatedly sacred sources of a pilgrimage 'souvenir':

TOURIST: How do we get to the church?
GUIDE: Which one?
TOURIST: The one with the holy water.
GUIDE: You get holy water at both the Anglican and the Catholic churches.
TOURIST: Which is the nearest?

DIMENSIONS OF PERFORMANCE

As we shall see, some pilgrims play with sacred boundaries in ways rather more skilful and self-conscious than the tourists mentioned above. We argue that a useful way to characterize variations in attitude and performance is along a dimension indicating distance from perceived orthodoxy in liturgical practice. The variations we have observed have been suggested to us as a result both of accompanying pilgrims round the shrines and talking to them either informally during their stays in Walsingham or in recorded interviews, often away from the village.[4]

Canonical enactments

Perhaps the 'ideal type' of the conventional pilgrimage to both Anglo- and Roman Catholic shrines is provided by the annual, parish-based visit. These are often carried out over a given weekend and consist of a number of generally invariant elements: a series of Masses; carrying out the stations of the cross; a procession incorporating the Virgin or Host (Figures 2.1 and 2.2); confession and prayers for intercession. In the Anglican shrine, pilgrims will also be sprinkled with holy water from the Saxon well. Such pilgrimages are ideally to be experienced collectively by a group of people who are likely to know each other well during their everyday lives, who tend to come to the site at the same time each year. As one Anglican pilgrim put it, describing how her parish would be leaving Walsingham the next day, but would already be anticipating its return:

> Quarter to two tomorrow afternoon, we all assemble around the Holy House and we have our prayers of departure which is very sad. . . . But we always say – right, next year.

In such cases, coming to Walsingham provides more than a sense of stability, however. It also invests the activities of the parish with translocal significance – and one that can only be provided by a national pilgrimage

Figure 2.2 Procession with Virgin, about to set off from the centre of Walsingham down the Holy Mile to the Roman Catholic shrine

site. A Roman Catholic resident of the village, who has also been engaged in the work of the Anglican shrine, notes:

> A lot of parishes look to Walsingham. It's a great experience for them because they come from a parish where possibly not very many people go to church, and maybe they feel it's a bit of a struggle to keep what they feel is important going there. . . . When they come on their annual pilgrimage, it's great because a whole lot of them go; there's a programme laid on. . . . Then they go down to the parish church Mass on a Sunday, and the church is bursting with people, and they suddenly think, my goodness this is wonderful, you know? Now we can go back and hang on.

For Anglo-Catholics in particular, the sense of collective validation that pilgrimage can bring is important, given that they are likely to perceive themselves as a beleaguered minority within the contemporary Anglican church. However, for both Anglo- and Roman Catholics, various ritualized means of linking their own parish indexically with the site exist. Candles may be lit in remembrance of people or groups back home, or the names of particular people invoked during the recitation of 'Hail Marys'. The performance of stations of the cross at both shrines links a parish not only with a national centre of faith, of course, but also with a biblical narrative which is both recalled and enacted. At such times, a priest might use short homilies spoken at each station to reflect upon matters related to the local parish or particular members of his congregation. This sense of the need to use performance as a method of investing 'everyday' religious practice with wider significance is described by an Anglican priest (himself a regular visitor throughout his career, with a variety of parishes), who states:

> Well I think why people like coming here, and . . . people [from my parish] have been coming 40–50 years, is that it's both unlike home, in the sense that Walsingham is a village not a bit like [industrial town in the north of England], but on the other hand the religion is something which fits. There are so many things I suppose which people take for granted, or don't see the point of at home. You come here and it begins to fall into place. . . . After a while you realise that what you do back [home] in say a church that was built at the end of the last century has been going on in some of these churches for seven or eight centuries, and it makes you feel that you are part of something which is more than . . . just local, just the way we do it, just the way people have been doing it in my lifetime.

In this description, echoed by other pilgrims to Walsingham, we see the idea of a parish observing itself performing pilgrimage in a highly charged liturgical context, and coming therefore to see itself in transcendent terms. Part of the power of the visit comes from the way local and national forms of worship parallel or 'fit' each other. It is also the case, however, that for some pilgrims Walsingham is a place to be seen by others – to demonstrate to the church and the world that one has chosen to go to such a sacred centre. This element of demonstration takes on an element of defiance among Anglo-Catholics who go to the more controversial Anglican shrine, and is made explicit on days of the Anglican national pilgrimage, when those processing through the streets have to run the gauntlet of evangelical Protestants who stand in the centre of the village and accuse them of idolatry.

Conventional parish pilgrimages vary in the extent to which they incorporate wall-to-wall liturgy. Some fill every moment of the day with sacred activities. Others explicitly incorporate periods of leisure, although such periods of fun, while seen as a necessary part of the experience, tend to be kept separate from strictly liturgical activities. One middle-aged Anglican woman, Beryl, states:

> The essence of a good pilgrimage in my eyes ... is that ... you can involve the reverence of the shrine ... [but also include, at other moments] ... the fun that we have. I mean this afternoon I organized a walk, and there were eighteen of us went on this walk even in the rain. And we went up to St Peter's in the fields, went in there, and ... looked at the architecture and everything, and then we walked up to the National Trust Craft Centre, had coffee there, and then walked on the old road back into Little Walsingham. . . . And it was wonderful.

Apart from stressing that the 'fun' is complementary to rather than mixed with the liturgy, as well as mentioning that her definition of pilgrimage has received 'official' approval, Beryl also takes care to note the large numbers who went on the outing, implying as she does elsewhere that collective action during the trip provides an important indication of group solidarity. Her commitment to the pilgrimage as involving periods of serious, even solemn moments that are orchestrated by the shrine and its officials is also indicated by the following description of how she felt when she first entered the Anglican shrine and Holy House:

> Absolute awe. A very old priest friend of mine ... met me at the gate there, and he said, right, this is your first time, come on in. And he took me into that Holy House, and I think every candle was lit, and I just stood there, in awe, and I felt enveloped, completely, and that's all I can say. And I felt this was my, you know, place.

Beryl expresses eloquently sentiments that are evident in other parish pilgrims' accounts, in which Walsingham is valued less as a liminoid opportunity to play with identity (cf. Turner 1982) than as a means of locating self-identity and ritual performance within a wider, amplified liturgical frame. As one Anglican priest put it, describing his first visit to the national pilgrimage, what was striking about the pilgrimage experience was its scale and intensity as much as the form of worship:

> I think I would say that while I was mesmerized of course by seeing hundreds of priests . . . and you know bishops concelebrating and all that – it was marvellous, it was everything a genuflectious youth would want. Benediction given simultaneously in three places: I was beside myself with excitement!

The importance of physical confirmations of faith should not be under-estimated in a branch of Christianity that stresses the sacramental means of achieving grace. For many Anglo-Catholics, Walsingham achieves a kind of holiness precisely because it provides the correct material background to performances of pilgrimage. Thus, one middle-aged man who has actually retired and come to live near Walsingham describes how the beauty and liturgical perfection of Walsingham led, at least in his memory, to a focusing on the village that required few other distractions: 'I mean, we used to come to Walsingham for donkey's years every year and never move out while we were there. We'd have a week and we'd never go out of Walsingham.'

Both the couple described above and many who go on formal parish pilgrimages attempt to locate themselves as exactly as possible, theologically and spatially, within a particular religious tradition. Indeed, a priest who currently works at the Anglican shrine referred in an interview to the difficulties involved in persuading visiting parishes to allow him to be experimental with liturgy. Each performance is to be like a 'token' replicating an original 'type' (cf. Lewis 1980), while descriptions of their experiences by such pilgrims tend strongly to affirm the idea that a 'communitas'-like solidarity is generated among those who go.[5] The literal and metaphorical location of the self within tradition allows the performance of pilgrimage to act for some like a form of restricted ritual code, an embodiment of collective belonging to particular forms of religious authority and stability.

Performing irony

Many other dimensions of participation than those described above exist, and they involve a much more complex attitude towards engagement in canonical ritual forms.[6] A number of pilgrims, *pace* Rappaport (1974: 31), may regard participation in pilgrimage to Walsingham as implying something less than a public acceptance of liturgical order. Instead, participation can imply to the self and even to some of one's fellow pilgrims a form of ironic engagement that comes close to parody.[7] One trainee priest noted:

> I think it's really great, I love it. I mean it's not, lock stock and barrel my cup of tea, but that colour and commitment and enthusiasm are really wonderful. Yes it is quite vulgar, extremely vulgar in places, but I mean fairgrounds are vulgar, and I think there's a great deal of overlap between Walsingham and a fairground.

If for some pilgrims, such as those examined in the previous section, it is necessary to distinguish the fun part of the pilgrimage from its serious side, here the ludic aspect of the experience is incorporated *into* the interpretation and positive evaluation of pilgrimage liturgy. What is evoked here is less a sense of awe and more one of wry amusement in an unconscious echo of the shrine priest who referred to Walsingham as a Christian theme park. This pilgrim described himself as a loner, and moreover one not particularly wedded to Anglo-Catholicism. His engagement with the shrine had little to do with the articulation of group identity and much more with a form of self-realization. He described the experience of going to Walsingham – itself an unusual event for him – as 'a point of departure if you like rather than something that I sought and wanted to immerse myself in', and indeed at one point he actually left the village to engage in a 'slightly strange caper in the Norfolk countryside one night', involving a visit with a friend to a night club. Significantly, however, such an act was regarded only partially as a rebellion against the formality of shrine liturgy; in another sense he saw himself as acting perfectly within the spirit (as well as the temporal frame) of pilgrim-age, engaging in an intense if not conventionally sacred experience with a chosen companion in a context very different to that of his quotidian existence. Another pilgrim referred, in the same vein, to a walk he had taken with a companion along a nearby beach. Such an event, during which the two had talked in ways they would never have done at home, was the high point of his visit to 'Walsingham'.

The description of Walsingham as vulgar is strikingly common among certain interviewees. Yet it is usually not intended as a simple criticism of the site, but is more an acceptance of the appropriateness of vulgarity in the set-apart context of a pilgrimage. This appropriateness seems to lie in the playful aspect it lends to ritual performance. Here is another reflection on the pilgrimage experience, again from a young man very involved in the Church of England:

> I think the whole idea of it being a sort of religious holiday is important, that you can go and do . . . things you wouldn't normally do in church. You can cross yourself hugely, and genuflect at every available shrine, and you can do sort of High Church stuff, get a feeling for it in a way that you can't elsewhere.

The pilgrim does not see his religious identity as essentially bound up with High Anglicanism. Rather, the pilgrimage allows him to engage temporarily in forms of 'ritual excess'. His viewing of the experience as somehow less serious than normal ritual is reinforced by his perception that the pilgrimage mixes sacred and secular genres of performance:

> It's very theatrical. . . . There is in it something quite self-conscious. . . . I can't take it too seriously. . . . It's two-dimensional in the way that

camp is often two-dimensional. . . . It's in good bad taste. . . . You know, you can enjoy it and enter into it, but you never need take it too seriously. But I do know that people do take it seriously.

Or again, describing being sprinkled at the Anglican shrine:

It was quite moving. . . . There was a man taking photographs of us as we went through the well . . . and I felt that was a bit out of order really. . . . But that's part of the whole two-dimensional thing about it. I mean you're at a moment of great intimacy and spiritual intensity and there's this flash. And I think there's something about that, about Walsingham, that's sort of consonant with that.

In one sense, this pilgrim's perception of what he is doing is similar to that of the 'parish' pilgrims, in that going to Walsingham encourages a certain degree of self-consciousness whereby he is forced to consider whether he 'fits' within the religious tradition on offer. He is, however, far from feeling the need to engage conventionally in canonical forms of worship; rather, his involvement seems akin to watching himself as he passes through a hall of distorting mirrors, each presenting him with an image of himself that is an amusing self-parody. Ritual here seems to be about a temporary dwelling in an alternative role, a means of experiencing the world of a liturgical 'other' without permanently crossing the boundaries into that world. The young man is actually rather surprised when a part of the liturgy proves to be emotionally charged. Other pilgrims express this ambivalence at the way Walsingham combines affect with spectacle by comparing it to the experience of inhabiting, for a brief period, a fictional, Chaucerian world of conviviality and self-conscious spirituality.

Similar attitudes are evident in comments on the tourist/pilgrim shops in Walsingham. The question is easily raised whether the shops are selling portable embodiments of the charisma of the place or knick-knacks, valued not least because their tastelessness has a ludic if not ludicrous quality, like a stick of rock bought from a seaside resort. Such purchases express the ambiguity of the whole experience for some – they are fun, but not the kind of thing one would indulge in at home. In this sense, the very fact that people feel free to buy goods from religious traditions other than their own is also significant: a number of interviewees have bought icons even though they are not Orthodox, for instance, implying that they feel free to experiment with other religious genres without necessarily being seen entirely to endorse them.

The ludic element of pilgrimage need not be expressed through a revelling in vulgarity, however. Instead, the mixture of genres – secular and sacred, theatrical and liturgical – made available on pilgrimage can be exploited with rather more gravity. One Roman Catholic pilgrim, for instance, talked of a weekend visit with a group of fellow theology students, most of them

Anglican. She described a performance of the stations of the cross put on by two of her party, who had previously been drama students:

> This particular weekend it had been snowing, and I think it had snowed the day before and there was ice and still a bit of snow around. . . . And [the people who were arranging the pilgrimage] organized these stations of the cross all around the streets and country lanes. . . . And . . . instead of having visual markers as you would do in the gardens, they acted out the scenes of the stations without announcing them first. . . . I thought 'Oh, this is a bit different from hot, dusty Palestine. . . . It's going to be a bit funny walking around all these slushy, cold, Norfolk country lanes, pretending that we're dying of the heat in Jerusalem.' But what they actually did was cleverly use the conditions we were actually in – the cold, the damp, and snow – to make the points, to incorporate them into the devotions. And there was one point . . . on the corner of the road. . . . The man who . . . was playing the part of Jesus – he was only wearing shirtsleeves . . . and he fell over in the mud, and just got covered. . . . And he got up and angrily said 'Oh, I've had enough of this, I'm not going on with it . . .' And everybody was just terribly awkward and thinking 'Oh no, what's going to happen next?' And just as he was saying this, one of the students who was standing in the crowd of us . . . he just walked out of the group standing there, and took off his coat . . . and put it on him, and suddenly we all realised that was Simon of Cyrene taking the cross. . . . It was extraordinarily effective.

This example refers to a collective experience, as the boundaries between drama, liturgy and 'real life' are skilfully broken down. The effectiveness of the performance seems to lie in its geographical and liturgical variations on standard enactments of the stations. Convention is made to refer indexically to the unique group of pilgrims present – a group that may never gather again in the same way, unlike the parishes described earlier. Most strikingly, of course, the boundaries between performance and audience are transgressed through an action that appears out of place, but is then reassimilated within sacred narrative, as the identity of Simon of Cyrene is established. The device of making the audience/participants feel that the actors have come out of character has an effect very different to usual notions of the way ritual works: it explicitly incorporates the unexpected. The result is not so much irony as 'serious' play.

One can re-examine this analysis in the light of Peacock's (1990) argument, developed partially in relation to primitive Baptists, but also supposedly the general traditions of western salvation religions, that the notion of performing the sacred is almost an oxymoron. For Peacock, to perform is a sign of inauthenticity, an indication of the triumph of stylized form over meaning. What is going on in the theatrical performance of the stations of the cross is admittedly a partial denial of the legitimacy of fixed ritual located in the conventional spaces of Walsingham. Yet the ritual is very far from the conscious denial of dramatic form and cultivation of spontaneity character-istic of, say, primitive Baptism. In one sense the ritual focuses attention on itself as performance, an activity staged for the group clearly different from anything done before or since, but explicitly modelled on and parallel with following the stations of the cross. The enactment of the stations thus presents an ambiguous Janus-face to convention: it takes place at one remove from the Anglican or Roman Catholic site geographically and liturgically, yet is sufficiently close to be encompassed by the space and time of a pilgrimage to Walsingham. It would not have been the same if it had been staged one winter afternoon in the London districts of Islington or Putney. The event thereby remains faithful (albeit probably unwittingly) to one tradition at Walsingham, that of transformation through a kind of semi-replication – a practice we have also seen in the various versions of the Holy House, or multiple images of the Virgin. After all, Walsingham itself – 'England's Nazareth' – has made its name as an East Anglian appropriation and transformation of a place in Palestine: the village provides not merely a flexible stage for pilgrimage performances, but also easy if vicarious access to a mythically charged, biblical landscape.

The kind of performance being described here is therefore a little different from the revelling in campness described earlier. Both forms of play provide ways of distancing oneself from convention, but to be camp is merely to exaggerate the traditional forms of liturgy, whereas this performance actually recreates liturgy. Interestingly, the latter, perhaps because it is so much more personalized in form, seems largely devoid of irony – extraordinarily effective rather than two-dimensional fun.

Neither set of attitudes is revolutionary, however, in the sense of imple-menting a permanent transformation of official pilgrimage liturgy: rather, both actually require the presence of canonical forms as symbols and actions against which to define themselves. Such canonical forms are useful re-sources, therefore, but are not to be taken as the only divinely sanctioned means to achieve powerful religious experiences. Indeed, it seems significant that so many of those interviewed even regarded the original legend of Mary sending a message to Richeldis, or the early history of the site, as essentially irrelevant to the site's importance for them. The significance of pilgrimages for more 'playful' visitors lies in its ability to become a cipher for the cultivation of powerful personal or group experiences. Like 'parish' pilgrims, they see Walsingham as providing an arena for the consolidation of social relationships. However, they are less concerned with the collective affirma-tion of commonality in belief, faith and practice, and more interested in a celebration of idiosyncratic, perhaps temporary social formations (such as the particular group of Anglican and Roman Catholic theology students men-tioned above, or relationships between just two people) or even in the cultivation of entirely personalized experiences.

Thus both kinds of pilgrim are likely to agree that Walsingham acts, as one interviewee put it, like a 'pressure cooker' for human relationships, but their forms of sociality and, often, frames of ritual performance are likely to differ. One pilgrim, a deaconess who is opposed to the shrine's opposition to women priests, noted how she had spent much of her time meditating on her own in the Holy House; only towards the end of her interview did she actually remember that her pilgrimage group had included not only personal friends, but also an entire parish from south London, so little an impact had the latter made on her memory of her visit. She also stated of the site:

> I have a sneaking suspicion that Walsingham is probably like Scottish culture and Celtic Christianity. They're both inventions of the nineteenth century. . . . I don't think it matters. I think it expresses something we want to express and can express through that place. . . . It would be false to say this is something we've inherited unchanged from the medieval period. Actually, we've invented it for ourselves.

Such a statement, especially from a member of the clergy, would probably seem puzzling to her fellow pilgrims from south London. Yet it states eloquently the idea predominant among some visitors that pilgrimage derives its value from being constantly reinvented in performance rather than becoming a fetishized container of fixed structures of authority.

CONCLUDING REMARKS

Hastrup notes that 'whenever we orientate ourselves in place, we actively constitute a space' (1994: 225). In this chapter, we have traced some of the ways in which various pilgrims to Walsingham use ostensibly the same site to constitute very different spaces for performance. 'Canonical' and 'ironic' forms of pilgrimage present alternative ways to incarnate symbolic action: in one, the individual and group attempt a perfect replication of sacramental liturgy; in the other, ritual practices are modified either through exaggeration or through more active types of transformation. Very broadly, it might be said that canonical ritual performance is partially about the self-conscious location of the particular (a certain group of pilgrims) in the general (the authorized rituals of a nationally renowned site of Christian worship). On the other hand much ironic ritual performance is about making the general (the liturgical forms offered by the shrines) adapt to and accommodate itself to the particular demands and experimental whims of the group or individual.

While the presence of irony implies a degree of deliberately cultivated fun as well as a mixing of performance genres, it should not be assumed that the presence of entertainment and theatre necessarily implies a lack of performative efficacy. For some of the pilgrims we discuss, certain rituals only become effective when invested with a certain playfulness and distance from conventional forms, while liturgy as well as drama are only valued in so far as they can provide effective means through which to express personal meanings or ritualize particular social formations. Schechner (1993: 27) has noted how play, as a western category, has often been tainted by implications of unreality, duplicity and inconsequentiality. Like him, we argue that it can, however, be valued by some performers of ritual precisely because of its provisionality, its ability to experiment with alternative forms of identity and action. Handelman (1990: 63–6) also discusses play in relation to ritual, linking it with qualities of indeterminacy and process. Again, in some ironic pilgrimages we see how ambivalence as to the status and value of conventional liturgy is translated into performances moving between genres of the conventionally sacred and secular, the predictable and unpredictable, the newly created and the traditionally inherited.

Of course, pilgrimage is likely to provide fertile ground for any researcher interested in the role of play in ritual, given that as a rite of passage it tends to incorporate ludic elements. However, our paper attempts to separate out particular context- and culture-bound aspects of the ludic in pilgrimage ritual. What is striking about canonical pilgrims is the way they regard much of what they do at Walsingham as an earnest reassertion of orthodoxy. In a national context where Anglo-Catholicism in particular, but also Christian commitment in general, are relatively peripheral activities on an everyday level, going to Walsingham provides the opportunity to take a holiday from being liturgically and spiritually marginal, in the company of an unusually high concentration of like-minded others. The playful aspects of such pilgrimage thus tend to be sharply separated from the serious business of engaging in powerfully charged liturgy. When viewed in the light of such attitudes, ironic pilgrims – somewhat ironically – seem almost more conventional as pilgrims given their Chaucerian stress on secular fun combined with spiritual devotions.

Our distinction between the canonical and the ironic has some resonances with Turner's (1982) differentiation between liminal and liminoid realms of experience. Walsingham offers to certain pilgrims something of the obligatory, corporate, cyclical elements of the liminal, in both its celebration of the official liturgical year and its incorporation of regular annual visits by parish groups. It also provides space for more obviously optative, liminoid and even commoditized forms of liturgical as well as touristic freedom. The distinction can also be phrased in relation to Walsingham in terms of an ideal-typical contrast between 'tradition' (which, even if 'invented', sets a value on a supposed continuity with the past) and 'heritage', a consumer-friendly, postmodern pastiche of styles (cf. Chaney 1994). Along with other contemporary ritual forms (cf. Boissevain 1992, Crain 1992), pilgrimages to Walsingham are partially supported and revived by the practices of a modernity shading into postmodernity, such as the cultivation of leisure, consumption and the commercialized 'staging' of culture, and are thereby sometimes transformed into objects of play, displaced from conventional temporal or liturgical frames.

Pilgrims to Walsingham are not the only contemporary participants in ritual forms to use irony and/or pastiche consciously in order to cultivate personally meaningful experiences and performances. Bowman (1993), for instance, describes how Glastonbury, itself a pilgrimage site, provides a kind of multivalent, shifting, spiritual service industry for its many Christian and New Age visitors. Luhrmann (1989) argues that part of the attraction of pagan movements lies in their capacity to allow practitioners to combine religious traditions in novel, often deliberately theatrical combinations, in order to create an imaginatively satisfying link with the past. An examination of ritual performance at Walsingham may thus lead into much wider, comparative considerations of the role of the personal and the institutional, the innovative and the apparently fixed, in the simultaneous enactment and transformation of cultural forms.

NOTES

1   As Brook points out, the outstanding term in French for watching a play is 'assister' – a creative collaboration of performers and their audience (1968: 155–6). To an extent much greater than with a theatre audience, pilgrims to Walsingham write their own scripts and perform their own ritual plays, which may or may not intersect with official ceremonial.

2   Processions to the priory ruins on major pilgrimage days attract thousands of visitors.

3   The Orthodox are actually granted a small space in an upper room of the Anglican shrine church.

4   It can be argued that the narrative reconstruction of a performance is very different to the performance itself. However, as noted, we have combined interviews with observation of and participation within rituals. In addition, interviews give us access to points of performance that pilgrims feel to have been especially significant.

5   One of us was present when a parishioner and a priest attempted to explain the significance of Walsingham. The parishioner, having described the perfection of the place and her parish's annual pilgrimage there, was clearly both discomfited and annoyed when her own parish priest proceeded to describe the generational differences between pilgrims and expressed his opinion that a number of previous administrators and guardians of the Anglican shrine were slightly lunatic.

6   Some similarities should become evident with the notions of restricted versus elaborated codes in ritual (developed by Douglas (1973), drawing on Bernstein's (1965) work on language). Canonical performances are 'restricted' in the sense that they assume that all participants will be party to the same essential assumptions about the nature of their faith. Ironic performances are more geared to the articulation of unique experiences within the performance of ritual itself. It is tempting to claim, in line with the Bernstein/Douglas argument, that differences in ritual can be related to class differences between ritual performers at Walsingham. Undoubtedly, 'parish' pilgrimages tend to have a large number of working-class participants, whilst the more innovative or ironic forms of participation we describe have often come from more clearly middle-class sources.

However, rigid distinctions along these lines should be avoided, not least as the same person may engage in both forms of pilgrimage at different times in her or his life.

7 The terms 'canonical' and 'ironic' are used by the authors, rather than pilgrims themselves. They are intended to indicate one – but not the only – dimension of contrast between styles of performing pilgrimage at Walsingham. By its very nature, the category of 'ironic' pilgrims is extremely internally heterogeneous.

REFERENCES

Bell, C. (1992) *Ritual Theory, Ritual Practice*, Oxford: Oxford University Press.

Bernstein, B. (1965) 'A socio-linguistic approach to social learning', in J. Gould (ed.) *Penguin Survey of the Social Sciences*, London: Penguin.

Bloch, M. (1974) 'Symbol, song, dance and features of articulation: is religion an extreme form of traditional authority?', *European Journal of Sociology*, 15: 55–81.

Boissevain, J. (ed.) (1992) *Revitalizing European Rituals*, London: Routledge.

Bowman, M. (1993) 'Drawn to Glastonbury', in I. Reader and T. Walter (eds) *Pilgrimage in Popular Culture*, London: Macmillan.

Brook, P. (1968) *The Empty Space*, Harmondsworth: Penguin.

Chaney, D. (1994) *The Cultural Turn: Scene-Setting Essays on Contemporary Cultural History*, London: Routledge.

Coleman, S. and Elsner, J. (1995) *Pilgrimage: Sacred Travel and Sacred Space in the World Religions*, London: British Museum Press, Cambridge MA: Harvard University Press.

Crain, M. (1992) 'Pilgrims, "yuppies", and media men: the transformation of an Andalusian pilgrimage', in J. Boissevain (ed.) *Revitalizing European Rituals*, London: Routledge.

Douglas, M. (1973) *Natural Symbols: Explorations in Cosmology*, London: Barrie and Jenkins.

Duncan, C. (1995) *Civilizing Rituals: Inside Public Art Museums*, London: Routledge.

Eade, J. and Sallnow, M. (eds) (1991) *Contesting the Sacred: The Anthropology of Christian Pilgrimage*, London: Routledge.

Gross, D. (1971) 'Ritual and conformity: a religious pilgrimage to northeastern Brazil', *Ethnology*, 10: 129–48.

Handelman, D. (1990) *Models and Mirrors: Towards an Anthropology of Public Events*, Cambridge: Cambridge University Press.

Hastrup, K. (1994) 'Anthropological knowledge incorporated: discussion', in K. Hastrup and P. Hervik (eds) *Social Experience and Anthropological Knowledge*, London: Routledge.

Lewis, G. (1980) *Day of Shining Red: An Essay on Understanding Ritual*, Cambridge: Cambridge University Press.

Luhrmann, T.M. (1989) *Persuasions of the Witch's Craft: Ritual Magic and Witchcraft in Present-Day England*, Oxford: Blackwell.

Peacock, J.L. (1990) 'Ethnographic notes on sacred and profane performance', in R. Schechner and W. Appel (eds) *By Means of Performance: Intercultural Studies of Theatre and Ritual*, Cambridge: Cambridge University Press.

Rappaport, R. (1974) 'Obvious aspects of ritual', *Cambridge Anthropology*, 2(1): 3–69.

Sallnow, M. (1981) 'Communitas reconsidered: the sociology of Andean pilgrimage', *Man*, n.s., 16: 163–82.

Schechner, R. (1993) *The Future of Ritual: Writings on Culture and Performance*, London: Routledge.

Schieffelin, E. (1995) 'On failure and performance', in C. Laderman and M. Roseman (eds), *The Performance of Healing*, London: Routledge.

Turner, V.W. (1982) 'Liminal to liminoid, in play, flow and ritual: an essay in comparative symbology', in *From Ritual to Theatre: The Human Seriousness of Play*, New York: PAJ Publications.

—— and Turner, E. (1978) *Image and Pilgrimage in Christian Culture: Anthropological Perspectives*, Oxford: Blackwell.

Wolf, E. (1958) 'The Virgin of Guadelupe: a Mexican national symbol', *Journal of American Folklore*, 71 (1): 34–9.

Chapter 3

Ritual, performance and media in urban contemporary shrine configurations in Benin City, Nigeria

Charles Gore

This chapter looks at initiation at urban shrine contemporary configurations in Benin City and considers Van Gennep's ideas of rites of passage as applied to initiation. This chapter suggests that this approach has become a ubiquitous anthropological truism which provides a limited understanding of the local contextualizations of such traditions of ideas and practices. It further suggests that any anthropological approach to ritual and/or performance must take account of human agency in the constitution of these traditions and how individuals relate them to other contexts of ideas and practice. Ritual ideas and practice are situated in different contexts in Benin City. They articulate notions of kingship; they underpin the legitimacy of inheritance; and they are found at shrines throughout the city. These different contexts contribute to a notion of an identity shared by Edo-speaking people – irrespective of an individual's acquiescence in or even rejection of such ritual ideas and practice.

The chapter then considers social constraint and argues that, in fact, it is a constituent of any tradition and enables the creativity of human agents in their participation and development of that tradition. It further suggests that ritual and performance cannot usefully be separated out conceptually at these shrines. The chapter concludes by looking at the role of video at these shrines and the way its uses link up with regional and local conventions of ideas and practice of television in Edo state.

BACKGROUND

Benin City, the capital of Edo state, is located in the tropical rainforest belt of southern Nigeria. It is the urban centre of the Edo kingdom, which has a core Edo-speaking population dispersed in several hundred village settlements about Benin City, and also a more extended regional sphere of influence. The ritual and political head of this kingdom is the Oba of Benin descended from the founder of the dynasty, who came from the sacred Yoruba centre of Ife sometime prior to the fourteenth century. The kingdom was annexed in 1897 by the British, who banished the reigning Oba, but the office was restored in 1914 with the accession of his son. The authority of this office is rooted in the pre-colonial traditions of the Edo kingdom, but it is also situated in the relationships that were established by the colonial and post-colonial governments after its re-establishment. Indeed under the military rule exercised in Nigeria at the present time the role of the Oba in local and federal state affairs constitutes one of the few legitimate exercises of civil authority.

The ritual authority of the Oba is predicated on the legitimacy he derives from *erinmwin*, the spirit world. The word *erinmwin* itself is the plural of *orinmwin*, corpse or dead body (Agheyisi 1986: 111). It is a fundamental assumption in Edo traditions (and has a wide regional currency) that *erinmwin*, the spirit world, to which the deceased belong is in close and intimate contact with the material world, *agbon*, events in which it intervenes and determines. Indeed notions about events in the material world are considered to be predicated on relations to *erinmwin*, the spirit world, although the ways in which these are interpreted by individual agents are open to social negotiation and contestation.

Much of the basis of Edo traditions and its notions of legitimacy are defined in terms of relations of a gerontocracy, both the living and the deceased. However, the extent and depth of lineages remain limited, as rights of inheritance and any offices pass from father to eldest son upon performance of funerary rites during which the son incorporates his late father into the ancestral shrine. Similarly, land rights are vested in the community of a village, rather than in its component descent groups, and these are distributed by its elders to both members of the community and outsiders (Bradbury 1973: 51). All sections of society participate in the worship of deceased predecessors, whether these are in respect of family, ward, guild or village, chieftaincy association or society, trade guild or the kingdom itself. Hence legitimation is situated in and by the spirit world.

In the instance of the Oba of Benin, his unique and exclusive relations to the spirit world are exercised not only on his behalf or that of his family but also for the various groupings of the city of Benin and the various parts of the Edo kingdom. Indeed the relations of the Oba to the spirit world are varied and extensive – both in deities which are exclusive to him and in others which are maintained in conjunction with particular social groupings, such as the village communities outside Benin City. His legitimacy is not only maintained by his office, and the offices that depend on it, but also validated by the actual person of the Oba, who stands in a series of unique relations to the different constituencies of his domain. These relations are defined primarily in the spiritual terms in which their legitimacy is grounded. This can be seen, for example, at the coronation and installation of an Oba in the way in which his person is redefined in terms of his now unique (and diverse) relations to different communities in the kingdom (Nevadomsky 1984: 48–9). Similarly, in many of the annual rites that are held at the palace (such as *Igue*, for example) the actual person of the Oba is sanctified and inculcated to fortify his unique relations to the metaphysical and physical domains over which he has authority.

The continuance of the Obaship in the colonial and post-colonial eras was fostered by the British and the subsequent Nigerian governments to legitimate and articulate national governance in both the urban and rural areas. The ritual linkages that this form of kingship maintained with its outlying rural communities provided a legitimacy of rule for the penetrations of the nation state, but also, conversely, provided a basis upon which a local ethnic identity is grounded in relation to access to the resources of that nation state by Edo-speaking peoples. This is a process that continues with the creation of Edo State in 1992 from part of Bendel State, with the reallocation of jobs and resources (determined by the federal allocation of state funding) to the advantage of members from within the newly formed state.

Local traditions of ritual ideas and practices articulate notions of kingship and form a basis for local political action within Edo state. Sometimes they extend beyond, as in 1991 when Chief Oyegun won election for governorship of Edo state for the Social Democrat Party (SDP) during the (soon to be annulled) 'transition to civil rule' campaign. Mr Lucky Igbinedion, the defeated National Republican Congress (NRC) candidate, appealed to the national military council to invalidate the election on the grounds that the SDP campaign had continued until the day prior to the voting day; this was banned under the rules for election of state governors. The claim of violation of the campaign rules was made because of a television broadcast by Chief Isekhure on behalf of the SDP on the day prior to these elections. It was argued that not only did this invalidate the campaign but that Chief Isekhure, as the religious representative of the Oba of Benin, had coerced the population into voting for the SDP through the Edo fear of the local 'ju-jus' – a term used to describe indigenous Edo shrines by the national press in their reports of the case.

In the legal case that followed, the Oba of Benin was summoned to the court to testify by Mr Igbinedion – an unprecedented step to take, as it contested the official status of the Oba as a 'first-class traditional chief',[1] officially outside of national politics. However, Mr Igbinedion lost his case, and his actions, in any event, alienated the local populace whose support he would require to contest a new election.[2]

SHRINES IN BENIN CITY

Benin City and the palace of the Oba are marked out by shrines which articulate the role and traditions of the Oba and his predecessors as rulers of the city and kingdom. Throughout the city there are also domestic shrines, found in many households despite the active proselytizing of Christianity in all its forms during this century. Apart from the ancestral and other shrines devoted to the domestic household, there are also personal shrines set up by individuals to various deities and other spiritual agencies with which they have entered into a relationship. Some charismatic individuals develop their personal shrines to attract a following of devotees and clients, and this enables them to practise full-time as Ohens, priests, in competition with other Ohens. These Ohens are characterized by personal and privileged relationships with the deities and other agencies in the spirit world. This is grounded in the presuppositions pertaining to relations to the spirit world, which in the instance of the Oba of Benin are constituted as an exclusive category through his office and person and are articulated by the institutions that underpin him.

Urban shrines in Benin City may be developed from personal shrines inherited from within the family, from communal village shrines, and in some instances from the importation of a shrine from another region or community. The means by which deities and shrines are acquired is often due to the complex biographies of the individuals concerned. Usually the shrine is owned by the Ohen within some area of his or her compound or dwelling place.

One local way of conceptualizing Ohens is that they are born into the world with the deities, and it is this personal relationship that they use in the spirit world to effect results in the physical one. The notion that some individuals are born with certain deities, which they are compelled to recognize, is part of a wider conceptualization that all individuals are born with part of their person known as *ehi* remaining with Osa, the supreme deity, who is the final arbiter of the material world (*agbon*) and the spirit world (*erinmwin*). *Ehi* guides the person through the world and determines some of the constraints of possibility in that person's life. This is not a predetermination of possibility but an active interaction between the *ehi* and other agencies in the spirit world, and the individual as he or she deals with events in the material world. *Ehi* is a constituent of personhood in this form of conceptualization of the spirit world. *Agbon* and *erinmwin* are not completely distinct domains: some entities transcend the boundaries presumed by the terms themselves, such as, for example, *ehi* and the deities, though this also suggests that the very notion implied in the term 'boundary' does not give an adequate description of this fluidity and flexibility.

The Ohen builds up a regular clientele through the development of a community centred on his or her particular shrine. There is the appropriate day of worship at the shrine, where regular devotees and casual onlookers can participate in the activities of worship. Song, dance and music are key constituents of worship of the deities. The Ohen is possessed by the deities with which he or she is in a special relationship, while dancing and singing to the distinctive music produced for each of the deities. Other devotees and visiting Ohens can also be possessed as they perform, and possession can occur spontaneously to any onlooker or participant as well – irrespective of whether they have been initiated or not to that deity. The events elaborated during worship vary considerably from one Ohen to another.

Membership of a shrine gains for an individual the protection of the Ohen, who can intercede on the individual's behalf in the spirit world. The Ohen provides protection but also offers an overlapping range of expertise and services that support the individual. This sense of protection and support is important, as life is insecure in Benin City, where the low average income (of about 300 *naira* a month in 1991) precludes access to many of the costly resources available in the city, such as hospital medical care. In the event of illness the expense of consulting an Ohen is far less than that of the medical services,[3] and in crises payment may be deferred or negotiated when funds are unavailable.[4] Ohens have a considerable knowledge and expertise in the use of plants for both their spiritual efficacy and their physical properties in the treatment of various illnesses. In terms of local conceptualizations of agency, the underlying spiritual as well as physical causes that produced an illness are addressed by the Ohen (for another example, see Hobart 1990: 90–135).

ONE ANTHROPOLOGICAL APPROACH TO RITUAL IN SOCIAL PROCESS

Ritual has been a subject of continual preoccupation among anthropologists as a phenomenon for the ways it can be used to highlight aspects of the society in which it is found. For the anthropologist it is a visible marker of complex social processes that situate the individual as a participant of a social grouping or community.

One approach to ritual has been to focus on the social dynamics of its processes and the type of transformation that it engenders. In his pioneering study, *Rites of Passage* (1960 [1909]), Van Gennep examined the changes of role and status that an individual undergoes within social groupings. He conceptually distinguished a process of separation, followed by transition (described occasionally in terms of opposition or liminality) and then incorporation. He noted that the period of transition, however fleeting, entails a different categorical status that is resolved through a renewed social incorporation of the individual at the completion of the event. Analytically this model of social process is able to consider transformations that occur in the social process and provide a means for cross-cultural comparison with events in other societies.

Turner further developed this approach by focusing on the symbolic articulation of ritual events for participants. He emphasized that the period of transition was the means to effect ritual transformation, and linked the dynamics involved in the symbolic process to the category of liminality. He elaborated this category in conjunction with a notion of 'communitas', whereby the liminal event undergone by social groupings levelled out social disparateness – however limited or constrained its context within a given society (Turner 1974: 200–1). However, this means of conceptualization of separation, liminality and incorporation has become a ubiquitous anthropological truism.

Ritual and performance at the urban contemporary shrines of Benin City have a 'classic' fit with this anthropological approach, particularly when applied to a specific context such as initiation through which an individual acquires a shrine. Some aspects of this fit are now briefly sketched out. But this chapter will then suggest that this anthropological approach (with its development by Turner (1974)) often uses taken-for-granted categories that do not give an adequate account of local contextualizations of ritual ideas and practice, constituted over time in this example from Benin City.

THE INITIATION CYCLE AT URBAN SHRINES

An individual sets up a shrine during the course of initiation to a particular deity. The shrine and its efficacy are dependent on a number of key objects which define and articulate the relations of the initiate with that deity, such as the installation of the pot, *uru*, with water drawn from the river, the leaves associated with that deity which have been macerated in this water and so on. Other artefacts, such as statues, are embellishments which are introduced at shrines after initiation to enhance its prestige. They remain an elaboration or a reiteration of the basic and fundamental relationship between the initiate and the deity, although indicating the mutual benefits of the relationship as the material success brought by the deity provides the means to embellish the shrine.

Many of the rites undergone can be delineated as rites of separation from the existing status of the individual and the secular world in which he or she participates. Initiation and any other important ritual commence with purification, *ihonmwengbe*, which prepares the participants, especially the principal protagonists, removing any ill intentions and impurities from the body that may otherwise desecrate the shrine.

During the initiation, an individual stays at the shrine of the officiating Ohen. When not performing some ritual, such initiates remain in seclusion and do not have contact with individuals outside the shrine – except on the payment of a fine. The initiates' links to the spirit world are emphasized by a strand of young palm frond, *ome*, tied about the wrist. In some shrines the initiates remain hidden under a white or red cloth (depending on the deity) and a bell is rung to warn the uninitiated not to look at them. All these events mark out the initiates in their role of transition. Set sacrifices are made on the appropriate days of the initiation, from which the initiate offers a small prepared meal to the deity. This underlines the personal and mutual support that is given in the relationship with the deity.

At the beginning and end of each day the initiate is bathed with a mixture of leaves dedicated to the deity and coated in native chalk. As the rituals progress, the initiate is infused with the presence of the deity both through the ritual actions that are undergone and through the power of the various leaves. At set intervals public celebrations are held where the initiate dances to the music of the deity and subsequently to the other deities. It is through dance that the deity makes its presence public. During these performances the initiate is possessed by the deity as he or she dances to the drumbeats and songs of the deity – *ebo zoy*, the deity chooses, describing the act of possession by the deity. The initiate is encouraged by the assisting Ohens and devotees who sing and beat calabashes with strung beads, *ukuse*, and by the increasing tempo of the drumming. The ritual events that occur and the possession by the deities, which overwhelm the initiate at key moments, can be classified as liminal characteristics with a 'destructuring' of social processes into 'communitas', emphasized by Turner (1974: 274).

Subsequent to the first public celebration, the initiate calls out the specific name of the deity that has possessed him or her. There are many names for each deity which describe a particular attribute or power of the main deity or one of the supporting ones. The calling of the name is the key event in the initiation cycle.[5] The final act of the initiation is the sweeping away, *ikpolo*, in which the material evidence of the rites of passage of the newly reincorporated individual are removed.

The novice is expected to serve the initiating Ohen for a further period of two (or three in the Edo numeral system) years as an assistant or helper, *owaise*, after which time another thanksgiving celebration is held. Each year an annual festival, with a day devoted to each deity acquired, is given by the Ohen, which becomes more elaborate as he or she becomes successful. Indeed an Ohen can demand attendance and material support (whether money or in kind) from those Ohens that he or she has subsequently initiated.

This brief description of initiation at urban shrines can easily be arranged and mapped out into the pattern that Van Gennep (1960 [1909]) depicts and cross-culturally compared with events in other societies. Similarly, Turner's (1974) focus on the transitional aspect of initiation as a liminal state that ultimately fosters a state of 'communitas' within the given framework of ritual ideas and practice provides one model of the processual dynamics of the events depicted. The conventionality of this ethnographic example of the mapping out of initiation is a tribute to the success of Van Gennep and Turner's ideas.

However, despite their emphasis on the transformational process of ritual events, these approaches take little account of localized indigenous strategies in the framing and contextualizing of such events. They present a conceptual representation of which Bourdieu's observation is perhaps a reminder:

The anthropologist's particular relation to the object of his study contains the making of a theoretical distortion inasmuch as his situation as an observer, excluded from the real play of activities by the fact that he has no place (except by choice or by way of game) in the system observed and has no need to make a place for himself there, inclines him to a hermeneutic representation of practices, leading him to reduce all social relations to communicative relations and more precisely, decoding operations.

(Bourdieu 1977: 1)

Indeed what is evident in these approaches is the elision of the ways in which local agents creatively construct and constitute these events, in relation to the various traditions of ideas and practices articulated both within the urban shrine configurations and outside them.

LOCAL CONTEXTS[6]

Each deity has its separate form of initiation, which requires its own distinctive set of knowledge that remains exclusive to those who have been initiated. These sets of knowledge are based on both commonalities of ideas and practices pertaining to a deity, as well as on the cumulative experiential knowledge gained by each Ohen in the unique individual relationship with that deity. Such knowledge is acquired from a variety of sources: the various Ohens who conduct the initiations, divination and oracle, as well as dreams which provide a link between the individual and the spirit world through which the deities communicate directly. Indeed the diverse ways in which this knowledge is obtained contribute to wide variations in how initiation is performed and is dependent on the particular Ohens who preside over the initiation.

This range of variations involves several factors. Ohens from different areas have developed differences in how particular sets of knowledge are constructed. The names and attributes of plants can vary from one area to another. There can be different ways of conceptualizing about a deity, its ordering in the spirit world and the various practices that are particular to it. There is also the extent to which an Ohen has been instructed in the practices and knowledge of the deity both by the Ohens who conducted the initiation (a process that can take several years) and by their own development and understanding of the deity in the ideas and practices they have accumulated both prior to and since initiation. This last factor is important, as the personal relationship that the Ohen has with the deity empowers and legitimates all practices of the Ohen, whether these conform to prior practices or introduce innovations. This is explicitly recognized by Ohens, who claim a unique knowledge and practice that is different to other Ohens' – even when the practices appear quite similar. Indeed very similar practices can be used to very different purposes by different Ohens.

This knowledge linked to particular deities is reserved exclusively for initiates of that deity. But the situation often arises where members of a shrine gather the materials for initiation despite being non-initiates themselves. Through these means they tacitly acquire much of the knowledge necessary for a particular set of practices. Similarly, as members of the shrine, they have less restricted access to activities conducted by the Ohen, with whom they are in a close relationship through membership.

Also, some songs at public performances can refer to, and be part of, a set of practices (such as initiation) and consequently are accessible to individuals, such as casual onlookers, who are otherwise excluded from these contexts. Publicly restricted knowledge can be tacitly known both by individuals who participate in the institutions of shrines and by those outside them who are publicly excluded from this knowledge. This can also be utilized as a means of recruitment of new followers and clients. Despite the emphasis on and, indeed, the advantages of sets of knowledge as a covert resource, they do not remain confined to these means of regulation and ordering.

This tacit acquisition of knowledge of the deities can vary from shrine to shrine, depending on the Ohen concerned, but the power or capabilities inherent in the usages of this knowledge can only be enacted by initiates, who have acquired the spiritual authority to intervene with these powers. For example, a native doctor may have the appropriate knowledge of the leaves prior to initiation, but it is considered that these will not work until he or she has performed the initiation washing of hands, *okpobo*. Similar notions prevail with regard to the deities and the leaves which are used in association with them. Thus initiation or membership to a group or community is legitimated not so much by the gaining of access to particular sets of knowledge but by the public recognition and conferment of the social capability to enact the power that access to these knowledges confers – a point clearly delineated by Van Gennep's conceptual approach (1960 [1909]: 13).

These sets of knowledge are gained by an individual through specialized and privileged access. They are considered to be owned uniquely by the individual who has them. They are a resource that has taken time and expense to acquire from those already in such a privileged position. During initiation the first people ever to have initiated are always acknowledged and their aid and assistance are requested in the spirit world (indeed a ranking of professional seniority is measured from the dates of initiation). This knowledge is not disseminated publicly without some form of gain for the individual divulging it. The failure to contribute adequately (or even a lack of generosity) during initiation and afterwards may be met by an exclusion from access to this knowledge. Thus notions of knowledge and power are often bound up with access to resources and the ability to withdraw that access. These sets of knowledge are used to gain privileged relations with respect to other individuals and so are a means to power (Foucault 1980: 97–9).

With initiation, there is an acknowledgement of the possibilities of an individual being born with deities, which provides one means of articulating events and experiences. When deities are not recognized by such an individual, they are considered to subject that individual to great suffering and hardship. This can range from a variety of illnesses – barrenness in women, strange behaviour, perceptions of another unrecognized world (aspects of the spirit world), disappearance into that spirit world for often lengthy periods of time – to personal misfortune and poverty. However, past experiences are articulated to this means of conceptualization by the Ohen and then utilized as skills with which to assert spiritual capabilities and powers. For example, a skill in dancing when young may then be reorganized within the role of an Ohen to demonstrate evidence of exceptional capabilities and powers in the spirit world. Similarly, an ability to see events in the spirit world, whether in dreams or in waking life, is problematical if not legitimated in some way. This is particularly acute if it occurs in childhood, as the child may be diagnosed as a witch, as under attack from witches or as a person who is linked to spirits from the river, *ogbanje*. However, these events can be developed by an individual as a legitimated past experience through initiation as an Ohen. Thus the process of initiation, and after, can become a means of rearticulating experiences and capabilities. It can also consolidate or enhance status as an Ohen.

The legitimation provided by the deity provides the means both for the constitution of a configuration of various traditions of ideas and for their conventions of practice (such as dance, song, possession, prophesy and so on) as a unity within the framing of the urban contemporary shines.[7] This framing is underpinned by the key legitimacy of the spiritual agencies with which the Ohen has personal relationships.

Although initiation is the public recognition of this unity and can be incorporated within a Van-Gennep type of schema, it is the localized strategies of individuals over time that constitute urban shrine configurations. This is not to propose a syncretic view of these ritual ideas and practice but to provide the means to discern its different elements, which can be constructed locally in various ways by different Ohens, according to the unique exercise of their individual skills. An understanding of these traditions and the configuration of the urban contemporary shrines that provides the unity of framing has to take account of the agency of practitioners in the acquisition of these skills and, moreover, the continuance, change and innovation in these ideas and practices over time.

Similarly, this offers a critique of models of liminality. Although initiation is the representation par excellence of liminality, its conceptual application also can be deconstructed. Possession and dance,[8] two elements that seem to present the ultimate exemplars of this paradigm, can be construed within the framing of the conventions of ideas and practices at these urban contemporary shrines.

Possession is an event that is established within the particular framing of its conventions of ideas and practices. It is encouraged in non-initiates as a means of creating a special relationship with the deity and, despite being defined in terms of its spontaneity, is bound by the conventions of its ideas and practice. It is brought out in an individual and co-ordinated by the presiding Ohen, who guides the possessed individual during its initial appearance, its presence in and as dance, and its eventual departure when the possessed individual retires to the inner shrine to pay homage to the deities. This is a public recognition that the deities are calling the individual to worship them through initiation. There is then the recruitment of the individual through initiation at some later date, when the novice has already gained some skill in the movements and dance steps of the particular deity involved. During initiation there is further reinforcement of these skills.

For example, in an initiation into Ogun in August 1996 the two initiates were instructed to dance to the rhythms of the deity at the beginning and end of every day as a separate event, in order, in the words of the Ohen, 'to catch the steps'. This is a cumulative and experiential acquisition of the conventions of possession. At a public afternoon ceremony these two initiates called out the Ogun names, Oguname, Ogun of water, and Oguneren, Ogun of fire, which were conceptualized by the presiding Ohen and other participants to describe the fluid and slow movements of the first initiate[9] and the heated and more erratic movements of the second. Furthermore these identities were linked to the heavy cloud cover that had threatened rain during the first initiate's performance and was immediately succeeded by intense sunshine on the entry of the second initiate.

However, individuals can also appropriate ideas and practices from other contexts. In dance at shrines there may be reference to other traditions of practice, such as the use of syncopated stepping motions of a particular fashion in disco dancing, which is used by some younger Ohens (1991–5) as a means of leaving the public arena. In some instances, other more long-standing traditions of dance and music such as *egbo*, a praise song and dance form, may be introduced into the proceedings to please the deities and onlookers. But the context of the dance, the music, its rhythms and the use of particular instruments associated with the deities distinguish it from some other traditions.

These local contextualizations and their relations to other traditions of ideas and practice suggest that the conceptual approach adopted by Van Gennep and the development of liminality by Turner provide a limited understanding of such traditions of ideas and practices. Furthermore, local notions of personhood as developed by Ohens in their unique and exclusive relation to their deities present almost the opposite of Turner's 'communitas' – a 'communitas' that is dependent on European notions of the person as an individual entity (Carrithers *et al.* 1985). These local contextualizations in Benin City further suggest that any anthropological approach to ritual must take account both of the intentions of human agents in the constitution of these traditions of ritual and of how they creatively articulate such traditions to other contexts of ideas and practice. As already noted, Van Gennep's and Turner's approach to ritual has become a ubiquitous anthropological truism, which often permeates anthropological discourse and ethnographic description as part of the subject and not in its actual siting as part of the conceptual framing.

However, this example of the urban contemporary shrine configurations suggests an alternative conceptual approach to ritual using a paradigm perhaps more familiar to the discipline of history of art[10] (see further Baxandall 1972, Picton 1990, 1995: 84–5; but also in anthropology Barth 1993). This approach centres on the agency of practitioners and conceptualizes the urban contemporary shrine configurations as a tradition of ideas and practices with its associated conventions. However, it is also a configuration of ideas and practices, many of which are not at all easily susceptible to verbal exegesis (including song, dance, possession and so on), and which are not only *of* this ritual tradition but are also *in themselves* traditions of ideas and practices with their own accompanying conventions. This conceptual framing provides a means to analyse localized contextualizations and situate human agents, their intentions and strategies in the constitution of the urban contemporary shrine configurations, its perpetuation and change over time, as well as, equally importantly, its relations to other traditions both in Benin City and beyond (Gore and Nevadomsky, 1997).

CONSTRAINT AND CREATIVITY IN RITUAL/PERFORMANCE

During public events the fundamental criterion for an Ohen is the ability to perform. It is during the Ohen's performance of the dances that the deity asserts itself and this is assessed by onlookers. They will evaluate these skills critically and distinguish the exceptional performance of an individual possessed by the deities. However, different qualities of a performance are evaluated and appreciated in different Ohens.

Ohens can dance in quite different ways to the same sequence of a particular deity's music. The use of styles of dance by the performer can be informed by the conventions of other local (such as village) and regional traditions of dancing. The emphasis is on the individual skill of the performer and the way in which different elements of the performance are combined together. However, one Ohen may emphasize the ability to dance, whereas another may emphasize skills in song or other ways of constructing the performance, such as prophesy or dramatic events. Ohens who are skilful dancers may combine together the different dance patterns of the deities to general appreciation. Such skill is a suggestion that the Ohen is pre-eminent in the ways of the spirit world.

The word *gbe* describes all the actions of the Ohen whether of singing, dance or prophecy at these public events. *Gbe* can be translated to many different contexts (Melzian 1937: 68–9), as 'kill', 'beat', 'dance' and so on. It most closely corresponds to the word 'perform', with an implication of the performer's being tested. Jealous onlookers are considered to threaten the performing Ohen spiritually and, indeed, to slip and fall to the ground during these ritual events presages the death of the performer. As a local conceptualization, the distinctions of ritual and performance interpenetrate because all actions of the Ohen and other participants are framed by the context of the spiritual legitimacy of the deities. A separation of ritual and performance denies local means of conceptualization of agencies in the spirit world that intervene in the material world, which engenders the performative constituent of ritual.

The notion of being challenged in the public arena is part of the competition between charismatic Ohens for followers and clients. They provide unique and personal services that foster individuation and innovation, legitimated by the personal relationship they have with their deities (as has been noted previously), in order to attract these followers and clients with their contemporary needs and requirements.[11] However, they are also constrained by the conventions of ideas and practice of the traditions that they utilize in its construction. The need to assert their unique and individual capabilities if unmediated by these traditions leaves them acutely vulnerable to accusations as quacks and fakes (indeed in performance Ohens will sing of the other fake Ohens in order to accentuate their own validity).

Hence there is a creative tension between the need to accentuate individual capabilities and yet retain commonalities of ideas and practice with other Ohens which would otherwise jeopardize their claims to legitimacy. It is this constraint that provides the dynamic for innovation and individuation within urban contemporary shrine configurations, and provides a framing in which individuals develop the conventions of the various traditions of ideas and practices configured within it.

An example of this can be seen in an individual Ohen's development of the dress tradition of the *adaigho* that Ohens wear for public performance. It usually has various sown or appliqué designs. These represent artefacts used in the practice of Ohens. It also contains medicines, some hidden and some incorporated into the cloth, as well as actual cowrie shells, which are sown on to represent the wealth and success of the Ohen that has been brought by his or her deities (cowries at one time were a form of currency). In this instance the Ohen commissioned a printer to produce an exclusive cloth for him to use at his annual festival in 1991. The exclusive design had the cowries printed onto the cloth along with the particular colours associated with his deities. The cost for such an exceptionally small print run was 20,000 *naira*, which in itself testified to the success of his deity. But the constraint of the customary convention of cowries in the dress was used to provide a distinguishing individuation within that tradition which proclaimed a unique status compared to other Ohens.

VIDEO AND TELEVISION: A CONTEMPORARY PRACTICE

Since 1989 there has been a boom in the setting up of enterprises offering video filming services for public events, due to the low cost of capital outlay and the fast return on it. Video has become extremely popular, as it provides access to an (often bootlegged) international portfolio of entertainment (as much from Taiwan as from the USA) that compares favourably with federal state television. With access to privately owned generators, it is also resistant to the transmission failures to which the national communication networks are susceptible.[12] Finally, it provides access to a low-cost medium for the filming of social events.

In 1990 the use of video to film was an innovative practice at urban shrine configurations. It was viewed with suspicion by some participants, both for the technical inconvenience it caused in the form of lighting and camera requirements and in recording aspects of events that were exclusive to some participants, such as initiation (particularly as the video operator often had few social links to the events taking place). However, within two years video cameras had become commonplace at shrines, particularly on important occasions such as annual festivals.

As such filmings are commissioned by the Ohen of the shrine, they are articulated within notions of ownership of the shrine (which includes ownership of photography and video filming). Video recording of events such as initiation is also bounded by this notion of ownership, although inadvertent exposure remains a possibility (video footage from public events at shrines, including initiation, albeit more exceptionally, has appeared on local television).

Familiarity with the technical requirements has led to participants now taking some account of the presence of the video operator, although it is a partial accommodation as events take place in the round with spectators encircling the main participants. The use of video filming shifted very rapidly from being a particular record of the event to an almost mandatory assertion of the importance of the individuals participating (Figure 3.1). Indeed an Ohen now loses status if there is no filming of the annual festival, and members of a shrine budget for its cost in their preparations for the festival. In terms of content, the most prominent features of this filming are the amount of real time expended and the emphasis on the numbers of participants, particularly the more eminent visitors. The more that the event is recorded in real time (this is often a 14-day affair in the case of annual festivals), the more prestige and status are asserted.

Figure 3.1 Video recording of Ohen Adigbe at his annual festival

The conventions of filming in Benin City differ substantially from media conventions in Europe and the USA. This cannot be attributed to the limitations (technical or otherwise) of a 'home-grown' market and audience, as there is familiarity with European and US production values through access to the latest videos worldwide. But the production of local videos is situated within a different context, where local strategies of enhancement of status and prestige are the basis of much social action and events. What is critical in this video filming is the span of continuous real time devoted to the individuals and events depicted (rather than production values in editing or fluid and stable camerawork). Video film is used to quantify as well as assert the social importance of an event and its participants compared to other individuals and similar events (Figure 3.2). These events are frozen on film to be replayed against other recorded events. This emphasis on real time militates against the use of many western editorial media conventions, as real-time representation is almost invalidated if the interludes and lulls (if not occasional tedium) of lengthy social events are elided. (Conventions of jagged and oddly angled camera shots also represent these social longueurs.)[13]

This real-time convention is used in federal and national state television, where representatives of the federal state or national government are accorded full real-time transmission. This can be seen in the early example in this chapter of the Oba of Benin appearing in court, which was broadcast

Figure 3.2 Audience and participants videoed at a night performance

immediately in real time. The Oba appeared to answer questions in court wearing ceremonial red robes, which in the context of ritual ideas and practice articulates notions of public performance in testing or challenging circumstances (indeed, it is sometimes contextualized as going to war). This ritual context was further extended by the father of the losing governor candidate, himself a prominent chief of the Oba of Benin, appearing during the hearing in red chiefly attire – an attire that itself presented a challenge or further affront to the authority of the Oba of Benin.

Despite the inherent regulation of federal state television in Edo state, its dependence on sponsorship for local programming (usually filmed in video) has provided a medium that is amenable to representations of local issues and concerns. The conventions of real time and camera angles provide a format for the easy assimilation of diverse and often disparate video material from other sources, which in Europe or the USA would be rejected as not conforming to the conventions entailed by western production values.

The use of the television medium to present local issues in Edo State can be seen in the following example. There has been a large increase in the number of charismatic independent churches since the beginning of the 1990s. Many of these are individual enterprises that have set up in response to the generally insecure conditions of the declining local economy. In the competition for followers these independent churches have used evangelical methods of conversion, and verbal and physical attack on non-Christians, to differentiate themselves from the more conservative mainstream churches and the urban shrine configurations. These attacks had become so virulent by the end of 1994 that there was a movement to promote 'Edo traditions', which were considered to be under threat from this fervid evangelism. It resulted in the sponsorship of a weekly video television programme promoting the urban shrine configurations and their local means of worship.

The low-cost use of video cameras and its overlap with television production has created an increasing diversification of the social contexts in which it is used. This has provided a medium that centres on local criteria and interests. Despite the penetrations of world satellite television programming, the medium of local television (particularly in its relationship to the low-cost use of video) in Edo state remains resistant to the diverse processes of international media globalization. This resistance hinges on its constitution as an autonomous regional and localized tradition of television that is concerned with its local contexts of significance, of which ritual ideas and practice are but one example.

CONCLUSION

The example of urban contemporary shrine configurations in Benin City suggests that approaches to ritual have to take account of local contextualizations. Ritual and performance are analytic categories constituted in western discourses. What is understood as ritual by these discourses is constituted through human agency as situated social practice. As all the examples in this book demonstrate, ritual and performance are variable categories. Furthermore, their construction is dependent on the particular ways in which they are constituted and framed in relation to their own historical trajectories as well as to other traditions of social practice.

NOTES

1 This refers to a ranking of comparable chieftaincy titles from different regions throughout Nigeria.
2 For further examples of how ritual ideas and practice have been utilized in local and federal state politics, see Bradbury (1968: 215–50).
3 The difference in cost between consultation of Ohens and medical doctors is increasing as the Nigerian economy has declined.
4 Some shrines have monthly co-operative saving schemes, where each month the pool of contributions by members is drawn by a different member and provides a contingency fund against sudden financial difficulties.
5 Ritual events within the initiation can be further classed into a succession of subgroupings of rites of passage. The name-calling of the deity can also be a rite of incorporation, signifying the successful attainment of a personal relationship with the deity.

6 'Local contexts' refers to Fardon's discussion of the use of local/global pairings to signal the provisionality of identities and to provide a means of avoiding the reified boundings of society and culture (1995: 1–22).

7 This unity of framing, albeit provided by a spiritual legitimation, has many similarities with Wulff's development of frames (this volume).

8 Possession and dance as categories are distinguished in these local contexts. Individuals dance in the course of worship without being possessed. Possession takes place during particular segments of dance but can also occur without the necessity for dance.

9 A graduate of theatre arts, University of Benin, and a skilled practitioner of the slow and stately movements of courtly dance at the court of the Oba of Benin, which is taught within this university course.

10 This is meant in a postmodern sense. Historically art history has essentialized a particular conceptualization of the person, encapsulated in notions of 'genius' derived from the development of the Romantic tradition. However, it has focused on agency and event in the production of works (which can include ritual – or indeed performance art) as a trajectory through time and its use of traditions, historical or reinvented, (Hobsbawm and Ranger: 1983), from which the individual can appropriate.

11 The matters which Ohens address on behalf of their clients deal with the whole gamut of their clients' lives, ranging from illness, death and witchcraft to job procurement, court cases, visas to travel abroad and so on. These matters are not compartmentalized into ritual and non-ritual areas.

12 The advent of international satellite TV programming in the early 1990s is still confined to the elites, as the capital outlay for satellite dishes is substantial.

13 Sheila Petty discusses this use of real time in relation to the production of African cinema (1992: 26)

REFERENCES

Agheyisi, R.N. (1986) *An Edo-English Dictionary*, Benin City: Ethiope Publishing.

Barth, F. (1993) *Balinese Worlds*, Chicago: University of Chicago Press.

Baxandall, M. (1972) *Painting and Experience in Fifteenth-Century Italy*, Oxford: Oxford University Press.

Bourdieu, P. (1977) *Outline of a Theory of Practice*, Cambridge: Cambridge University Press.

Bradbury, R.E. (1968) 'Continuities and discontinuities in pre-colonial and colonial Benin politics (1897–1951)', in I.M. Lewis (ed.) *History and Social Anthropology*, ASA monograph 7, London: Tavistock Press.

—— (1973) 'The Kingdom of Benin', in P. Morton-Williams (ed.) *Benin Studies*, Oxford: Oxford University Press.

Carrithers, M., Collins, S. and Lukes, S. (eds) (1985) *The Category of the Person: Anthropology, Philosophy, History*, Cambridge: Cambridge University Press.

Fardon, R. (ed.) (1995) *Counterworks: Managing the Diversity of Knowledge*, London: Routledge.

Foucault, M. (1980) *Power/Knowledge: Selected Interviews and Other Writings 1972–1977*, ed. Colin Gordon, London: Harvester Press.

Gore, C.D. and Nevadomsky, J. (1997) 'Practice and agency in Mammy Wata worship in southern Nigeria', *African Arts* 30 (2): 60–9.

Hobart, H. (1990) 'The patience of plants: a note on agency in Bali', *Review of Indonesian and Malaysian Affairs*, 24: 90–135.

Hobsbawm, E. and Ranger, T.O. (eds) (1983) *The Invention of Tradition*, Cambridge: Cambridge University Press.

Melzian, H. (1937) *A Concise Dictionary of the Bini Language of Southern Nigeria*, London: Kegan Paul, Trencil, Trubner.

Nevadomsky, J.N. (1984) 'Kingship succession rituals in Benin. Pt. 3: The coronation of the Oba', *African Arts*, 17 (3): 48–57.

Petty, S. (1992) 'African cinema and (re)education: using recent African feature films', *Issue: A Journal of Opinion*, XX/2: 26–30.

Picton, J. (1990) 'Transformations of the artifact: John Wayne, plastic bags and the eye-that-surpasses-all-other-eyes', in C. Deliss (ed.) *Lotte or the Transformation of the Object Durch 7/8*, Austria: Kunstverein.

—— (1995) 'Dialogue', *African Arts*, 28 (3): 84–5.

Turner, V. (1974) *Dramas, Fields and Metaphors: Symbolic Action in Human Society*, Ithaca NY and London: Cornell University Press.

Van Gennep, A. (1960 [1909]) *Rites of Passage*, trans. M. Vizedom and G. Caffee, Chicago: University of Chicago Press.

Chapter 4

From ritualization to performativity
The Concheros of Mexico

Susanna Rostas

My concern in this chapter is to assess anew the so-called 'ritual process'. I suggest that we do not need to make a distinction between ritual and performance although, as the title of the book implies, we frequently conceptualize them as disparate entities. I do not look then at how these two reifications may be seen to be interrelated but, as my ethnography will show, explore why they are not distinct. The Concheros hold all-night vigils and on the following day a dance. It could be said that the vigil is more of a ritual than a performance but it has performative aspects, while the dance is perhaps more of a performance than a ritual, although during a dance there are periods of ritualization.

The performative as an aspect of enactments has largely been ignored until comparatively recently. Turner explored with Schechner the possible continuities between the rituals that he had witnessed in Africa and the cultural performances of the theatrical world. But despite this wider purview, he remained enamoured of or entrapped by the structural stages he had utilized in his earlier work and more especially the dichotomy between structure and anti-structure (Turner 1982, 1986, Schechner and Appel 1990). Tambiah (1985 [1981]) suggested that ritual has a performative side that should be looked at in conjunction with the more formalized dimension: the repetition of invariant and stereotyped sequences. More recently, the prescribed aspect of ritual or ritualization has been explored in some depth by Humphrey and Laidlaw (1994), but much less attention was given to the often more 'masked' or intentional element which I call 'performativity' (Humphrey and Laidlaw 1994: 69, 263, Goody 1977: 32).

In this chapter I employ 'ritualization' and 'performativity' as processual terms for different forms of human agency that indicate a tendency towards a particular kind of action or activity. I will be arguing that both are likely to be found in any enactment which will be constituted by more or less of one with respect to the other (and much else besides). I will be suggesting that they can occur separately or alternately (more or less rapidly), but that predominantly they occur together when, under certain conditions, other additional states of being can then emerge. The chapter is at an exploratory stage and 'ritualization' has been formulated in more depth than 'performativity', on which I take a more tentative stand.

ETHNOGRAPHIC BACKGROUND

The Concheros meet to perform a circle dance and to hold all-night vigils at frequent intervals throughout the year. They hold four major dances in locations that are the sites of both Catholic churches and pre-Hispanic temples, the former usually having been constructed from the latter. The major dances are held on significant dates in the Catholic calendar, while each group also holds smaller dances, often as frequently as once a week, to dance for some significant event in its own tradition, to honour a saint's fiesta or that of an Aztec deity, or to perform by invitation on a cultural occasion in some new location.

All the groups, of which there are many, dance the same dances and sing the same songs, but there is considerable divergence in the clothing worn. This variety is indicative of the range of ideas held as to what the dance signifies and how indigenousness should be represented, although all groups, except possibly the most rural, are vociferous in their various ways that the dance is about the regeneration of Indianity.

THE VIGIL

A vigil is a more private and informal affair than a dance, which it frequently precedes. Special clothing is not worn and the participants dress up warmly in preparation for the long hours of work ahead throughout the night. Arriving at the house where the vigil is to be held in twos and threes, they bring with them candles and large bunches of flowers of all types and colours; carnations, roses, lilies, *cempasuchil* (marigolds). These are handed to the *saumadora*, who cares for the incense burner, over which she passes them following a three-dimensional form as she presents them to the four winds (which are roughly equivalent to the four cardinal points).

The vigil opens usually at about 11 p.m., with the playing of the *pasion* on the *concha*, an instrument that is special to the Concheros, made from the carapace of an armadillo (and it this that gives them their name). The *pasion* is said to call up the spirits (*animas*) of the dead (dancers). Thereafter the *saumadora* can begin to direct the main work of the night: the building of the flower form which is accompanied by singing backed by music also played on the *concha*. During the work, there are brief breaks during which people can talk, get something to drink and stretch themselves, but when the music begins again, it indicates that work is about to be resumed. Talking must then stop and all those present sing the *alabanza* (a song of praise or hymn) appropriate to that phase of the vigil, as they focus their attention on those who have been asked to lay out the flower form on the ground. The overall design is usually that of a cross with four or more arms of equal or unequal length, while the details will depend on the flowers available and the suggestions of the *saumadora*. Once the form has been completed, prayers are said, and words of thanks –presented as short impromptu speeches – are offered to the assembled company by those who have been asked to perform this task. At this stage, the assembled company normally moves elsewhere to eat, before returning for the next phase of the work, the tying of these same flower-heads to the *bastons* (rods), which is also accompanied by singing. In the following stage, as dawn approaches, these are then used to cleanse those present, by passing them over their bodies, first their fronts, heads and backs and then their arms.

The participants now usually snatch a little sleep before breakfasting and then dressing up for the day's dance. An hour or two later the house is usually the scene of frenetic preparations as the dancers struggle to take off the warm layers of clothing before dressing themselves up in their more minimal and highly decorated costumes elaborated especially, usually over a long period of time, for the dance. Finally a conch shell is blown to attract everybody's attention: the moment has come to go out to dance.

THE DANCERS

But who participates in such events? The Concheros come from all walks of life. Some are rural peasants, others urban workers, whilst the largest contingent are middle-class town and city dwellers. Rural dancers can offer little exegesis as to why they dance; the dance and its attendant vigils are part of the Catholic tradition in their locality and it is one that has run in their families for many generations (Rostas 1996). For urban proletarians, with a little education, the dance is more clearly about indigenous identity. Some come from rural families who dance, but more frequently they have come across the dance since they have moved to the city and it is thus something that they have chosen to become involved with. For the middle group, which ranges from people who have clerical jobs, to professionals, to those involved in the arts – professional dancers, potters, actors, painters – the dance is understood rather differently again. Far fewer of such people come from families who have traditionally danced. This group of dancers have more self-awareness than the members of the two earlier groups. They see the dance not only as a re-presentation of an indigenous past that is rapidly disappearing but also as a way of re-enacting or recreating something essentially Mexican, with which they feel a particular affinity. It is too a means to personal fulfilment through the experience of the dance, a way of building or changing their consciousness in the longer term.

For upper middle-class housewives with time on their hands or the more numerous young interested in the esoteric, the dance is a conscious search for enlightenment, a way to get a 'high', and often just one amongst many 'paths' that they may follow, others being Sufism or Buddhism (for example). In addition there are the 'New Age' dancers, who claim that their main concern is with ecology and attaining a balance with nature by means of a certain lifestyle. But most importantly there are those who in the interests of 'Indianity' are rejecting the Catholic church completely and attempting to recreate a pre-Hispanic form of religiosity based predominantly on elements taken from the Aztec past. These dancers call themselves the Mexica and their number has been growing rapidly since the early 1990s (Rostas 1991, 1993). For the Mexica, it is not so much that they assume 'Indianity' only when they dance, but rather that they lead their everyday lives in such a way that such claims form an inherent part of their quotidian discourse and practice. Most are members of a social movement that calls itself *mexicanidad* and the dance is but one of their interrelated activities. The Mexica are increasingly bringing the dance into the public arena. By not only freeing it of Catholic elements but cleansing it also of Hispanic influences, the Mexica are fulfilling a felt want in Mexican society in the wake of the so-called celebrations for the five-hundred-year 'discovery' of the Americas of 1992.

Traditionally the dance has not been performed for an audience: if there are onlookers well and good, but to be watched is not essential to or part of the intention behind the dance, although, as I shall be discussing in this chapter, the Mexica are beginning to change this. On the other hand the Concheros, although few in number, have a relatively high profile in the arts world in Mexico City. Their dance has strong links with professional theatre and dance: the latter have both been influenced by and influenced the Concheros at times in the past; for example, the Ballet Folklorico has several dances in its repertoire that have come directly from the Concheros' tradition.

The main activities discussed in this chapter, the vigil and the dance, are linked closely with the other activities in the everyday lives of those involved. The Concheros tend to socialize with each other and spend time discussing the dance, enquiring about arrangements and commenting on other dancers' performances both in and outside the dance. They also do this both before, after and occasionally during both vigils and dances. For the purposes of this chapter I shall limit my purview to the above two distinctive ways of 'going on'[1] that the Concheros evince, manifested under particular but rather different conditions. The many kinds of group outlined above, and individuals within them, give a range of different meanings to their dance, but in this chapter I am concerned primarily with the processes involved in their activities, rather than with meaning and symbolization.

RITUALIZATION/PERFORMATIVITY

I have already indicated that, as an analyst, I am tempted to describe the vigil as more of a ritual than a performance and the dance as more of a performance than a ritual, but the Concheros themselves do not talk about the two events in these terms.[2] The Concheros, being enactors, do not make these distinctions. For them a vigil is known as a *velacion* and is seen to be 'work'; it is above all a 'sacrifice' and frequently referred to as such. A dance, however, is talked about as *una danza*, and if one goes well it will tend to be described as a 'conquest'; which certainly implies more than just discharging one's duties; that is, it is perhaps more than a ritual, rather it is a performance.

But to talk of ritual and/or performance for the Concheros gives us descriptive categories, which reifies them and tells us very little about process. Rather 'ritualization' and 'performativity' indicate a tendency towards a particular kind of action. They do not describe the action *per se* but indicate a propensity for the action during any particular part or phase of activity to be of a particular kind. The terms can be used to highlight important differences in the activity or action and are useful as tools in my analysis of the Concheros, both for any one group of Concheros and for drawing distinctions between the different types of group described above. I will now outline how 'ritualization' and 'performativity' will be used in this chapter.

To begin from our everyday usage of these terms: when we say that something is being done as 'a ritual', or rather 'ritualistically', we tend to mean according 'to the book', according to convention or tradition, possibly rather emptily, without innovation or meanings supplied individually (or communally) by those carrying out the activity, which because of its habitual nature can be seen as 'ritual' (Boudewijnse 1995, Asad 1993: 58). Thus 'ritualistic' can have the meaning of being empty of conscious intention; perhaps, at the extreme, even of becoming, and thus being, completely without meaning. In this case, 'ritualization' might be used to describe the process whereby an action that had once had meaning has now become empty: ritualistic.

That is not precisely how I will be using 'ritualization', but is certainly linked to it. For ritualization is to do with the quality which an action can come to have, a special way in which any act may be performed. It indicates a way of acting that is non-intentional, that does not depend on the agent's intention in acting, that is habitual – or has become part of the habitus, to use Mauss's and then Bourdieu's term (Bourdieu 1977) – that can be done with half one's attention on it, or with the mind on other matters. It is the rendering of acts that could be intentional, non-intentional, that makes ritual, ritual. So ritualization does not describe the action *per se*, but the way that an(y) act may be carried out, the occasional modification of that intrinsic feature of action, intentionality; in religious activity, the special way that it is performed. It is the conforming to conventions that makes the act a ritual act (Humphrey and Laidlaw 1994).

Ritual action is stipulated and not necessarily accomplished by processes of intentional understanding, thus it does not imply that any particular beliefs, ideas or values are held by the actors. It is necessary to look at the quality of ritualized action itself rather than to ask about the beliefs, attitudes or purposes which those who perform ritual might or might not have. The relation between intention and action is transformed because of the adoption of a 'ritual stance', the making of a ritual commitment (Humphrey and Laidlaw 1994: 94, 88) or the 'ritual ruling' (Lewis 1980). What the actors' action should be can be described as prescribed: it is ready made and precedes the conduct of those who come to perform it; 'ritualized action is stipulated . . . by constitutive rules which establish an ontology of ritual acts' (Humphrey and Laidlaw 1994: 89). This provides the 'identity' for ritual acts in the absence of intention. By choosing to adopt the 'ritual stance', the actors accept that they will not be the authors of their actions, although they themselves are carrying them out. Thus in my terms the actors deny their ego, or in Humphrey and Laidlaw's they remove 'the sovereignty of [themselves] as agent[s]', for in ritual 'you both are and are not the author of your acts' (1994: 96, 99).

People learning ritual acts start by copying, reproducing what they have been taught by others, which requires thought about what is actually being done. But later what they do or what happens can be described as 'making manifest' (Humphrey and Laidlaw 1994: 102); when practices have become embodied and can be reproduced spontaneously and without thought, in the appropriate setting. Such acts are perceived as discrete, named entities, and 'the sense that in doing them, one is doing more than one seems', accounts for much of the 'felt power' of ritual (ibid.: 101). It is 'because [such] acts are felt, by those who perform them to be external, [that] they are "apprehensible"' (ibid.: 89): they can then be scrutinized and reassimilated to the actors' intentions. Ritualization, in sum, involves a modification of the normal intentionality of human action: it 'effects a subtle yet pivotal transformation in the relation between intention and action'(ibid.: 88).

Performance, on the other hand, in everyday life, at the extreme, often has the sense of putting more into something (in a self-conscious or intentional way) than is absolutely necessary; of loading an act with meaning, even of overdoing it, of above all insisting on 'meaning to mean'. So if someone makes rather a fuss over something, or a scene to melodramatic effect, we might say that 'that was quite a performance'. Performativity is thus a measure of the effort (or energy or affect) put into an action.[3] Performativity entails action that is not prescribed, the deployment of consciously formulated strategies. It implies individuality and resourcefulness as put into the movement: it can be seen as creative. On the whole it is the performativity that gives an enactment its zest, that makes ritual and/or performance interesting to watch.

Some part of any activity is habitual (involves ritualization), in that it has been done like that before, or there is a script to follow, or there are actions that are prescriptive. But that is not the whole story. For it to be a 'good performance', some intention, some effort must be put into it. Emphasis must be put on the use of personal energy or effort or power: something over and above the 'conventional' must be added to it. In Spanish the verb *animarse*, meaning to animate oneself, expresses an important aspect of performativity. In this sense performance can thus be good or bad. Ritualization on the other hand is ritualization, whether it is carried out well or not; and the context in which the latter occurs usually makes it inappropriate to have expectations or to make judgements about it.

THE RELATIONSHIP BETWEEN RITUALIZATION AND PERFORMATIVITY

Ritualization and performativity can be looked at analytically as discrete processes but in an enactment they will tend to be activated in sequence or together. In an overall sense, the action will begin with a period of predominant ritualization followed by predominant performativity. Thus at the beginning of a vigil or dance, ritualization occurs before performativity comes into play, but towards the end of a vigil when the flower form has been built, the construction of which has strong performative aspects, the ensuing activity then becomes increasingly ritualized. Or, as the dance proceeds, a period of ritualization may be re-energized by a spurt of performativity; as when a dancer pushes herself or himself to her or his limits, thus restimulating those around her or him (and I say more about this later). Or a period of performativity is recontrolled by one of ritualization. Throughout the activity there is an apparent oscillation from the one to the other: in fact this is a movement that occurs frequently, repeatedly, even continuously throughout both a vigil and a dance.

But this is perhaps only at one level. At another level performativity and ritualization can and do act together, and this becomes especially the case as an enactment proceeds or builds up. So for example, when, after years of dancing, the ability to act non-intentionally can be achieved in the way a dancer dances, a further state of intentionality can then come into play that emanates from that earlier ritualized state and merges with it: this could be the desire or intention on the part of the dancer to put more effort into the activity, or to change the direction of what he or she is doing, or to add new flourishes or steps. So that *in toto*, the actors are in part involved in acts that they themselves are not aware of authoring but onto which they superimpose some further action and into which they channel their conscious intentions. So the dancers do not just let themselves be danced, let their bodies flow with the dance, but they can, at the same time, have the conscious intention of putting something more of themselves into it, of pushing themselves as far as they have pushed themselves in the past; to the limits (or beyond) of their inculcated habitus. This then is not a dichotomy, rather this distinction is closely linked to Hastrup's idea of double agency (this volume) where the actor as agent both 'is' and 'is not'. The training (of an actor or dancer) permits the enactor to perform between identities as a double agent, which makes it possible to work on 'being' and 'becoming' simultaneously.

I would suggest that ritualization can occur without performativity. The example here would be of someone carrying out ritual actions either extremely passively or only intellectually: that is in their head, which we might want to call mental performativity (such as in a Quaker meeting). But on the whole, to attain ritualization, a degree of corporeal performativity seems to be necessary. The aim of the dance for the Concheros is to achieve the two together: a successful dance is when ritualization and performativity can be made to act together or in parallel. It is, however, possible for performativity to act in an opposing sense to ritualization and I shall give an example of this below. It is also possible for performativity to occur without much ritualization: so for the Mexica, the dance is becoming more concerned with what they communicate outwardly than with attaining a state of ritualization, at least as the Concheros understand it.

To look at these differing ways of enacting, that is the possible combinations of 'ritualization' and 'performativity', I want to return to the dancers whom I left changing into their dance clothes after an all-night vigil in order to go out to dance.

THE DANCE

The Concheros travel to the site of the dance in formation: two lines following the banner carried by the lieutenant, with the *jefe*, *saumadora* and those who are taking responsibility for the dance, known as those carrying 'the word' (the *palabras*). The nomenclature of the Concheros is predominantly militaristic: a leader high up in the hierarchy is known as a general (although most are more simply known as *jefes*); the dancer who metes out discipline is called the sergeant; the one who bears the group's standard is the lieutenant, while the dancers themselves are the foot soldiers. En route, the *palabras* will be active in between the two lines, setting the pace for the slow, forward-moving dance steps. If there has not been a vigil, the dancers will change their clothes at the location where they are to perform.

The site of the dance having been reached, the two columns proceed into the church to pray and to sing an *alabanza*, often to Santiago (St James). Outside again, the columns then move through a complex ritual formation to encompass the four winds (equivalent here in space to the four cardinal directions). Further prayers are said, including the Lord's Prayer, and then the petition for permission is sung. By this later means, permission is requested to dance in that location from God the Father, the Son and the Holy Spirit and more especially from the conquering souls of the four winds (*las animas conquistadores de los cuatro vientos*). These are considered to be present during the dance, invoked specifically by the *saumadora*. Then when the dancers have fanned out and are in circle formation facing inwards, the *jefe*, *saumadora*, the three *palabras*, and any visitors who have come without their group will render holy or take over the space of the circle. This they do by presenting their *conchas* to the four winds, a process linked to further prayers. Then, and only then, can the dance begin. Thus a fairly complex process of ritualization is gone through by the dancers, involving a combination of bodily activity, singing and prayer, which is linked to the framing of the space, for its reclassification can be said to mirror the mental reclassification of ritualization.[4]

During a dance men and women, placed alternately in the circle, perform together while the leader of the group takes up a position in the centre with the *saumadora* beside him or her. There are about fifteen dances named after Aztec deities, animals and agrarian activities (Rostas 1991). Each has a similar structure: the opening sequence, followed by variations, between each of which the opening sequence is once again performed. Before any one dance can begin, there is a repetitive period of ritualization, known as the *permiso*, in which the dancer moves his or her body slowly and surely first in a turn to the left and then to the right, after which the form of a cross is traced out on the ground with the toe of the right foot, followed by the stamping of the left three times and then the other way around. The *permiso* takes about two to three minutes to perform and is followed by the shouting out of '*el es dios*' by the leader, to which all the dancers respond in unison with the same words. '*El es dios*' translates literally as 'he is God' and is (I have been told) an invocation to the deity of the dance to enter the dancer; an indication that what is about to happen is occurring by consensus and not according to the dictates of one person's will. It is an indication that each dancer is ready to take the next step in ritualization, to hand over his or her individual will to that of the deity: that the 'ritual stance' has been adopted.

For every dance, one dancer is invited into the centre to perform, so that all the dancers can follow his or her example: this process is usually initiated by the first *palabra*. The actions of this dancer are in a way rather like those of the conductor of an orchestra; each dancer in the circle knows his or her steps (more or less well depending on his or her experience), but gains his or her sense of the timing of the dance not just from the music but also from the speed at which this dancer executes that dance. The analogy of an orchestra is helpful too in understanding that the dancers are facing into the centre, focusing their attention on the person dancing in the centre, not outwards to the onlookers, although they are vaguely conscious of how their 'orchestration' of the dance is blending in with that of their neighbours on either side. After the first dance, the *palabra* asks dancers one after another to come into the centre of the circle to perform 'their' dance. By 'their' dance is usually meant the dance that any particular dancer performs best, that she or he feels greatest affinity with, that she or he has developed certain elaborations for, that are well tried and are now part of her or his habitus or 'ritual stance'. Although she or he may still have to put that extra attention into them, she or he is beginning to enable her or his ritualization not to be dominated by performativity.

From now on there is no pre-set or preferred order in which the dances must occur. A particular named dance may be danced several times during the course of the morning, or once only or not at all. Nor is there any predetermined idea of who will be leading them.[5] When asked to come from the periphery and enter the circle to perform 'his or her' dance, it is up to each dancer to animate the others in the circle (so that they will be inspired to follow the example by giving as much of themselves as possible to the dance). If this works for everyone then ritualization and performativity

Figure 4.1 A dancer playing her *concha* as she dances: she balances ritualization and perfomativity expertly and transcends frequently

augment one another and can be said to be occurring in parallel. Needless to say this is very rare, and I will return to this later on.

More frequently, those dancing are at such different levels of proficiency that in a large circle of dancers there will always be someone who could be said to be hindering the ritualization of the whole. But the dance is not exclusive but inclusive; the more dancers the better, even if their dance is only rudimentary. Further, the dancers are in no way linked physically. Although ideally they are placed in the circle, men alternately with women, there are often unequal numbers or the dance begins before the dancers can position themselves in the preferred order. Each dancer, although part of the circle, is in his or her own dance space and free to dance in his or her own way, providing this conforms with the tenets of the group; individual dancers do sometimes transcend while those around them do not (Figure 4.1); I say more about this below.

But although this is what most might hope to achieve, it is not necessarily the overall purpose or work of a dance. The role of those who 'carry the word' is to take responsibility for the dance, to encourage and look after the dancers; to be able to sense what is happening to all the 'personnel', even those who are not fully in view. As one informant put it, the role of the *palabra* is to ensure that all can follow what is being enacted, that the obligations are carried out as they should be according to tradition and that harmony is achieved (Figure 4.2).

I turn now from practice to the tenets of practice. The maxim of the Concheros is 'Union, conformity, and conquest' (*union, conformidad y conquista*); these precepts appear on the banners of some groups and are repeated frequently amongst the dancers. They indicate the type of work that everyone in the circle needs to do to ensure that the group achieves a good outcome. Although 'ritualization' and 'performativity' are my analytical terms and are not used by the dancers, they relate as indicated below to the desired states of the dancers. The exegesis of 'union', 'conformity' and 'conquest' is verbal and ongoing; their interpretation varies to a degree from group to group and between individuals. 'Union' refers to the initial enactment of asking permission, to the process of ritualization before each dance begins, and to the further, shorter periods that occur throughout the dance. It refers too to the initial disposition to participate in the dance, to act communally or non-intentionally in the same way as everyone else. 'Conformity' refers to the type of harmonious enactment that is achieved by the circle as a whole when each dancer has divested herself or himself of her or his ego so that she or he can be 'obedient': that is, no dancer dances in such a way as to belittle the dancing of others. Performativity, although present, is carefully controlled. Lastly, 'conquista' refers to what the dance communicates to those involved, to what the dance does to you or teaches you, and what it says or does (possibly) to those watching, if there is anyone watching: for these people might in the future want to come and join the

Figure 4.2 Ritualization at the end of a Conchero dance: two groups that have danced together separate

dance. In principle the dance is not performed to be watched but is rather a learning experience, linked to humility.

It is perhaps easier to illustrate what is meant by this by giving an example of its non-achievement. Thus when a dancer who is a visitor from another group is asked, as a matter of courtesy, to perform 'his or her' dance in the centre, he or she may dance in such a way that the group's dancing is disrupted. The way this particular dancer performs is novel and challenging to the others in the circle, and although they attempt to follow, they cannot keep up: especially if it is a man, either he may move too fast or his footwork may be so complex that the familiar timing of that dance to which they have become accustomed is overridden. What has become the 'ritual stance' for that one visiting dancer (and probably others too in his own group), who has danced for many years in this manner, is experienced by those in this particular circle (some of whom may be comparative neophytes) as performative intentionality rather than ritualization animated by a measure of performativity. He thus draws the main body of dancers out of their state of ritualization and into a self-conscious state of performativity, where they are trying desperately to do something new without the benefit of practice. David Parkin has called this a 'tangled state', what happens 'when participants interfere in each other's interpretations of the ritual "ruling"' (1992: 24). A breakdown of the dance may then occur, with everyone moving at different times, in different ways and directions, and rather than that particular dance producing a sense of 'unity' linked to 'conformity', it will terminate in disarray and disruption. In this case the 'interference' may not have been wholly intentional, but the leading dancer has not modified his dance to suit the circumstances (their idea of union) and so has not enabled either 'unity' or 'conformity' (let alone 'conquest'); he has not in other words fulfilled his responsibilities.

This situation can be remedied by the first *palabra* asking a dancer to enact the next dance whom she or he knows from experience will be easy to follow, but the desired state of ritualization can also be restored by the permission (*permiso*), enacted by all the dancers before the next dance starts. Thus although much of the dancing has to do with the combined effects of performativity and ritualization, before every dance begins there is a calm, ritualizing sequence that enables the state of the dance to move towards 'union' and 'conformity' once again.

On the other hand, if the first *palabra* (or *jefe*) senses that the dancers are tired, and that the dance is beginning to be lacklustre in quality, she or he may ask a dancer to come into the circle and really let himself or herself go in order to energize the others. A female informant described one such dancer. Apparently, many think of him as a show-off, as one who likes to 'move a lot and . . . flaunt his brilliance'. However, she went on to say that a time comes in the dance when, after many hours of dancing, although you may begin to feel exhausted, it is necessary to go on, to tap another level, to generate a further source of energy. If a dancer such as the one described above is invited into the centre he enables such a transformation to occur. His dance, which appears to be mere performativity to an outsider, is in reality the action of ritualization linked to performativity. According to the same informant, by dancing in the centre but close to those most depleted, he 'lifts them up'.

TO TRANSCEND

When ritualization and performativity are acting together in some kind of balance, or rather when that intermixing that is right for any particular dancer is attained, the point is reached at which a dancer can begin to transcend to another state of consciousness. One informant described for me this new state of being. She starts by saying that the keeping going in itself stimulates you and:

> you forget your exhaustion, you forget about the outside world, you dance, you forget about being exhausted . . . Suddenly you are filled with good emotions; you want to smile, laugh, or shout something completely spontaneously . . . [such as] 'no, we're not alone, we're all together'.

What the above dancer is describing seems to be a non-everyday psychological state on the way to trance, but not actually trance itself. Transcendence is perhaps a term best left to resonate. However, Turner has explored the term 'flow', used by Csikszentmihalyi. He characterizes it as that 'holistic sensation present when we act with total involvement', a state that seems to need no conscious intervention on our part, when what we experience is 'a unified flowing from one moment to the next, in which we feel in control of our actions, and in which there is little distinction between self and environment; between stimulus and response; or between past, present, and future' (Csikszentmihalyi, as quoted in Turner 1982: 56). The state is summarized by Turner as one in which there is no dualism; that is, there is a merging of action and awareness made possible by the centring of attention on a limited stimulus field. Unlike 'communitas', flow is an individual experience; you may be experiencing it, and your perceptions seem to indicate that others are too, but you can never be sure: it is elusive, rather like the state of being in love and akin to the Christian state of grace. 'Communitas', sometimes referred to as anti-structure, is a term of Turner's which I have carefully avoided using in this chapter. It is a state or space rather than a process and is communal rather than individual; thus ritualization can be seen as a tendency towards 'communitas', but is not 'communitas' itself.

It is in this new state of being that, as one informant said, the dance begins to talk to you:

> the leader introduces you, presents you to the dance. It is the dance who teaches you and who adopts you as her apprentice. It is the dance who chooses you, the dance becomes your mistress . . . and talks directly to you, to you alone, not to the group.

Not everyone can attain this state or status, but some can and do. Most dancers are not destined to become the apprentices of the goddess of dance: this is a state they never experience. For the majority the dance is something that they do for a variety of completely other reasons.

THE PREDOMINANCE OF PERFORMATIVITY

This brings me back to the Mexica, the dancers who promote 'Indianity'. The Mexica's dance is not fully approved of by many of the main groups of Concheros; for although they dance the same dances they do not on the whole adopt the 'ritual stance' familiar to the Concheros. Their dance style is seen to be a concatenation of performative aspects, such as flamboyant clothing and overly expressive footwork combined with little desire to find the energy of the godhead, that at-one-ment (atonement (Ness 1992: 11)). Many Concheros are concerned that what the Mexica are doing with the dance is not what it should be about at all.

A sense of 'union' and 'conformity' is rarely achieved by the Mexica, and their dance does not appear to be about 'conquest', at least in the sense predominantly held by the Concheros. The Mexica have largely truncated many of the preliminaries of 'ritualization' discussed above; they do not present themselves to the four winds in formation, they do not entone the same prayers, and they do not enunciate 'el es dios' at the end of the permission, for obvious reasons: for they want to commune with the various Aztec deities, not the Christian God.[6] Further, they dance the 'permission' more as an exercise in individual prowess than as a sequence of movements that leads to harmonious interdependence or what Tambiah has called 'interpersonal orchestration' (1985 [1981]: 138). If we can talk of 'ritualization' for the Mexica, each dancer's is so individual that it does not seem to produce what the Concheros understand by 'union'.

Their performativity is not one controlled by ritualization: it has little to do with the Concheros' idea of 'conformity'. The Mexica's desire is to assert the self rather than to deny it. They dance in an egocentric and competitive manner. Few women dance in their groups, as the dance is usually so rapid that many cannot keep up. It is not unusual to see a dancer performing in the centre of the circle dressed in impossibly huge plumes, the speed and intricacy of whose dance is such that virtually no one in his group can follow his pace. Rather than animating the rest of the dancers, his dance turns them from being co-performers to disempowered strugglers, in a state of 'entanglement' (Parkin 1992). This could be called empty performativity or what bystanders watching in Mexico often call 'show',[7] for it is performativity not built on the ritualization common to other groups of Concheros, which is effectively a ritualization that is similar for all those in any one group.

Nor are the Mexica interested in finding that balance between performativity and ritualization when transcendence can begin to occur, which is ultimately what the Concheros mean by conquest. 'Conquest' for them is not to do with the control of the human impulses of egoism, ambition for power and pre-potency (as one informant defined 'conquest' for me) but rather the reverse (Figure 4.3). The Mexica undoubtedly get a 'high' from dancing, which seems to me to have much less to do with consciousness raising and much more to do with the production of endomorphins, the outcome of pushing the physical body to its limits, as do athletes: although to be fair, their production is probably also important in the Concheros' dancing. But the Mexica's dance, rather than bringing out the best in them, seems to bring out the worst: to enhance their competitiveness. A huge number of fights occur not only between groups of Mexica dancers but between individual dancers in the same group, both before and even after a dance and often in public places, to the acute embarrassment and shame of groups of Conchero dancers present. Further, I was often told by Mexica dancers that the energy

Figure 4.3 A moment of extreme performativity at the end of a Mexica dance

of the circle is disrupted if someone enters it during a dance, that such an act brings dancers 'down': whereas various Concheros told me that a dancer should be unaware of what is going on around him or her.

The Mexica are more interested in making a political statement: their way of dancing, rather than reinforcing the values of the tradition, is leading to the politicization of the dance within those constraints to which they still adhere. I have already mentioned that the Mexica's aim is to free the dance from any links with the Catholic church, but they aim also to reject any part of the practices which might be considered to be Spanish. Thus they do not enter churches before they dance, their prayers are either non-existent or (invented) Nahuatl ones, Nahuatl being the language of the Aztecs, which many are learning and from which they frequently adopt names, such as Moctezuma or Cuahtemoc. The *concha*, so central to the tradition of the majority of dancers, is rejected by the Mexica because of its European origins and instead they play their music on instruments (predominantly percussive) of known pre-Colombian origin; the *huehue* (drum), the *teponaztli* (slit drum) and small pipes and rattles.

CONCLUDING REMARKS

This chapter has argued that an analysis of the activities of the Concheros makes it difficult to differentiate ritual from performance. A distinction can be made between a vigil and a dance as events, although as indicated the one merges into the other; it could perhaps be said that a vigil is the process of ritualization prior to a dance on the following day, which is more performative. This, however, would be to simplify complex activity. For in both, ritualization *and* performativity occur, the latter alternating with or emerging from the other after the initial process of ritualization has been attained. During a vigil and more particularly a dance, periods of ritualization are followed by periods of performativity, which in turn lead to periods of ritualization balanced by performativity.

What each group does with the dance varies considerably. But to generalize, the country groups of Concheros perform with a predominance of ritualization and the minimum of performativity. To achieve 'union' and 'conformity' is for them all-important, and their 'conquest' is primarily a spiritual one; their identities are well established and taken for granted, while those in Mexico City are more involved in identity politics. Many city groups and especially those with middle-class dancers have long since subverted the rural ways. Their dance has much more performativity to it; costumes are more varied, different ways of sequencing certain steps are explored. They are to an extent open-minded about the content of the dance.

As already indicated, the Mexica have little interest in ritualization. 'union' and 'conformity' have been abandoned in favour of 'conquest', but conquest which is based in pure performativity. The title of the chapter refers in part to the fluctuation between ritualization and performativity (and vice versa) that occurs throughout a dance, but more particularly to the changes that the Mexica appear to be making to the practices of the Concheros. Although the Concheros argue that the Mexica's dance has little to do with 'union, conformity and conquest', as already indicated the Mexica would deny this. They claim that the precepts need to be given new meaning; that the end of the twentieth century is a time for outer conquest, not for a search for inner harmony. But they tend to say that they do not make claims to being Concheros; and indeed they seem not to be!

ACKNOWLEDGEMENTS

I would like to acknowledge not only the support of the British Academy and the Nuffield Foundation, who have made several short fieldwork trips for this project possible, but also all those who helped me in Mexico City. Gratitude goes also to the other contributors, and to Felicia Hughes-Freeland for organizing the conference and realizing this book. Currently I have a grant in aid of research to assist in the preparation of a book on the project from the Leverhulme Foundation.

NOTES

1 This Wittgensteinian designation is used by Humphrey and Laidlaw to classify the kinds of action carried out during ritual (1994: 89).
2 There is no equivalent term for performance in Spanish; the verb closest to 'to perform' is *disempeñar* ('to act' or 'to discharge'), but Mexicans do not talk about a dance performance as a *desempeño* (although the word exists) but as an *estreno* (for the first night) and thereafter as a *funcion* or *representacion*.
3 If, for example, I take washing up: this is precisely the kind of action that is done ritualistically; it is done frequently, usually in the same way, with attention but not conscious intention, other than that of getting the dishes clean, which has become an embodied, habitual activity. If someone carries out this action rather more dramatically than is strictly necessary for the task, with expansive movements and rather amusingly or angrily, for example, then we might want to classify this as 'performance', and look more closely at the performativity, the non-conventionality of the act, the non-habitual nature of it, even at its creativity.

   That household activity can involve 'ritualization' is indicated by George Herbert's poem 'The Elixir', in which he points out that any task can be done 'as for' him (God). Thus he declares that:

   > A servant with this clause
   > Makes drudgery divine:
   > Who sweeps a room, as for thy laws,
   > Makes that and th'action fine.
   >   (Herbert 1995: 189)

4 Framing is clearly linked to ritualization; it can be seen as marking it but is not part of it, it does not account for it. Framing can be seen as an external reclassification which mirrors the internal psychological processes involved in ritualization (cf. Humphrey and Laidlaw 1994: 75, 105).
5 Humphrey and Laidlaw discuss how the order of ritual acts is unimportant in the work that they carried out with Jains in India (1994: 126); unlike the order of events in everyday life, because the activity is non-intentional, ritual acts can occur in any order. For the Concheros, the order of ritual activity in the initial process of setting up the dance, which I have called the process of overall ritualization, is important because these acts by their performance enable people to begin to act non-intentionally. But the dance itself is more performative and although ritualization is still going on, it does not matter in which order the dances are performed
6 Various Mexica told me that the pre-Colombian deities are not different gods but

should rather be seen as different forms of energy. As members predominantly of a younger generation of dancers, (and admirers of Carlos Castaneda), they talk about the dance in terms of energies and are more inclined to conceptualize the dance as an 'energy field' than are other groups.

7 Occasionally bystanders ask if what they are witnessing is 'puro show'; that is they use the English word 'show' in their question and seem to be saying; is this dance anything other than showing off?

REFERENCES

Asad, T. (1993) 'Towards a genealogy of the concept of ritual', in *Genealogies of Religion: Discipline and Reasons of Power in Christianity and Islam*, Baltimore: Johns Hopkins University Press.

Boudewijnse, B. (1995) 'The conceptualization of religion', *Jaarboek voor Liturgie-Onderzoek*, 11: 31–53.

Bourdieu, P. (1977) *Outline of a Theory of Practice*, Cambridge: Cambridge University Press.

Goody, J. (1977) 'Against "ritual": loosely structured thoughts on a loosely defined topic', in S.F. Moore and B. Myerhoff (eds) *Secular Ritual*, Assen, The Netherlands: Van Gorcum.

Herbert, G. (1995) *The Complete English Works*, ed. A.P. Slater, London: Everyman.

Humphrey, C. and Laidlaw, J. (1994) *The Archetypal Actions of Ritual*, Oxford: Clarendon Press.

Lewis, G. (1980) *Day of Shining Red: An Essay on Understanding Ritual*, Cambridge: Cambridge University Press.

Ness, S.A. (1992) *Body, Movement, and Culture*, Philadelphia: University of Pennsylvania Press.

Parkin, D. (1992) 'Ritual as spatial direction and bodily division', in D. de Coppet (ed.) *Understanding Rituals*, London and New York: Routledge.

Rostas, S.E. (1991) 'The Concheros of Mexico: a search for ethnic identity', *Dance Research*, 9 (2): 3–17.

—— (1993) 'The Mexica's reformulation of the Concheros' dance; the popular use of autochthonous religion in Mexico City', in S. Rostas and A. Droogers (eds) *The Popular Use of Popular Religion in Latin America*, Amsterdam: CEDLA.

—— (1996) 'The production of gendered imagery', in M. Melhus and K.-A. Stolen (eds) *The Power of Latin American Gender Imagery*, London: Verso.

Schechner, R. and Appel, W. (eds) (1990) *By Means of Performance: Intercultural Studies of Theatre and Ritual*, Cambridge: Cambridge University Press.

Tambiah, S.J. (1985 [1981]) 'A performative approach to ritual', in *Culture, Thought and Social Action: An Anthropological Perspective*, Cambridge MA: Harvard University Press.

Turner, V. (1982) *From Ritual to Theatre: The Human Seriousness of Play*, New York: PAJ Publications.

—— (1986) *The Anthropology of Performance*, New York: PAJ Publications.

Chapter 5

Perspectives towards ballet performance

Exploring, repairing and maintaining frames

Helena Wulff

REFRAMING BALLET PERFORMANCE: MANIPULATION

At the world première of the short ballet *Firstext* by William Forsythe at Covent Garden, the stage was opened up and the stage manager and stage hands could be seen at work in the backstage area, as the audience slowly moved into the auditorium. Suddenly, at 7.30 sharp, when the performance was scheduled to start, the House lights were turned off. A large part of the audience stumbled in the dark. When they finally found their seats, the auditorium was lit up again, brighter than the stage, and this is how it stayed for the rest of the ballet. On stage, the line 'The Organization of Culture' was projected on the backdrop, and below a fire spread in a groove along the entire stage, finally to be extinguished by a lid that was placed over the groove.

A woman dancer entered in silence, dressed in short trousers, sleeveless shirt, and socks. Down on the floor, she started to bend her legs, seemingly beyond human imagination and capacity. A cracking sound suggested that her legs really were breaking. Then a side curtain slammed down. There were false starts of Bach music and fire-cracker sounds. Except for a few scattered laughs, the audience seemed to be in a state of shock.

In this chapter I investigate how ballet performances come about through the management of different perspectives and their frames by a number of agents. The frames may be explored choreographically, and they sometimes need to be repaired, as well as maintained. I draw mostly on ethnography of the Royal Ballet in London and Ballett Frankfurt in Frankfurt-am-Main, and to some extent of the Royal Swedish Ballet in Stockholm and the American Ballet Theatre in New York.[1] Contrary to the general approach in dance anthropology my focus is on the dancers, choreographers, technicians and ballet directors backstage, not the dance on stage. Since there are connections between social life backstage and illusion on stage, I include some observations of performances, however. I also take the audience, not least critics, into account, since they are there when the performances happen, more or less involved in the making of them. Backstage ethnography around performances, especially the narrow liminal zone in the wings, will anchor the production of the framed illusion on stage socially. After commenting on the concepts of ritual and revelation in relation to ballet performance, I conclude by discussing the creation of ballet art from the dancer's point of view, containing three different levels: frame maintenance, audience awareness and acting.

FRAMING BALLET PERFORMANCE: CONVENTIONS

Most anthropological studies on theatre, dance and performance have dealt with traditional societies and are associated with ritual. Many rituals contain sequences of dancing which are thus examples of performative behaviour. Charles Gore (cf. his chapter, this volume) exemplifies how skilled dancing in the public ritual of the Ohen in Benin City is a way of showing spiritual excellence. Performative behaviour can also be found in everyday life, and the concept of performance has been applied quite extensively in a transferred sense.[2] For my purpose here, to analyse the social production of ballet performances, I find Richard Bauman's definition of performance as 'an aesthetically marked and heightened mode of communication, framed in a special way and put on display for an audience' (1992: 41) appropriate.

The idea of frame in social acts is often referred to Gregory Bateson and his metacommunicative message 'this is play' (1972: 177–93), which may be challenged more or less explicitly. Influenced by Bateson, Erving Goffman (1974) analyses framing of theatrical performance (and even mentions ballet in passing), yet when it comes to ballet performance, Barbara Myerhoff's (1990: 247) suggestion 'Let's pretend' is more accurate. As much as play is used as a metaphor in performance studies, its joyous connotation does not cover the range of existential themes around life, love and death in the motifs of ballets. And as my opening vignette suggests, framing as well as reframing may be fragmented in ballet performance; the audience at Covent Garden reacted in different ways to Forsythe's new frame.

Built in the early eighteenth century, Covent Garden has been demolished twice by fire. The present Victorian building originates from 1858 (Koegler 1987). The auditorium is furnished in red velvet and some gold, evoking memories of Great Britain at the height of its imperial power, as well as that of significant ballet events and renowned dancers and choreographers. When Covent Garden was reopened after World War II, the Royal Ballet had a sensational international breakthrough with the *Sleeping Beauty*. Nearly twenty years later, Rudolf Nureyev danced here for little over a decade, making a dazzling impression not only on balletomanes but also on those ordinary theatre-goers who watch ballet performances occasionally.

The 1994–5 ballet season at Covent Garden opened with a gala performance of a new production of the *Sleeping Beauty*.[3] Choreographed by Marius Petipa to music by Tchaikovsky, the *Sleeping Beauty* had its world première at the Maryinsky Theatre in St Petersburg in 1890. The performance at Covent Garden took place in the presence of Princess Margaret, president of the Royal Ballet. The princess is an ardent ballet lover of many years' standing, and can be seen incognito at performances. She is reputed in the ballet world to be quite knowledgeable about ballet. This November evening, as the audience – in tuxedos and evening dresses in the stalls, or in blue jeans on the higher balconies – made its way to their seats, the expectant atmosphere was building up. A low murmur of voices, and the unharmonious sound of musicians tuning up their instruments in the orchestra pit, mixed with the sweet smell of theatre make-up.

The stalls circle was decorated with flowers to honour Princess Margaret. When the auditorium was filled, there was a pause, the audience rose – and the princess entered. The orchestra played 'God Save the Queen', and the audience sang. And then the performance started with the prologue, the christening of Princess Aurora.

In the first interval, the audience streamed out to the foyers, under the huge, sparkling crystal chandeliers: families with children, young and old couples, groups of friends, gay men. In the bars theatre-goers, balletomanes, critics and ballet people mingled, standing in line, talking in groups, exchanging greetings, meeting and avoiding glances. Those in the boxes remained seated, as salmon and champagne would arrive on order.

Three hours later, when Princess Aurora had married Prince Florimund in the glorious grand *pas de deux* in the third act, the applause exploded. There were loud 'Bravos' and stomping feet. After the curtain calls, Princess Margaret rose. The audience applauded her; she had been given a small bouquet of flowers. She waved and left.

The day after there was a feeling of happy relief in the rehearsal studios at Covent Garden. The première had gone very well. The dancers were pleased with their achievement, and they had felt the audience responding well to them. The ballet management was quite content. Then the reviews started coming in. On the whole, the critics were not impressed, especially not by the lavish pastel set and costumes.

CRITICS: THE EVALUATING GAZE

The profound tension between the artistic and the critical attitude is explained phenomenologically by Bensman and Lilienfeld (1973) as generic and consisting of the artist's aim of hiding technique in order to create a 'natural' world of artistry that the critic demolishes by analysing the technique. This becomes especially evident in non-verbal and non-textual art forms that use images, since the critic is confined to words. Although those dance critics who are skilled writers are able to create depth and other dimensions through their texts, on the whole they have to deal with one component of a performance after another since there is a certain linearity about a text that cannot be avoided. (Neither can the particular size and form of the page.) Unless something exceptional has occurred, many reviews start with a general description of the set and the choreography, the plot, if there is one, or an interpretation of emotions that the steps can be seen to signify. Evaluations may be built in, or come afterwards. Then comes a remark about the music, and perhaps towards the end the costumes and the lighting may be mentioned. Some critics make a point of situating dance pieces in dance history, in ideas of thought or in the wider art world, as well as in social conditions. But again, contrary to a performance that offers a combined experience of different visual and aural components, a review usually only has room for one component at a time because of its textual nature.

In the conflict over interpretative authority between dancers and critics, the critics' stance tends to be that 'it's none of the dancers' business to read reviews!' since 'I'm not writing for the dancers, but for the readers of the newspapers'. This becomes quite paradoxical for two reasons. Firstly, from what I saw and heard as a participant observer in the ballet world, dance reviews may be skimmed over by the general cultured newspaper reader, occasional theatre-goers, and colleagues and fellow dance writers of the critics. Balletomanes read them to make sure that their idols are treated well. It is, however, the dancers who are the most avid review readers, scrutinizing especially the sentences about themselves most thoroughly.

The second reason why it is paradoxical that critics state that they do not write for the dancers is that they have an impact on dancers' careers. Terms like 'breakthrough' can provide dancers with the recognition (cf. Bourdieu 1993) that they have been striving for. Reviews also serve to confirm positions and add to loss of recognition. There are dancers who make a personal decision to stop reading reviews, but since they live in a social context where other people (mothers, friends, rivals, ballet directors) read reviews, they may find themselves in a situation when someone unexpectedly comes up to them and starts consoling them – or congratulating them.

Dancers often feel called upon to point out that 'critics don't know anything about ballet'. Dancers' experience is an absorbing, bodily one, often the result of having performed a number of roles in certain productions over a long period of time. Critics know other things: they tend, for example, to be more knowledgeable about dance history than dancers, and many of the seasoned critics have in fact seen a large number of companies in many more productions than the dancers have. After all, since the latter have to concentrate on their own dancing all the time, they do not have that much time to go to other performances in their own city or abroad.

It is a discrepancy between *doing ballet* and *watching ballet* that is at stake, although both camps contain diversified experiences. The same performance appears quite different to leading dancers who are responsible for solos, on one hand, and corps de ballet dancers, on the other. Critics usually acquire their recognition among editors and fellow dance writers by writing mixed reviews, more negative than positive, at least with regard to established choreographers and companies. The ambiguity of mixed reviews allows them, moreover, to be read in different ways. Some reviews contain contributions to internal debates among critics, and personal communications of various sorts. Personal alliances and animosities between ballet people and critics add to the layers of discourse in the ballet world.

Habitual balletomanes and occasional theatre-goers do not register the same features of a particular performance either. And even if they all happen to be touched by an unexpected creation of ballet art on stage, thereby sharing an intense presence, they will reflect upon this state in fragmented ways afterwards, depending on earlier experiences of ballet, art and life.[4]

If there was often an ambivalence towards critics in Stockholm, London, New York and Frankfurt, I noticed a totally different attitude among the Russian dancers that I talked to and interviewed in the companies. Having lived through the period of political oppression in the former Soviet Union, where dance reviews had to be in line with the party mood – and hence were always positive – these Russians found the reviews in the west refreshing and interesting to read. Horst Koegler (1995) mentions how critic Vadim Gayevsky wrote a book where he condemned Yuri Grigorovich, then chief choreographer at the Bolshoi Ballet: the book was withdrawn and the editor was fired.

AUDIENCE: BALLETOMANES AND THEATRE-GOERS

Since classical ballet is perceived as so-called 'high culture' taking place in grand opera houses that probably seem like impregnable strongholds for the uninitiated, it is often taken for granted that ballet dancers themselves are of culturally and economically comfortable middle- and upper-class backgrounds. The audience is lumped together with the dancers. This is a misunderstanding. Ballet dancers identify themselves primarily as artists, finding themselves caught in the tension between cultural capital and the market, not really comfortable with either of them. In fact, most dancers do not possess much cultural capital of their own – they just provide it for the audience. Historically, ballet audiences came about through the establishment of ballet societies and friendship circles that also contributed financial sponsoring to ballet companies, which they still do.

Although many members of ballet societies are more interested in the social life they provide than in ballet *per se*, true balletomanes can also be seen at their meetings. For balletomanes, ballet is an absorbing hobby. There are balletomanes who after years of admiration at a distance get to know their stars personally. Balletomanes are also known for taking dance editors and critics to task if their stars have suffered bad reviews.

Dancers make an important distinction between good and bad balleto-manes. One bad variety of balletomanes are those ballet fans who, I was told by ballet directors, choreographers and dancers, 'go to the ballet because they lead distorted lives, they are fanatics who pursue dancers' by way of obscene or pathetic love letters and dirty telephone calls. They can be found in the groups of people who wait for colleagues, friends and family outside the stage door after performances. Inside the theatre they are talked about in terms of 'the nuts at the stage door'. 'Followers', on the other hand, keep a respectful distance from the stars they admire, and tend to limit their expressions of appreciation to the auditorium, by applauding, shouting 'Bravo' and throwing flowers on stage. Ordinary theatre-goers without a special interest in ballet keep a low profile in the auditorium.

BALLET PERFORMANCE BACK STAGE

As in any theatrical stage performance, what can be seen of a ballet performance from 'up front' or 'out there', in the auditorium, is only half of it. Even experimental dance which breaks boundaries and plays with the frames of illusion (sometimes extending beyond the stage by dancing among the audience, even in the foyer during intermissions) originates from back-stage, from what is mostly hidden from the audience. When backstage areas are exposed in performances, everyone knows that they have been cleaned up beforehand, and many of the ordinary activities which would usually go on in the wings have been moved away.

Not only does the polished illusion on stage appear totally different for dancers when they are in it from what they see of the same production from the auditorium the next evening, they told me emphatically; there is also an intense world backstage, producing the performance both before, during and after 'the show'.

Many theatres get the dancers to sign in before performances, so that they can be called if they are late, or an understudy can be notified in time if someone is ill or injured. When I was on tour with the American Ballet Theatre I discovered, however, that it happened that some of the dancers signed in for each other. As they explained to me: 'he's on his way, he just has to wake up' or 'she's having a bath'. At Covent Garden, the stage manager 'goes around the rooms [the dressing rooms] at half [half an hour before performance]' to check whether anyone is missing.[5] The dancers are also supposed to inform the ballet management or a coach if someone is not present in time.

On a performance day the dancers are usually in the theatre about an hour and a half before the performance starts, taking temporary refuge in the dressing rooms or hovering in the canteen. Some can be found doing warming-up exercises in a studio, or going over variations they are soon to perform on stage. Messages are transmitted over the Tannoy system: 'Teresa to stage door! You have a visitor!', 'Joaquín, please call 154!', or 'Camilla, please contact Sophie Soloview!' can be heard over and over again, addressing different people, mostly dancers. Assisted by make-up artists, dressers and wig makers, the dancers are putting on make-up and costumes, and having their hair done or wigs put on. As the stage manager announces: 'This is your half-hour-call!', which in fact is called 35 minutes before the performance is scheduled to start, the dancers are dropping down to the stage. With full stage make-up and dressed in warm practice clothes such as worn woollen sweaters, leg-warmers and plastic trousers over their often ethereal costumes, they walk towards the rosin box to make sure they will have a good grip, which they try on stage right away by doing some combinations of steps behind the closed curtain. There is already an indistinct humming from the other side of the curtain as the audience is on its way into the auditorium. Outside the stage area, the stage manager is calling 'the quarter' – 15 minutes left to performance. The dancers are nervous, but focused. Now the stage manager summons 'the fiver' and the ballet directors and coaches, dressed up in dark suits and ties, black silk and velvet and high heels, come down on stage to see that everyone and everything is ready, and to show their presence and support. As they hasten to their seats in the auditorium, the House manager who is 'up front' tells the stage manager through their electronic communication to start the performance by turning the House lights down. The humming in the auditorium is lowered, then it stops. In breathless silence, thousands of people are waiting for the conductor to arrive. He is greeted by applause and bows to the audience. Then he turns round and starts the orchestra. The curtain rattles to the sides, and there it is – another world for the audience to recognize and discover.

In classical ballets, the ballerina is welcomed by applause on her first entrance. So are guest dancers who do leading roles. As the performance progresses into the first interval, 'the red light is on' over doors leading to the backstage area. This means that entrance is prohibited because of the risk of accidents when big, heavy sets have to be moved quickly on and off stage. This is stressful for the stage hands, who groan as they lift and push Renaissance stairs and court columns. There are signs of class opposition in their loud shouts, I believe, as they are warning each other, carrying pieces of set together, putting them down with a bang that echoes in the auditorium. It becomes even more evident when such 'mishaps' occur during performances. After the curtain call, when the leading dancers have received flowers and taken their bows, the curtain is closed. Then the ballet management comes on stage to give compliments and corrections to dancers who have done leading roles or solos, or who have had a debut. And then it is over – the dancers rush to their dressing rooms, tired, with smeary make-up and wet through. The tension is usually replaced by relief, but also many nagging thoughts about mistakes, such as crooked pirouettes and lack of rapport between dancers. For even if the audience seemed to enjoy the performance, the dancers and the ballet management have another scale of judgement.

Dancers are rarely completely pleased with their performances, not even top dancers at the peak of their careers.

Ballet performance and risk

Every performance is unpredictable. So much (dancing, set, light, music, costume) and so many people (including dancers and orchestra, about two hundred people are working frontstage and backstage during a full-length classical ballet) have to function for a performance to run smoothly. In order to handle the risk that a performance will not be successful, let alone leave dancers injured, many dancers follow a special routine on 'pre-performance days' by resting, meditating, praying, dieting or taking drugs of one kind or another. The stage fright culminates minutes before performance, then the dancers appeal to supernatural powers in order for the performance to go well. This behaviour may for example entail knocking on the floor three times (for it to hold), or on the scenery, or touching a special spot backstage (in the new opera house in Frankfurt, some dancers touched a red box that covered electric appliances) when the curtain is still down, while the music may have started. I have seen dancers from Catholic or Greek Orthodox families who declare that they have nothing to do with religion cross themselves in the wings seconds before they go on stage. Certain accessories like a pair of leg-warmers which one had happened to wear on a 'pre-performance day' when the performance went really well may be preferred after that, or a pair of pointe shoes (as long as they last). This can be explained by an awareness that chance or randomness may turn the performance one way or another. At the same time, this theatre behaviour is a kind of concentration cue. Although these tricks are mainly learnt from older dancers in the company, new habits are also picked up from guest dancers. There are special good luck expressions such as 'merde!' or 'toi-toi-toi!', which must not be answered back (especially not close to or on the stage), since that is believed to bring bad luck. So it is to say thank you for 'toi-toi' cards or presents, usually small dolls, soft toy animals or sweets that may refer to the ballet production in one way or another. Whistling backstage is another old theatre taboo that is still adhered to, or at least commented on as potentally harmful for an upcoming performance.[6]

IN THE WINGS: WATCHING, WORKING, WAITING

In the obscurity of the wings, with the heat from the spotlights close by and a smell of dust and old paint, there is a vibrating zone of intense social activity structured by the happenings on stage and the transformations of the dancers going back and forth to the stage (Figure 5.1). But other things are also going on in this narrow passage. There is a lot of waiting, not least for dancers between entrances, but also by technicians for their cues, and by dressers for

Figure 5.1 Royal Swedish Ballet: *Swan Lake* in the wings

dancers. They all learn the particular rhythm of a production and follow it through the music.

On their evenings off, dancers sometimes watch from the wings because they have nothing else to do, or because they have a friend in the perform-ance. They may also be in a different cast from the one that is on, or they may be in the process of learning a role that is danced by someone else. Spouses and friends, whether they are dancers, ex-dancers or non-dancers, may watch from the wings. Groups of dancers and other people from the house come there to give support to a young dancer who is doing a debut or who has been asked to dance at short notice because of an injury. Such support is expressed through good luck wishes, applause and compliments when the dancer comes back to the wings, as well as consolations when things have not gone so well.

All watching, however, is not benevolent. It happens that dancers who define colleagues as threatening take to a subtle but deeply stressful way of harassment: when the competitor is dancing a difficult variation of steps on stage, the rival tries to disturb her or him by standing in the wings on a spot where the dancer on stage has to look – and makes faces or waves. Established dancers, moreover, watch younger colleagues from the wings, to check on their potential as competitors. Between entrances dancers judge each other, discuss how their colleagues are dancing, and compare them with themselves. Envy is mixed with admiration and camaraderie.

The wings are also a place for intimate conversations between close friends, as well as soft flirtations between dancers; two boys or a boy and a girl who do not know each other so well. This is a space offering a temporary shelter from the exposure on stage, where muscles and facial expressions have to be controlled, and any physical pain must not show. In the wings, on the other hand, there is room to scream it out (since the music is so loud), weeping over an ugly arabesque or a bad day in general.

REPAIRING THE FRAME: MISTAKES

In the international ballet world, William Forsythe is regarded as one of the current innovators in ballet. In a fax to the Royal Ballet he described how he was sharing authorship with his dancers in Ballett Frankfurt: 'Not only are the dancers fluent in a movement coordination that evolves outside of the classical norms, but now they are also responsible for the co-construction of the movements and the phrases and the counterpoints thereof.'

In *Firstext* he was making fun of the frames of ballet performance, breaking them on purpose in his endeavour to create new ballet art. This strategy is of course more common in experimental dance and theatre, with already converted, knowledgeable audiences.[7] At Covent Garden the audience seemed to be particularly uncomfortable with Forsythe's use of silence. The audience remained silent, however, out of politeness. Yet the silence was undoubtedly diversified and contained different attitudes and stances: the reactions of horror were mixed with both amazement and wonder.

The conventional framing of ballet performances enacted beyond the time and place of dancers and audience in the theatre room can easily be disturbed by technical errors. Both ethereal and dramatic atmospheres on stage may evaporate because of a heavy bang backstage, or a mishap with a costume or set. It can be a dancer who loses a shoe, or a door that does not open, that turns a magnetic flow of feelings into awkward comedy. The spell is broken – and everyone present is painfully reminded of the fact that they are at a dance performance.

As a part of the reframing (cf. Turner 1982: 79) of ballet performances, and his boundary-breaking aim, Forsythe does not really distinguish between rehearsal and performance: at his base in the new opera house in Frankfurt he continues to change steps during performances. Technical errors do, however, also occur in Forsythe's open form. At the world première of a new ballet programme *Six Counter Points*, Ballett Frankfurt presented six short ballets. The performance the day after the première went well until the fourth ballet. When the curtain went up for *(Approximate Sonata)*, everyone who had been watching the rehearsals saw that a spotlight that was placed to light up a flag that projected a 'Ja' on the backdrop was far too strong. The small white light dominated the stage. The dancer, an American man, started his 'improv' (improvisation),[8] a jerky walk along a straight line towards the audience. He probably did not see the spotlight. Then everybody could hear William Forsythe's voice, calling the stage manager in his microphone from his seat next to the composer Thom Willems on the first balcony. Irritatedly, he demanded that the ballet should start over again. The audience giggled amusedly. The curtain went down, not only once, but twice, before the spotlight was corrected and the ballet could really start. Was this then planned? That the spotlight was too strong was not planned, but since Forsythe in fact could communicate with the stage manager without anyone hearing, he obviously chose to turn this technical error into another kind of 'improv'.

Curtains that unexpectedly go up and down have actually become one of the signature marks of Forsythe. What would count as a disaster in many, if not most, other ballet productions has become one way for Forsythe to explore and manipulate the frame. He did it on purpose in *Firstext*, albeit with a side curtain, and he does it time after time in *Artifact*, a full-length ballet that was first performed in 1984 and since then has been hailed as a masterpiece. When Ballett Frankfurt performed *Artifact* in Stockholm, the Swedish critic Gunilla Jensen (1994) described the curtain that went up and down here and there in the performance as 'a twinkling eye that sharpens the attention of the viewer'. When I did fieldwork in Frankfurt, Forsythe's stage manager told me that this curtain trick had in fact occurred to begin with because she once pushed the wrong button, causing the curtain to go down in the middle of a performance. And Forsythe had kept it as a gimmick.

It is, in fact, more common than not that something goes wrong during a performance. Most of the time, however, the audience does not notice. A dancer missing a step or two does not really belong to this category, partly because he or she can be 'rescued' by partners. I both observed and heard many stories about dancers falling on stage, but then getting up and dancing even better than before, knowing that they had the attention – and the sympathy – of the audience. It is supposed to happen to everyone at some point, yet it is often an upsetting experience.

Timing is crucial in ballet performance; entrances and exits have to be co-ordinated with the music. The dancer stands in the wings, listening to the music, waiting for his or her cue to enter. And then it is a matter of seconds. On stage, leading dancers can communicate with the conductor, at least they are able to see each other, and if things are at their best there is rapport between them. A late entrance may confuse successive cues, in the music, set or dancing. Some cues, like 'the vision of Aurora' in the second act of the *Sleeping Beauty*, are a short variation danced by a corps de ballet girl, but at the same time the cue for the dancer who dances Aurora to enter. In one performance at Covent Garden, the vision was forgotten, the corps de ballet girl was there, but there was no light on her, so the principal dancer who did Aurora that evening missed her entrance. Some cues are ordered by the stage manager over the electronic system to stage hands, others stage hands are responsible for themselves.

Entrances are sometimes missed because a dancer just forgets. In a performance of the *Sleeping Beauty*, one of the women principals was waiting in the wings for her solo in the third act, when she discovered that one girl who was to take part in a *pas de trois* was not there. On the spur of the moment she got into the costume – and did it! Meanwhile the missing girl was found in the shower, with wet hair.

There are also comic turns in stage errors, making the audience and/or the dancers laugh; a male dancer at American Ballet Theatre was wearing a wig with long black hair like the other boys in a group in the *Red Shoes*. In a fast movement his wig flew off. Beacuse of the speedy tempo and to the amusement of the audience, he had to finish the variation displaying a stocking that covered his hair. And in a performance of *Dances Concertantes* by Kenneth Macmillan at Covent Garden, one of the soloist women nearly lost her balance, stumbling as she was entering with two other women dancers. The next day she asked me if I had seen it. 'We were hysterical after that!' she assured me.

The ballet management in Stockholm was, however, not amused when the magnificient diadem worn by Gamzatti, the daughter of the rajah in *La Bayadère*, kept falling down over her face at the end of the first act. The make-up artist had not fastened it well enough. In a sense it was a kind of luck anyway that it started falling down in Gamzatti's fit of jealous temper against her rival, Nikia, the temple dancer, over a warrior, Solor, whom they both loved. The dancer seemed to emphasize her fury as she repeatedly pushed her diadem upwards.

Major injuries that happen unexpectedly on stage can cause actual dramas. An American principal was dancing Prince Siegfried in *Swan Lake* on a tour with the British Royal Ballet in Washington, DC. Suddenly, in the first act 'my knee collapsed, I had snapped a ligament'.[9] The stage manager also told me spontaneously about this incident. She said that the dancer had fallen with his back towards the audience, which meant that it did not see his grimacing. At moments like that, the stage manager is responsible for deciding whether to close the curtain or not. This time, it was closed, and the dancer was carried off stage. In the idiom of 'the show must go on' that structures the ballet world, a male dancer who was watching from the wings was asked to continue the performance. He had danced Prince Siegfried before, so the dressers put the injured dancer's costume on him – and 15 minutes later he was on stage.

RITUAL AND REVELATION

In the extensive debate over connections, similarities and influences – and the lack thereof – between religious and secular ritual, theatre and perform-ances in traditional societies and in the west, ballet may appear far removed, like a very special case of western high culture entertaining a small segment of the population. It is, however, not devoid of ritualistic aspects.

Ballet performances at Covent Garden are not rituals in the strict sense of the term, solving social conflicts and crises through communications about transformations that temporarily reveal central social structures, as do for instance a Hindu funeral in Trinidad (cf. Gerholm 1988) or the West Indian carnival in Notting Hill (cf. Cohen 1993, Wulff 1988). Yet ballet perform-ances fit into Victor Turner's (1964 [1957]: 20) original definition of ritual as 'prescribed formal behaviour for occasions not given over to technological routine, having reference to beliefs in mystical beings or powers'. For even if there is a reframing going on by manipulation as well as repairing of mistakes, the framing of ballet performances is certainly 'prescribed formal behaviour'. A 'technological routine' is indeed regarded as desirable, but is seldom realized during a performance; minor or major technical errors happen all the time. And there are certainly 'beliefs in mystical beings or powers' connected to ballet performances; not only is there pre-performance supernatural behaviour, but the plots of the Romantic classical ballets often feature the 'mystical powers' of witches, magicians and fairies as crucial for the course of events. Drawing on themes from folk tales, the classical ballets present universal human conditions, yet steeped in a highly specialized cultural idiom. There is an emic notion in the ballet world of ballet as an 'international language' because of its non-verbal character. The fact that 'international' only covers the west in this sense is hardly ever discussed, however.

The transformative quality of rituals is to be found in the liminality of the wings where the dancers go in and out of their roles, some for a split second, while others are already inside the role when they come from the dressing rooms to the wings. This temporary transformation of the dancers provides the stuff of 'Let's pretend' for the audience. There may be spectators in the audience who experience transformations, as well, but of a different kind.

Many people in the ballet world, not only dancers and choreographers, but also critics, balletomanes and ballet sponsors, recall having been spellbound by one sparkling ballet performance. In the ballet world there is an emic expression for extraordinary experiences of ballet art – 'ballet revelations' – that I remember as a heightened state of mind that resemble a religious conversion.[10] They can be a source of unprecedented empowerment (cf. Hastrup, this volume). They tend to happen to children, but they may hit adults as well. The point is that they make a lasting impression that cannot be outshone by later experiences of ballet art: ballet revelations are formative and may be the force that makes a ballet pupil decide to become a professional dancer, or turns a chance spectator at a ballet performance into a balletomane.

CREATING BALLET ART

Acting in dance performance is not as elaborate as in theatre performance, even if the leading roles have to be created quite carefully, not least when they are supposed to display some kind of personal development. Except for William Forsythe's interest in theatrical theorists, I never came across any systematic discussion of theories of acting in the theatres in line with Stanislavsky's system, for instance. It seemed to have informed coaches and other choreographers, however, especially Stanislavsky's idea that actors should use their 'emotional memory' (1967: 53–5) when they are on stage. Choreographers and coaches told me how they tried to get dancers to use their memories, and dancers did talk about how they applied their personal experiences when they were acting. A male principal who was dancing Romeo just days after his girlfriend had broken up with him confessed that in the scene where Romeo finds Juliet, thinking she is dead, he had shed real tears. And a male corps de ballet dancer was pondering over the fact that they were 'required to rape and kill – most of us have not raped or killed anyone!' Yet a woman principal in her early thirties, who had danced many of the leading roles in classical ballet, revealed that she did use her own experiences and mostly those of pain when she was dancing. At one point when she was dancing Manon: 'In the *pas de deux* towards the end, when she is dying', the dancer said 'I was such a mess, I was just hysterical because I felt as if I was really there. It took me about twenty minutes to recover afterwards!'

Otherwise, there is a kind of double consciousness, or 'double agency' as Kirsten Hastrup calls it (cf. this volume), in performing ballet roles: not consisting of a dual awareness of technique and artistry, since dancers say that ballet art comes about when they forget the technique and, at the same time as they 'become' certain characters, they are aware of the audience, of the fact that they are acting. Once when *Romeo and Juliet* was played in Stockholm, and the balcony scene was about to end with Romeo and Juliet kissing each other, as they parted a string of saliva grew longer and longer between their mouths. This the audience did not see. Instead it was over-whelmed by the touching emotions on stage, while the dancers had to concentrate very much on not bursting into laughter by the breaking of style in the situation. Here a third level in the double consciousness on stage appeared: on top of the acting and the awareness of the audience, the dancers had to make an extra effort to maintain the frame.

In conclusion, then, different perspectives towards ballet performance, fragmented as they may be by different occupations and positions in the ballet world, thus contribute to the making of ballet performances by establishing, manipulating, repairing and maintaining the frames around them. When frames are broken, whether by mistake or in artistic exploration, new ones are inevitably being created.

ACKNOWLEDGEMENTS

I wish to thank Felicia Hughes-Freeland for her thoughtful comments on an earlier draft of this chapter.

The chapter has grown out of my study 'A transnational ballet world: network and subculture in Stockholm, London, New York, and Frankfurt am Main'. The study, carried out between 1993 and 1996, was a part of the programme on National and Transnational Cultural Processes, funded by the Swedish Research Council for the Humanities and Social Sciences.

NOTES

1 Formal access to this closed world, as well as informal access to the different zones in the theatres (the studios, wings and green rooms, let alone the dressing rooms) were facilitated by the fact that I danced classical ballet for 15 years. Ballet is a non-verbal bodily experience that never subsides totally and although I had to stop dancing at the age of 17 because of a back injury, ballet is still in my body. I grew up in the ballet world learning the steps and the culture simultaneously. Dancers identify themselves as different from other people, and difficult to understand, but I was defined as 'a member of the family', someone who could have been a dancer. My status as an ex-native thus contributed to the process of getting access and to the kind of empathy I developed, which inform my theoretical position.

2 The concept of performance has a linguistic history to which Dell Hymes's (1975) definition relates when he points at the communicative competence of both performer and audience in performance, as well as the responsibility that the performer takes on in relation to the audience. Erving Goffman (1959) early identified aspects of everyday life as performance behaviour. Singer (1972) and Fabian (1990) are examples of anthropological monographies on theatre performance in traditional societies. Dance performances are analysed, more or less extensively, in Royce (1980 [1977]), Hanna (1979, 1988), Novack (1990), Ness (1992), Lewis (1992), Daniel (1995) and Savigliano (1995). In the expanding interdisciplinary field of dance studies, Foster (1986), Goellner and Murphy (1995) and Thomas (1995) are but a few who take performance practices into account.

3 This new production of the *Sleeping Beauty* had its world première in Washington DC, on a USA tour in April 1994.

4 For Lacanian analyses of ballet performances, see Rimmer (1993) and Foster (1996).

5 The stage manager is in charge of the technical side of performances backstage. It is called 'being on the book', since the stage manager follows the score of the ballet in order to know when to signal cues. Since technical errors do happen, and may be potentially dangerous, the stage manager is asked to do a 'show report' after performances; preferably this should then be a 'clean show report'.

6 Swedish ethnologist Kerstin Koman (1996) describes the folk rule against whistling on sailing ships because it was believed to stir a wind, even a storm, in the old days. Koman notes that there is still a resistance to whistling on board many contemporary Swedish merchant ships.

7 An interesting case of layers of framed illusion is provided by Carmeli's (1990) analysis of travelling circus performances in British towns in the late 1970s. They evolved around a play of the real when the presenter kept claiming that the performers and the tricks were real and at the same time impossible for anyone else to do.

8 Banes (1994) writes about how Merce Cunningham started working with chance methods in the early 1950s.

9 It took him two years to recover, but the fact that he did recover and is now dancing leading roles again is considered something of a miracle by himself as well as by his colleagues and coaches.

10 Experiences of ballet art can be phrased in terms of transcendence (cf. Fernandez 1986), even if this concept tends to illustrate the state of mind of performers (cf. Zarrilli 1990, Myerhoff 1990), not the audience.

REFERENCES

Banes, S. (1994) *Writing Dancing in the Age of Postmodernism*, Hanover NE: Wesleyan University Press.

Bateson, G. (1972) 'A theory of play and fantasy', in *Steps to an Ecology of Mind*, New York: Ballantine Books.

Bauman, R. (1992) 'Performance', in R. Bauman (ed.) *Folklore, Cultural Performances, and Popular Entertainments*, New York: Oxford University Press.

Bensman, J. and Lilienfeld, R. (1973) *Craft and Consciousness*, New York: John Wiley and Sons.

Bourdieu, P. (1993) *The Field of Cultural Production*, New York: Columbia University Press.

Carmeli, Y.S. (1990) 'Performing the "real" and "impossible" in the British travelling circus', *Semiotica*, 80 (3/4): 193–220.

Cohen, A. (1993) *Masquerade Politics*, Berkeley CA: University of California Press.

Daniel, Y. (1995) *Rumba*, Bloomington: Indiana University Press.

Fabian, J. (1990) *Power and Performance*, Madison: University of Wisconsin Press.

Fernandez, J.W. (1986) *Persuasions and Performances*, Bloomington: Indiana University Press.

Foster, S.L. (1986) *Reading Dancing*, Berkeley CA: University of California Press.

—— (1996) 'The ballerina's phallic pointe', in S. Foster (ed.) *Corporealities*, London: Routledge.

Gerholm, T. (1988) 'On ritual: a postmodernist view', *Ethnos*, 53: 190–203.

Goellner, E.W. and Murphy, J.S. (eds) (1995) *Bodies of the Text*, New Brunswick NJ: Rutgers University Press.

Goffman, E. (1959) *The Presentation of Self in Everyday Life*, Garden City NY: Doubleday Anchor.

—— (1974) *Frame Analysis*, New York: Harper and Row.

Hanna, J.L. (1979) *To Dance is Human*, Austin TX: University of Texas Press.
—— (1988) *Dance, Sex and Gender*, Chicago: Chicago University Press.
Hymes, D. (1975) 'Breakthrough into performance', in D. Ben-Amos and K.S. Goldstein (eds) *Folklore*, The Hague: Mouton.
Jensen, G. (1994) 'Koreografi som genetiska tecken: Vidunderlig variationsrikedom i Frankfurtbaletten under William Forsythe', *Svenska Dagbladet*, 3 November.
Koegler, H. (1987) *The Concise Oxford Dictionary of Ballet*, Oxford: Oxford University Press.
—— (1995) 'A life between art and politics', *Dance Now*, 4 (3): 88–93.
Koman, K. (1996) *Mynt under masten och vissla på vind*, Stockholm: Rabén Prisma.
Lewis, J.L. (1992) *Ring of Liberation*, Chicago: University of Chicago Press.
Myerhoff, B. (1990) 'The transformation of consciousness in ritual performances: some thoughts and questions', in R. Schechner and W. Appel (eds) *By Means of Performance*, Cambridge: Cambridge University Press.
Ness, S.A. (1992) *Body, Movement, and Culture*, Philadelphia: University of Pennsylvania Press.
Novack, C.J. (1990) *Sharing the Dance*, Madison: University of Wisconsin Press.
Rimmer, V. (1993) 'The anxiety of dance performance', in H. Thomas (ed.) *Dance, Gender and Culture*, London: Macmillan.
Royce, A.P. (1980 [1977]) *The Anthropology of Dance*, Bloomington: Indiana University Press.
Savigliano, M.E. (1995) *Tango and the Political Economy of Passion*, Boulder CO: Westview Press.
Singer, M. (1972) *When a Great Tradition Modernizes*, New York: Praeger.
Stanislavsky, K. (1967) *On the Art of the Stage*, London: Faber and Faber.
Thomas, H. (1995) *Dance, Modernity and Culture*, London: Routledge.
Turner, V. (1964 [1957]) 'Symbols in Ndembu ritual', in M. Gluckman (ed.) *Closed Systems and Open Minds*, Edinburgh: Oliver and Boyd.
—— (1982) *From Ritual to Theatre*, New York: PAJ Publications.
Wulff, H. (1988) *Twenty Girls*, Stockholm Studies in Social Anthropology 21, Stockholm: Almqvist and Wiksell.
Zarrilli, P.B. (1990) 'What does it mean to "become the character": power, presence, and transcendence in Asian in-body disciplines of practice', in R. Schechner and W. Appel (eds) *By Means of Performance*, Cambridge: Cambridge University Press.

Chapter 6

From ritual sacrifice to media commodity

Anthropological and media constructions of the Spanish bullfight and the rise of women performers

Sarah Pink

'Isn't she attractive, she's truly beautiful . . .' marvelled the masculine voice of a male television commentator as the televised performance of a woman bullfighter, transmitted from Peru, filled my small screen, '. . . we're not here to discuss her beauty!' his female co-commentator cut in: '. . . our role is to observe her ability as a bullfighter'.

I snatched a pen to scribble a note of their dialogue on the corner of a bullfighting supplement lying on my Cordoban dining table: perfect for an anthropologist seeking public reiterations of contemporary debates about gender!

INTRODUCTION

In this chapter I discuss the contemporary successes of women bullfighters in 'men's' bullfighting leagues in connection with the interface between the live performed bullfight and the televised media bullfight. In a contemporary bullfighting context that encompasses both live and media events I situate women's popularity by exploring how their performances are interpreted in both these domains. Finally I argue that the meanings invested in women performers and televised bullfights can be understood with reference to styles of domestic and public consumption.

The research: televisions in the field

I lived and researched in Córdoba, Andalusia, from 1992 to 1994. The fieldwork focused on 'women and bullfighting' but incorporated a wider project on gendered identities. In addition to participating in local social life and interviewing, I spent many hours watching television in my home, in bullfighting clubs and with informants in their homes, thus situating media within local ethnography (see Hirsch, this volume). Television and the press provided a variety of representations of the bullfight while also constituting media through which they are experienced. The media were a resource of information and experience accessed by informants and researcher, although with different methods and motives.

THE CONTEMPORARY BULLFIGHT

In the 1990s the Spanish bullfight features in the domestic and public leisure of its *aficionados*. Throughout the year, live bullfights are screened regularly on television. Televised bullfights are recordings or direct transmissions of live performances to which audience participation is fundamental: 'studio bullfights' are not recorded for television. At the height of the summer season, weekend performances are held concurrently in many cities, towns and villages in Spain, southern France and Portugal. In the winter the emphasis shifts to Latin America. Performances are well supported by a public of men, women and children of all ages. Bullfighting generates capital and employment within the 'bullfighting world' itself and the media; this economic dimension is crucial to understanding the context in which performers succeed or fail.

Matadores (literally killers) usually commence their careers in their early teens as *becerristas*, who fight yearling animals. Some progress to the 'novice' *novillero* category fighting 3-year-old *novillo* bulls. This stage is divided into two steps. For the latter, the bulls are stronger and heavier and the *novillero* is assisted by two mounted *picadores* (see below). Many reach the first stages but few *novilleros* eventually take the *alternativa* to fight 4-year-old bulls (*toros*) and graduate to professional *torero* status.

Most performances take place in the late afternoon and last for two hours. In a standard bullfight three performers each kill two bulls; twenty minutes is allowed for each animal. The performance commences with the entry of the *alguaciles*, mounted officials, followed by the three *matadores* and their respective teams of assistants; three *banderilleros* on foot and two mounted *picadores*. The performers salute the *presidente* who governs the performance, and retire to their ringside position. On the release of the first bull the bullfight begins. The assistants 'test' the bulls with their capes whilst the *matador* contemplates its characteristics, before performing several cape passes himself until the president calls for the *picadores*. With the assistance of the *matador* and *banderilleros* the *picador* attracts the bull to charge him so that he may spear it, weakening its shoulder muscles and lowering its head. The *banderilleros'* stage follows: their task is to insert six decorative spiked sticks (*banderillas*) in the bull's shoulder muscles. Taking one *banderilla* in each hand the *banderillero* runs towards the bull, leaping to one side to place the *banderillas*. Finally the *matador* takes the red *muleta* (cape) and sword to confront the bull alone. After a series of passes he kills the bull. The audience expresses approval or disapproval throughout the bullfight and requests that trophies of the bull's ears or tail be awarded to a successful performer. During the victory lap the *matador* is thrown gifts, hats, flowers, etc., and the dead bull is dragged away by the mule team.

Bullfighting is dangerous. Not all performers are successful and while bullfighters are rarely killed they are frequently injured.

WOMEN BULLFIGHTERS AND THE BULLFIGHT AS RITUAL

'Traditionalist' bullfighting discourse stresses gender-role segregation and excludes women performers;[1] its iconography centres on the triumphant masculine *torero* figure (Pink 1997a). However, during my fieldwork, when the 1993 season closed six women were active in the *novillero* league and Cristina Sánchez had maintained a position amongst the top ten *novilleros* with *picadores* throughout most of the year. In 1996 Cristina became the first woman bullfighter to take the *alternativa* in Spain and thus become a *torero*.

Anthropologists have interpreted the live bullfight as ritual. Pitt-Rivers defines the bullfight as a 'ritual sacrifice' (1984: 29), a symbolic language, which has survived in 'rational' modern society.[2] Following Turner (1967), Pitt-Rivers regards ritual as better 'read' or understood by an outside observer. He appreciates that symbols are 'polysemic' but assumes the fixity of meaning within cultural or temporal boundaries (1984: 30–1). I would argue that what Pitt-Rivers postulates as an 'objective' anthropological interpretation of the relationship of the bullfight to a homogeneous 'Spanish culture' is unfounded: his reading of the bullfight is no more 'true' than Spanish culture is homogeneous.

According to Pitt-Rivers (1984), the bullfighter commences the performance symbolizing a feminine role; during the bullfight he becomes increasingly masculine, to kill the bull finally as a 'superhero' who violates the taboo of raping a menstruating woman (apparently now symbolized by the bull, which is transformed into a metaphorical female). Cambria justly criticizes Pitt-Rivers for extracting 'certain aspects from the bullfight (which he confesses, he used to frequent . . . thirty years ago)', imposing a 'sexual/ religious interpretation' on them and applying 'them to Andalusian men and the relations between the sexes in that southern region of Spain' (1991: 221).

Douglass also compares the kill to copulation, extending her analysis to the media: 'Television in Spain now shows bullfights regularly and repeated instant replays of the kill are shown: the torero's blade goes in and out and in and out, for all to see; a kind of televised copulation' (1984: 254). Douglass's treatment is inappropriate. A repeated 'in and out' (slow) motion of the sword does not dominate televised bullfights. The kill requires utmost skill and precision, and in my experience, *aficionados* appreciate the slow-motion televised kill to concentrate on technique; action replays are crucial for this. In this sense the televised kill constitutes not a sexual metaphor but a fragment of a media event.

Numerous anthropological and popular interpretations of the bullfight invest sexual meanings in the iconography of the bullfight. Nevertheless the bullfight does not essentially symbolize copulation any more than copulation represents the bullfight. Anthropological imputations of symbols render the bullfight meaningful in terms more significant for their own authors than for 'the culture' (cf. Fabian 1983: 125). Classification of the bullfight and other so-called Spanish 'traditions' as uncivilized throwbacks to pre-enlightenment Europe (e.g. Mitchell 1991) is equally problematic. This constitutes a selective 'othering' of certain aspects of Spanish culture that renders them uncivilized or primitive, both of which are inappropriate: 'there are different cultural definitions of being human, being male and being civilised' (Marvin 1986: 135). Moreover, multiple definitions of being human, male and civilized exist within as well as between cultures. Anthropological definitions of the bullfight as 'primitive' ritual represent anthropology's (former) preoccupation with the 'classification of primitive social types' (Friedman 1994: 6). These perspectives support ethnocentric impositions of symbolic interpretations that claim to reveal the non-civilized rationality of other cultures. They do not explain its social significance.

Other interpretations are more grounded in ethnography, but do not admit female performers. For Corbin and Corbin the theme of the bullfight is masculinity: 'the bullfight epitomizes the specifically male predicament and the means of overcoming it' – it is analogous to public competitiveness, where men are judged in terms 'of relative success in coping with difficulties' (1986: 109). In the 1990s women intellectuals, professionals and politicians are equally admired for problem solving in public domains in many urban (but also rural) situations. For instance, women prove their competence to deal with public and professional predicaments as they compete with men at work; thus Corbin and Corbin's model also applies to some contemporary femininities.

Marvin defines the bullfight as a drama about masculinity that provokes an emotional response and affects the performer emotionally (1988: 169), and a ritual in which 'meaning' is shaped by structure (1988: 167). Whereas Pitt-Rivers constructs the bullfight as 'the ritual revindication of masculinity' (1963 [1961]: 90) but regards women bullfighters as compatible with his reading of bullfight symbolism, Marvin demonstrates how women bull-fighters can disrupt the ritual structure of the event. According to Marvin's interpretation female performers (whom his informants considered inappropriate and out of place) cannot communicate the symbolic message of the bullfight: 'a statement in dramatic form of what it means to be a human male in this [Andalusian] culture' (1988: 142). Marvin argues that the emotional responses provoked in both performer and audience through the bullfight are dependent on the biological maleness of the bullfighter. When the performer is female this emotionally charged *ambiente* (atmosphere)[3] is absent.

IS WOMEN'S BULLFIGHTING RITUAL?

The theoretical assumption that the ritual structure of the bullfight prohibits the acceptance of women bullfighters excludes their performances from the category of 'bullfight as ritual'. However, the empirical presence of women bullfighters in this ritual appears to render invalid the anthropological interpretation of the bullfight as a ritual about masculinity. Women performers cannot adhere to the 'structure and formal characteristics' (Marvin 1988: 167) of the ritual because they are female. Do women subvert the ritual bullfight or do they create a different ritual?

It seems useful to interpret rituals as 'polysemic' in a way that neither Turner (1967: 50–1) nor Pitt-Rivers (1984) intended. The bullfight is a visual and emotional performance which may be interpreted subjectively in terms of a variety of gender models. By stressing differences *within* cultures and questioning gender categories a revised agenda may be set to enquire into the plurality of meanings of the performance for its participants (including the audience), rather than what the symbols say about *the* culture. There is much debate over whether women should bullfight (Pink 1996); Andalusian *aficionado*[4] opinion and gender models are plural. If the bullfight's message is 'what it means to be a human male in this culture' (Marvin 1988: 142) it corresponds with only one 'traditional' Andalusian masculinity and a binary model of gender. Instead I situate the bullfight in a context of multiple masculinities and femininities (cf. Cornwall and Lindisfarne 1994) to account for a variety of subject positions.

'Traditionalist' discourse remains relevant to Marvin's fundamental point that the *ambiente* of the bullfight changes with the biological sex of the performer. Communication between performer and audience, audience consensus, and the idea that the sex of female performers inhibits the production of the *ambiente* associated with a good bullfight are key issues. Therefore 'traditionalist' perspectives and lack of audience consensus present practical problems for women bullfighters.

RITUAL AND 'TRADITION'

Contemporary women's bullfighting raises two issues as regards 'tradition': what should be the limits of behaviour which adheres to traditional morality, and what measures should be taken to preserve the integrity of tradition? These questions are neither simply nor uniformly resolved. In some contexts women bullfighters convincingly appeal to tradition, claiming to participate in a traditional activity and to conform to the rules set by established tradition (see Hobsbawm 1983: 2),[5] but they defy a vital norm – that of the gender of the performer. On these terms the 'tradition' as structured procedure is untouched. Conversely, by defining that 'tradition' as a living event whose participants are part of its existence, the introduction of female performers challenges its established composition. Women bullfighters break 'the rules which permit or constrain . . . participation' (Lewis 1980: 12) but still insist that they perform the bullfight 'properly'. Lewis emphasizes that such customs are justified by tradition, in the sense that 'our ancestors have always done things this way' (1980: 12). Whilst arguments for the exclusion of female performers are sometimes justified by an appeal to tradition, this is not invariably accepted as legitimating an exclusionist policy that clashes with widespread values. Ultimately *aficionado* subjectivities construct the specific meanings invested in different gendered performers: some inform-ants found women's participation non-problematic, others feared it threatened the integrity of the event.

Contemporary local perspectives on the 'traditional' bullfight and other rituals must be located in a changing Andalusian context where gender roles performed in 'traditional' events are frequently at variance with the morality and aspirations of their participants (Pink 1997b). Whilst many *aficionados* criticize the 'traditionalist' gender roles they see as epitomized by male performers as 'sexist', this does not inhibit their appreciation of the profes-sional bullfight. This is congruent with Lewis's point that the very in-determinacy of ritual lends it significance and 'contains a way of seeing that ritual may survive, still seem worth doing, offering some feeling of con-tinuity, message and enrichment' for people throughout periods of social change (1980: 38). However, a woman's performance – if it is to be considered the same ritual – poses further questions about the relationship between ritual and society. Some people demand that the public 'ruling' (Lewis 1980: 19) of this ritual should be sufficiently flexible to correspond to non-'traditional' gender configurations. 'Tradition' fails to justify the rigidity of the 'ruling' against female performers consistently.

The bullfight is in an ambiguous situation: it is a 'traditional' ritual in a changing socio-cultural context. The contemporary success of women per-formers, critics, journalists, photographers and managers illustrates the way bullfighting culture is obliged to accommodate non-'traditional' gender models in a context of changing attitudes towards work and sexuality in Andalusia (see Pink 1997c). Furthermore, the bullfight is a 'living tradition' and a commercial enterprise, which must be both contemporary and 'tradi-tional' in order to satisfy its broad range of potential audience: it must be a marketable tradition.

MEDIA IN BULLFIGHTING

Media representations are inseparable from contemporary bullfighting cul-tures and identities. The media are connected socially, culturally, politically and economically to the definition and organization of live performances, and individual bullfighters' careers. Recently the ex-bullfighter El Cordobes signed a 'come-back' contract with a television company and bullring.

Although he eventually pulled out (precipitating a media event), the performance would have become an important media happening and live bullfight.
The transmission of live and recorded performances has become a competitive commercial enterprise. Some informants associated this with a
corrupt 'business' dimension of bullfighting that threatens the purity of art.
Others, like the journalist Carabias (1993), consider that the promotion, the
publicity, the generation of funds and the advantages of competition outweigh
the disadvantages implied by an increasing interdependency between media
and live events.

The media's ordering of the places, events and personalities of the
'bullfighting world' offers a spatial and temporal structure by which that
world can be interpreted as a cohesive whole and understood in its supposed
entirety. Its hierarchies are created in and by the media: explicitly in
published listings of performers' positions in the bullfighting league; and
implicitly as importance is conferred when a performance is televised.
Cordobans complained that as their *feria* bullfights coincided with a series of
important bullfights in Madrid, Madrid received not only better bulls but more
media coverage.[6]

The bullfight has also developed in relation to other technologies. Satellite
transmissions of Latin American bullfights bring distant arenas into domestic
spaces, and bullfighting package tours fly *aficionado* families to see local
heroes perform in Mexico. Distant and disparate elements of the 'bullfighting
world' are held together by the national bullfighting press and television.
Locally, in Cordoba during *feria* bullfights were broadcast daily on municipal
television – an arena of local public production and representation of
Cordoba's bullfighting identity (see Figures 6.1 and 6.2).

THE SETTING OF THE TELEVISION

Televised bullfights are viewed in a variety of locations – predominantly in
bullfighting bars, clubs or family homes. The televised performance is said
to lack the *ambiente* of the live performance and viewing is not necessarily
a social event: *aficionados* may attend bars to see bullfights on a subscribers'
channel which they do not have at home. On different occasions viewing may
be incidental, central to conversation, or in silence. Since many performances
are screened live in the afternoons while most people are at work, they are
often videoed and viewed later. Similarly in summer, when bullfights may be
transmitted simultaneously on four television channels, video is indispens-
able. During the winter season clubs screen videoed programmes to review
and debate the previous season. In this context, where television is financed
by advertising or subscription fees and viewing and video recording are
contingent on these economic elements, the televised bullfight moves into a
'commodity state' (cf. Appadurai 1986: 38, Morley 1995: 316). Access is
regulated, amongst other things, by money and social relationships.

Figure 6.1 and 6.2 Television cameras as part of the context of Cristina Sánchez's début with *picadores* in Valdemorillo, 1993: the media presence was silhouetted above my audience seat while the live performance unfolded below

The televised bullfight becomes woven into sets of public and domestic relationships in the contexts of family and bar. Once broadcast in the domestic space of the family home, televised performances are made meaningful in terms of family relationships as well as individual standpoints. Below I concentrate on 'watching television' as 'a domestic consumer practice' (Ang 1992: 132) to consider some examples of how the televised bullfight is 'domesticated into the society of family life and shaped by the complexities of family interaction' (Strathern 1992: ix). For one Cordoban student, televised bullfights invoked her resentment of paternal dominance and her father's monopoly of the colour television nearly every summer afternoon, preventing her from watching soap operas on another channel. In contrast, for *aficionado* families with a shared interest in bullfighting, televised performances and reports were family occasions connected later to peer-group discourses. An elderly woman with no desire to attend perform-ances alone followed the bullfight through televised performances. In these settings debates and discourses originating in the domestic context are entangled with interpretations of the content of television programmes. Television does not 'influence' passive viewers, but members of the domestic group (and those who pass through) co-operate in interpreting and debating the issues presented in television programmes. For instance, evaluations of televised women's performances may be related to family discourses and debates on gender roles. Performances viewed in domestic domains where particular gender roles are enacted and negotiated are incorporated differently from those viewed at the bullring, where (following Marvin) masculinity is (structurally) dominant. The television is often central to Andalusian do-mestic situations where gender roles are produced, reproduced and modified. Most homes have a television, and video access to televised bullfights neither is restricted to the wealthy nor signifies a public occasion, as in the 1960s when the bullfighter El Cordobes' first televised performance was viewed by most of his natal village clustered around the television in the local bar (Collins and Lapierre 1968). The media bullfight transgresses the temporal and spatial limits of live performance and permits daily and global access to bullfighting; time and location become encapsulated in media frames.

THE 'MEDIA BULLFIGHT'

Dayan and Katz suggest that when a ritual is televised 'An anthropological artefact, a ritual hybrid is thus born' (1987: 174). The media event is defined as 'altogether another experience' involving a new form of spectatorship (1987: 194). I focus first on the experiential aspect of live and 'media' bullfights.

In televised and live events sensory experience is organized differently. A general difference is indicated by the concept of *ambiente*. The live bullfight has been defined as a ritual performance in which *ambiente* is generated between performer and audience. *Aficionado* resistance to televised bullfights stresses their incompleteness: this standpoint states that television transmits colour but not art, depth, vibrations or emotion. Television directors and commentators are obliged 'to create a new spectacle – which will never be a complete taurine spectacle' and will attract a new type of public (Matilla 1993: 14). The media bullfight *can* represent a different 'completeness'. This was reflected in an appraisal of Tele Madrid's coverage of the San Isidro bullfights (published in *6 Toros 6* magazine in 1992) as 'a complete taurine programme which attempted to increase in type and style the number of *aficionados* who become involved in the bullfight by means of knowledge and participation'. The reviews, summaries, commentaries and interviews offered by these programmes were particularly praised. However, the ritual structure of the live performance is replaced in the media event by the structure imposed by television, and the performer's presentation of his or her communicative body-self is re-presented in media events. The televised bullfight is restructured and reframed by editors, camera people and narrators: this tailored event is presented as a complete package – its performers and performance become packaged commodities, intertwined with media narratives.

In common, television and women both threaten the ritual structure and dramatic narrative of the 'traditional' live bullfight; according to their critics neither can produce its *ambiente*.

MEDIA REPRESENTATION VS. LIVE PRESENTATION

Pitt-Rivers has suggested the biological sex of the performers is unimportant and, as in theatre, the gender of performers is interchangeable. This approach is flawed because Pitt-Rivers imposes symbolic meanings on the bullfight and fails to acknowledge fundamental differences between the bullfight and theatre. Moreover, he ignores the gendered nature of audience interpretations of performances and *ambiente*.

The bullfight is not 'staged'. Recognising difference between the actor and the *torero* is essential for understanding its emotive atmosphere. In the bullfight 'The role of the *torero* is much more closely tied to the man himself than the role of actor is tied to the person who is an actor.' The *torero* performs as himself – 'the role of *torero* is not thought to be separable from the man who is a *torero*' (Marvin 1988: 178–9). This contrasts with theatre, where the actor/character may be defined as a 'double agent' (cf. Hastrup, this volume). The actor 'uses his body primarily as a tool, as a means of expression (speech, mime, gestures)' and 'as an instrument in a re-presentation: standing *before* the audience (his concrete presence) but at the same time standing *for* something that is absent, that is his or her "role" in the play' (Falk 1994: 199). The bullfighter's body does not stand for absence, it is utterly present and at risk. In the bullfight mortal danger is present, not evoked as in theatre: 'excitement and emotion are generated because of the danger' (Marvin 1988: 179). In Marvin's analysis the performer must be male; the drama of the bullfight belongs to a wider representation of bullfighter's 'self' whose narrative extends out of the bullring into his everyday life: Marvin thus excludes female performers. However, I suggest that Marvin's definitions of masculine drama and experience are not exclusively masculine; *some* people assert that women also live such experience. Like the male bullfighter, the female bullfighter is no actor; through the drama of her performance she also acts her 'self', a woman who has succeeded in the public sphere and has become a bullfighter. Gender roles are contested in contemporary Spain – consensus over what constitute 'proper' women's roles exists neither in 'the culture' nor amongst bullfight *aficionados*. Thus for some, the bullfight represents a contemporary femininity.

Above I have discussed interpretations of the bullfight as a story that parallels cultural models of success. Simultaneously it is an event in which the skills of individual performers are judged. This constitutes a direct presentation (as opposed to re-presentation) of art, technique and knowledge, embodied in and expressed by human bodies. Women bullfighters act roles *in* not *with* their bodies. In the live bullfight the performer's is an experiencing communicating body, an expressive body (Frank 1991). However, for those who reject a female body as the bearer of 'masculine' accomplishments the equation of female body/feminine self/professional does not equal 'bull-fighter'; they claim that she cannot evoke the *ambiente* of a 'true' or 'pure' bullfight.

The structure and organization of televised bullfights deviate from the live performance and involve new characters and new discourses. Television provides both expert commentary and discussion and visual and graphic information about bulls and bullfighters. This introduces a relationship between the aural/oral and the visual whereby oral narrative predominates and the voice of authority replaces the more direct association of vision and knowledge characteristic of the live bullfight. The relationship between bullfighter and audience is mediated by a narrator and visual editing. The performer is dispossessed of the viewer's exclusive attention, a disembodied commentator's voice leads the performance and visual communication is punctuated by editing. The live performance and bullfighter are fragmented and reconstituted in the media bullfight: zooms to the bullfighter's feet indicate whether they are correctly positioned, cuts to the bullfighter's face 'show us' its expressions, or frames filled with celebrities or audience represent their presence. This facilitates a closeness not achieved at a live bullfight: a bull's head can fill the screen, allowing a close scrutiny of the animal impossible in a live situation. Similarly both closeness and distance are implied as bullfighters become television stars. Contact with bullfighters is represented through televised interviews and close-up shots, but distance is maintained since such communication is always mediated by television producers and journalists.

Whereas a successful bullfighter dominates both the bull and the event itself, the media bullfighter cedes control to the media crew. Whilst the bullfighter directs his or her live performance, the programme director takes charge of the televised performance. The televised bullfighter shares centre stage with commentators who define the performance and the issues. Moreover, television mutes the communicative bodies of live bullfighters; they cannot communicate directly with or receive responses from the television audience.

Other significant differences between live and media bullfights are manifest in the uses of and interfaces between image and sound. Amongst the legitimate sounds of the live bullfight are the officially sanctioned, 'traditional' double-step music played by a brass band, and unofficial but conventional audience participation. Music is not simply a response to the bullfighter's visual display, but comments on and compliments his or her performance. Music, moreover, contributes to the sensory experience of performance: music is thought to affect one's way of seeing the bullfighter's performance, making it 'look better' (Marvin 1988: 20). Generally music refers to the visual descriptively because it signifies that the visuals are impressive, but specific reasons for requesting music are more complex. For instance, a mediocre performance from a local 'hero' may be rewarded with *musica* whilst the superior bullfighting of his rival is received in silence. Such motives for requesting *musica* are 'conventional' but were usually explicitly stated as accusations of unfairness.

Conventional audience participation/response also refers to binary meanings to imply approval or disapproval; for example, *¡Ole!* or its absence. These commentaries are intended as expressions of audience consensus on performance quality, only elaborated on occasionally. Individual shouts of direct criticism of the bullfighter are usually regarded as inappropriate and those responsible criticized for their untimely intervention. The final judgement on a performance is represented visually and orally; the audience shake their white handkerchiefs and chant *oreja*, demanding that the president award a trophy. The president's interventions are visual: he displays an appropriately coloured handkerchief to signify his decision. Announcements are never made over a loudspeaker.

The relationship between image and sound differs in the televised bullfight. The audience may express extensive commentary, but cannot actively participate in the live event. The television audience receives detailed and continuous voice-over response to the live event plus selected images. The presence of spoken commentary on television and its absence in the arena indicate a key difference between the ways televised and live bullfighting are experienced. Commentaries that represent conventional audience consensus (at the bullring) and commentaries that presume distanced judgement (at home) parallel the contrast between presence/absence or participation/ distance and refer to different discourses. It is due to the spectator's participatory role in the live event that he or she is not in a position to commentate on it. In the experienced event there exists no 'voice of authority'; authority is inherent in the visual display.

Bullfighters' biographical narratives are woven into media events, often illustrated with photographs and presented as a prelude to the performance. Voice-over to performance also refers to the bullfighter's career and personal biography. Rather than presenting any bullfighter representing the drama of being a man (woman) in 'Spanish' culture, the media televises part of his or her own life – a personal instead of a general story. Dissected and reconstructed in the media, the dramatic continuity of Marvin's 'ritual performance' becomes obscured by slow-motion playback, commercial breaks, interviews and the authoritative voice-over. Close-ups of bullfighters' faces, emotions, feet or technique construct a different drama. The televised bullfight would tell another story; it is 'an other type of spectacle' (Matilla 1993: 14).

RITUAL/SPECTACLE?

In Parkin's terms the media bullfight may be rendered non-ritual due to the importance conferred on words, by which 'spontaneous' interviews and verbal 'asides' are spoken over images of the performing bullfighter:

> I have never come across a ritual in which the spatial movements and orientation counted for nothing and the words were all important. By contrast, I have never met a ritual in which the words, though sometimes claimed to be essential for proper performance, were not inscribed in spatially arranged phases and sequences.
>
> (Parkin 1992: 17–18)

However, live and televised bullfights do not fit a ritual/spectacle dichotomy for several reasons. Notably, *aficionados* apply the Spanish term *espectaculo* to imply that media bullfights as well as some men's and women's performances lack artistic quality. If a media bullfight is interpreted as 'respectful' representation of the live performance, it incorporates the ritual but is not the ritual itself. In this sense it is less a 'ritual hybrid' (Dayan and Katz 1987) than a televised interweaving of media and ritual agendas. The media performance should not necessarily be compared *negatively* to the live event as non-ritual.

It may be no coincidence that in this epoch of the televised performance women bullfighters are successful and accepted as never before. In the media bullfight the ritual structure and production of *ambiente*, which are problematic for female performers (or conversely which female bullfighters problematize), are less restricting. I propose that the interdependencies that exist between the successes of women as live and televised performers are key to understanding their popularity. Most of my informants based their judgements of women bullfighters on media reports and televised bullfights. During my fieldwork no women performed live in Córdoba, but through watching her televised performances and meeting Cristina Sánchez when she visited Córdoba my informants began to commit themselves to standpoints on her ability and potential. This inspired one informant to attend one of her performances in Malaga; others resolved to see her next nearby performance.

Success for all bullfighters is partially dependent on media coverage; the contemporary bullfight is a media phenomenon as well as a live performance. In this media context bullfighters take on something of a commodity status (and have fluctuating economic values) at certain points in their careers. Television is not a gender-neutral context and develops existing discourses that impinge on the media commodification of men and women performers.

GENDER ON TELEVISION: POWER, NOVELTY AND SUCCESS

The presence of a female body in the bullring (a space usually occupied by a male body) rarely passes without comment. In television narration this has been conceptualized in terms of 'the body of a woman' with the mind of a 'male' bullfighter. A feminine mind is thus dissociated from the sexed performing body as the media extends an invitation to gaze on a novel blend of masculine mind and female body.

During a woman's live performances men in the audience usually shout remarks about her physical appearance and 'sexiness'. More politely, two male commentators of a televised bullfight in Badajoz noted the attractiveness of Cristina Sánchez, announcing her as 'La guapa torera, Cristina Sánchez ... una bellisima mujer' ('The pretty bullfighter, Cristina Sánchez ... a lovely woman'), commenting over her performance: 'guapa de verdad, guapa, guapa' ('truly pretty'). The voice-over engaged in 'traditional' discourse that feminized her performance in relation to the masculine commentary. I spoke with informants who found such commentary variably amusing, sexist or inappropriate. The audience calls and commentator's remarks both represent 'tradition', but differ as they intersect with class, education and behavioural expectations.

Nevertheless a 'technological' context also permits other representations. Women's standpoints are often clearly expressed in the media and women bullfight journalists and critics also participate in these debates.

The woman bullfighter's plea of 'when I am performing see me as a professional, not as a woman' is not a simple demand for viewers to respond to if they are constantly reminded of the novel visual evidence that the person bullfighting is a woman. The opening scene of this chapter is exemplary: when a male voice spoke of Cristina's feminine beauty, he was swiftly interrupted by a reprimanding female voice stressing that their concern as commentators was with Cristina's performance. Competing ideas about how one should speak about and look at women form part of public political discourse in Spain, and may also be applied to the bullfight.

Commentaries, however, *usually* focused on Cristina's beauty and a 'historical tradition' of feminized bullfighting. The biological sex of a woman bullfighter is, when not unacceptable, made novel. Televised performances are heavily laden with many assumptions that problematize women bullfighters (or that make women bullfighters a problem for the bullfight).

The body of the woman bullfighter is on display; its shape is emphasized by the tightly fitting costume. The way in which one looks at a woman bullfighter, represented by the question over whether the audience should look at her body or her performance, is significant. Male bodies are similarly 'on show', but tend to be treated differently. For example, in 1993 during a televised performance a male bullfighter's trousers were torn by the bull's horn. Although he was not injured the tear revealed his penis, which, hanging outside his clothing for the remainder of his performance, was followed in a close-up shot. This clip was screened without public debate. Whilst 'traditionalists' insist that breasts are out of place in the bullring (Pink 1996), a penis, it seems, is well situated.

The reference to the body of a woman with the mind of a bullfighter/man classifies the woman bullfighter as a biological or medical-scientific novelty. Televised close-ups of Cristina Sánchez pulling what an informant labelled 'masculine' facial expressions whilst preparing for the kill could be interpreted as affirming such suggestions. In my experience, interpretations of her performance always referred to gender. Whether or not the femininity/ masculinity she embodies is problematic depends on the subjectivity of the viewer. Since television audiences do not necessarily trust the opinions of commentators and critics, the media bullfight provides a curious context for multiple evaluations of women bullfighters.

Televised transmissions introduce a way of watching the bullfight that involves variable forms of participation, a geographical 'closing' and greater accessibility. Cristina Sánchez has entered the bullfighting profession during this era and has been viewed by millions of television *aficionados*. There have been media opportunities to scrutinize her body, her face, her hairstyle, her bullfighting skills, and her father (who performs with her). Nevertheless male bullfighters are subject to similar scrutiny and the particular gaze of the viewer on the viewed varies not simply according to the sex of the bullfighter, but, in Strathern's words, 'in what kinds of bodies are the eyes [of the viewer] set' (1993: 42).

Women bullfighters are thus often constructed as (albeit successful) media novelties. Encased in this novelty veneer they may appear less threatening to masculine power holders: how many rare creatures with female bodies and male minds exist in a 'natural' world? Naturalistic metaphors suggest women bullfighters are unlikely to recur frequently, thus diminishing their disruptive potential.

If women bullfighters attract media attention, publicity, popularity and contracts through a combination of recognized skills and novelty value, this does not necessarily harm their career progression. Whilst this successful novelty category can be offensive to feminists, some performers benefit from dissociating themselves from feminism to align themselves with the 'traditionalist' domain they work in.[7] Cristina Sánchez, the most successful contemporary woman performer, was adopted by the media when she featured in a televised bullfight on becoming the top student of the Madrid bullfighting school. She has featured in press and on television and her performances have been praised for their technical and aesthetic value. She wins trophies, draws crowds and is competitively rated. Television does not implement this process but is an aspect of the culture in which audiences and contract makers act as decision makers. Nevertheless the media play an important role in facilitating her success. For every bullfight most *aficionados* attend they watch many more on television, and media representations inform *aficionados*' decisions about which performance to purchase expensive tickets for. Bullfighting shares characteristics with ritual, but is also a media event transmitted into the domestic space of many households and a commercial enterprise driven by market forces and advertising campaigns, and riddled with power networks and corruption.

Similarly the structures and routines practised by some viewers of televised bullfights in both bar and domestic contexts may be regarded a site of ritual activity. For instance, a glass of wine, a *tapa* and a particular group of people were required by some *aficionados* to 'complete' particular viewing contexts. Viewing, like live performance, offers individuals an opportunity to perform themselves. However, in comparison to the live bullfight, dramas of 'ritual' television viewing are small-scale and varied. Whilst different viewers share some cultural information and centre their activity on a common media narrative, their roles are less formally scripted than those of bullfighters.

There is no one key to becoming a successful performer in an expansive 'bullfighting world'. For example, whilst *ambiente* is central for the purist *aficionados* of live bullfights, the production of *ambiente* is activated not only by the performer, but through the dynamic between the performer, bull and audience. Furthermore, *ambiente* is not a fixed concept; as I have argued, the *ambiente* of a woman bullfighter's performance is likely to lack the audience consensus of that of a top man performer (although this may not necessarily be the case). The perception of *ambiente* is also a subjective act, and as subjectivities take different foci in the future, *ambiente* will be evaluated in different ways. Indeed some informants have already said that *ambiente* is produced in women bullfighters' performances, and on occasion consensus is apparent. However, division is rife and it would be incorrect to argue that women bullfighters are established or will become so.

CONCLUSIONS: THE BULLFIGHT CONSUMED

The relationship between the bullfight as ritual performance, the popularity of women performers, and the media can be usefully understood in the wider context of consumption and commodification. New communications technologies, global networks and increasing access to media performances have facilitated the development of a media domain of bullfighting culture in which some of its dominant discourses are played out. Television supports women bullfighters, but it is not gender-neutral and tends to reproduce current discourses and ideologies of gender. However, that it does so on a wider public stage and to a greater and more diverse audience is significant.

The media bullfight draws attention to the economic dimension of bullfighting culture. Financial relationships between bullrings and television companies, and the spending power and consumption patterns of *aficionados*, are significant. The bullfight is thus linked with the economic agendas of institutional, individual and family patterns of spending and consumption.

Home video recorders allow 'complete' media performances to be saved and their viewing fitted into the structure and routines of busy lives. Recorded performances become collectable commodities; recorded from television and archived at home. Advertising, frowned on in live bullfighting, is an integral element of the televised bullfight. The televised bullfight therefore unfolds in a context of consumerism, intercut with the commercial breaks that structure much Andalusian viewing. Some famous performances can be purchased. Series of bullfight videos are sold in kiosks or 'free' with collectable volumes. Many *aficionados* or bullfighting clubs are 'collectors'. Death, for example, is a marketable feature; a video of the death of one bullfighter was a popular conversation point. In 1992 the death of a *banderillero*, killed when a bull's horn pierced his heart during a performance, became a media death that was replayed in close-up and slow motion on the news. I viewed it on television in bars, in night clubs and at home. One family switched from channel to channel to catch it on 12 different news programmes in one day. Although initially conceived as complete, a televised performance can be separated into many parts. Some collections are thematic; for example, one *aficionado* video recorded hundreds of short takes of bulls entering the arena. Others collect recordings of particular performers or breeds of bull.

I have suggested that continuities between televised bullfights and the success of female performers partially explain women bullfighter's current popularity. When the live performance is represented in a media event the ritual statement of the performance is fragmented, reconstituted and rendered incoherent. To an extent the televised bullfight quashes the problematic relationship between ritual statement and contemporary culture, by forgoing atmosphere for technique and ceding the performer's control of the event to the media directors. Moreover, my research suggests that television *aficionados*' attitudes to and reviews of both performers and breeds of bull

develop in relation to, for example, media, publicity, economic considerations, and the social relations of both domestic and club-oriented television
viewing and discussion contexts. Various strands of television bullfight
culture are thus produced. The televised bullfight reflects an increasingly
national (and global) projection of the bullfight out of the local context. It is
a dynamic event, subjected to a variety of public gazes, and developing in
relation to discourses created in the societies on which it depends for its
audiences and performers.

NOTES

1 Although there is a 'history' of women performers they have rarely been accepted
   as valid bullfighters.
2 See also the Spanish anthropologists Romero de Solís (1992).
3 The term *ambiente* usually refers to a lively and social atmosphere and is not
   limited solely to performances or specific events. It is also used to comment on
   general atmosphere and, for example, can be applied to a city, or neighbourhood
   (see Marvin 1988, Díaz de Rada and Cruces 1994).
4 *Aficionado* when used to speak about bullfighting refers to a knowledgeable
   bullfight enthusiast.
5 Hobsbawm distinguishes between the rigid and repeated character of traditional
   activities and the more flexible 'custom'.
6 Interdependencies between live and televised bullfights appear similar to those
   developing for other events. The effects of television on 'traditional' events and
   the relationship between media representations and experienced events has been
   raised in media studies (e.g. Dayan and Katz 1987) and the anthropology of Europe
   (cf. Boissevain 1992; and see Crain 1992: 95).
7 Whilst dissociating herself from 'feminism' and 'feminists', Cristina Sánchez has
   expressed her wish to be accepted on the same basis as 'any' bullfighter and calls
   for a stop to the differentiation between male and female performers.

REFERENCES

Ang, Ien (1992) 'Living-room wars: new technologies, audience measurement and
   the tactics of television consumption', in Roger Silverstone and Eric Hirsch (eds)
   Consuming Technologies: Media and Information in Domestic Spaces, London:
   Routledge.
Appadurai, Arjun (1986) 'Introduction: commodities and the politics of value', in
   Arjun Appadurai (ed.) *The Social Life of Things: Commodities in Cultural
   Perspective*, Cambridge: Cambridge University Press.
Boissevain, Jeremy (1992) 'Introduction', in Jeremy Boissevain (ed.) *Revitalizing
   European Rituals*, London: Routledge.
Cambria, Rosario (1991) 'Bullfighting and the intellectuals', in Timothy Mitchell
   Blood Sport: A Social History of Bullfighting, Philadelphia: University of Penn-
   sylvania Press.
Carabias, Jose Luis (1993) 'Zapping Taurino', *Aplausos*, 832, 6 September.
Collins, Larry and Lapierre, Dominique (1968) *Or I'll Dress You in Mourning: The
   Extraordinary Story of El Cordobes and the New Spain he Stands For*, London:
   Weidenfeld and Nicolson.

Corbin, John and Corbin, Marie (1986) *Urbane Thought: Culture and Class in an Andalusian City*, Aldershot, Hants: Gower Publishing.

Cornwall, Andrea and Lindisfarne, Nancy (1994) 'Introduction', in Andrea Cornwall and Nancy Lindisfarne (eds) *Dislocating Masculinity: Comparative Ethnographies*, London: Routledge.

Crain, Mary (1992) 'Pilgrims, "yuppies" and media men: the transformation of an Andalusian pilgrimage', in Jeremy Boissevain (ed.) *Revitalizing European Rituals*, London: Routledge.

Dayan, Daniel and Katz, Elihn (1987) 'Performing media events', in James Curran, Anthony Smith and Pauline Wingate (eds) *Impacts and Influences: Essays on Media Power in the Twentieth Century*, London: Methuen.

Díaz de Rada, Angel and Cruces, Francisco (1994) 'The mysteries of incarnation: some problems to do with the analytic language of practice', in Kirsten Hastrup and Peter Hervik (eds) *Social Experience and Anthropological Knowledge*, London: Routledge.

Douglass, Carrie (1984) 'Toro muerto, vaca es: an interpretation of the Spanish bullfight', *American Ethnologist*, 11: 242–58.

Fabian, Johannes (1983) *Time and the Other: How Anthropology Makes its Object*, New York: Columbia University Press.

Falk, Pasi (1994) *The Consuming Body*, London: Sage.

Frank, Arthur, W. (1991) 'For a sociology of the body: an analytical review', in Mike Featherstone, Mike Hepworth and Bryan S. Turner (eds) *The Body: Social Process and Cultural Theory*, London: Sage.

Friedman, Jonathan (1994) *Cultural Identity and Global Process*, London: Sage.

Hobsbawm, Eric (1983) 'Introduction: inventing traditions', in Eric Hobsbawm and Terence Ranger (eds) *The Invention of Tradition*, Cambridge: Cambridge University Press.

Lewis, Gilbert (1980) *Day of Shining Red: An Essay in Understanding Ritual*, Cambridge: Cambridge University Press.

Marvin, Garry (1986) 'Honour, integrity and the problem of violence in the Spanish bullfight', in D. Riches (ed.) *The Anthropology of Violence*, Oxford: Blackwell.

—— (1988) *Bullfight*, Oxford: Blackwell.

Matilla, Jose Luis (1993) 'Corridas de toros por television', *El Ruedo*, 87, 1 January.

Mitchell, Timothy (1991) *Blood Sport: A Social History of Bullfighting*, Philadelphia: University of Pennsylvania Press.

Morley, David (1995) 'Theories of consumption in media studies', in Daniel Miller (ed.) *Acknowledging Consumption*, London: Routledge.

Parkin, David (1992) 'Ritual as spatial direction and bodily division', in Daniel de Coppet (ed.) *Understanding Rituals*, London and New York: Routledge.

Pink, Sarah (1996) 'Breasts in the bullring: female physiology, female bullfighters and competing femininities', *Body and Society*, 2(1): 45–64.

—— (1997a) 'Photography and the world of bullfighting: visual histories of success', *History of Photography*, 21(1): 54–9.

—— (1997b) 'Topsy-turvy bullfights and festival queens', *Social Anthropology*, 5(2): 159–75.

—— (1997c) 'Female bullfighters, unemployed feria queens and women who want to fly: gender, identity and the Andalusian labour market', *Self, Agency and Society*, 1(2): 90–107.

Pitt-Rivers, Julian (1963 [1961]) *The People of the Sierra*, Chicago and London: University of Chicago Press.

—— (1984) 'El sacrificio del toro', *Revista del Occidente*, 36: 27–47.

—— (1993) 'The Spanish bullfight and kindred activities', *Anthropology Today* 9(4): 11–15.

Romero de Solís, Pedro (1992) 'De la tauromachie considérée comme ensemble sacrificiel', *Information sur les Sciences Sociales*, 31(3): 531–50.

Strathern, Marilyn (1992) 'Foreword', in Roger Silverstone and Eric Hirsch (eds) *Consuming Technologies: Media and Information in Domestic Spaces*, London: Routledge.

—— (1993) 'One-legged gender', *Visual Anthropology Review*, Special Issue: Feminist Approaches to the Visualization of Culture, 9 (1): 42–51.

Turner, Victor (1967) *The Forest of Symbols: Aspects of Ndembu Ritual*, Ithaca NY and London: Cornell University Press.

Chapter 7

'A oes heddwch?'

Contesting meanings and identities in the Welsh National Eisteddfod

Charlotte Aull Davies

The demarcation between ritual and theatre is far from clear cut and is bound up as much with the context of performance as with its content. Beeman has suggested it applies on two primary dimensions: 'efficacy vs entertainment in intent, [and] participation vs observation in the audience's role' (1993: 379). These dichotomies appear to have been formulated primarily with theatre in view. They become more problematic when theatre and public spectacle are taken as similar performance activities (Schechner 1988). Public spectacles, in contrast to theatre, appear to incorporate rather more of the characteristics of ritual on these two dimensions. In the first place, while their role as entertainment is undoubted, many carry out as their central activity the recognition of individual accomplishments in ways that alter permanently the social status of those so exalted. Furthermore, participants, and more particularly organizers, often regard them as having a serious purpose of collective representation, as well as individual recognition, at least equal in importance to their entertainment role. The second distinction between audience observation and participation can be justified for public spectacle only by taking a single aspect, its ceremonial focus, as its entirety; although audiences may be primarily observers in formal ceremonies, they are participants in the surrounding activities and informal performances that make up a spectacle.

This rather arbitrary separation of ritual and public spectacle, and the linking of the latter with theatre, may be due in part to the relative paucity of studies of both theatre and spectacle which concentrate on 'performance per se: its structure, its cultural meaning apart from other institutions, the conditions under which it occurs, and its place within broad patterns of community life' (Beeman 1993: 370). This chapter explores the nature of spectacle by examining the performances which constitute the Welsh National Eisteddfod with particular reference to the two dimensions noted above: the role of spectacle in formulating, maintaining and projecting collective identity; and the importance of the nature and participation of the audience in this process.

It is often claimed that public spectacles are expressions of collective identity; 'spectacle is a public display of a society's central meaningful elements' (Beeman 1993: 380). For example, DaMatta's analysis of Carnaval concludes that 'it was not Brazil that invented Carnaval; on the contrary, it was Carnaval that invented Brazil' (1984: 245). Similarly, Schechner (1993: 97) argues that the Yaqui ceremonial of Waehma built around Easter-week observances is what makes them Yaqui. Clearly such interpretations of the relationship between a given spectacle and a society's fundamental identity bears a resemblance to Turner's (1969) discussions of the creation of 'communitas' in and through ritual. However, there is a danger of overlooking the degree to which such spectacles encompass competing performances and identities or even mobilize a collectivity to challenge existing power relationships (cf. Cohen's 1993 analysis of the Notting Hill Carnival). Baumann (1992) has argued that ritual in plural societies is often far removed from the Durkheimian expectations either that it unites a community or that its performance is primarily inward directed towards community members. On the contrary, ritual may express conflict and desire for cultural change rather than any celebration of the community as currently imagined or constituted, and in so doing it may involve outsiders, either actually present or as absent categorical referents (1992: 102–5). Such features would seem to be even more salient as regards the nature of spectacle. These observations also direct attention to the nature and role of the audience in spectacle. It will be argued that spectacle should not be viewed simply or even primarily in terms of its ceremonial focus. In fact spectacle includes its audience in very complex ways. It is affected by the nature of the audience, both the actual crowds who watch and those who are imagined to be observing. Furthermore, the audience is part of the spectacle, is itself spectacle, and its ways of participating – audience performances – may reconstruct the nature and meaning of the spectacle itself (cf. Leach 1984; Schieffelin, this volume). Finally, the spectacle should be seen as dynamic; if indeed it is a site for contesting meanings, it may itself alter in meaning over time and be constituted of different activities and different audiences (Boissevain 1992; Morgan 1983).

THE WELSH NATIONAL EISTEDDFOD

Originally, an *eisteddfod* (the word means 'a session') was a gathering for literary and musical competitions which had been announced in advance. The first recorded *eisteddfod* was held in 1176 by the Lord Rhys at Cardigan Castle, although this was certainly not the first *eisteddfod*. The tradition of *eisteddfodau* waxed and waned with the fortunes of a bardic tradition which depended primarily on a Welsh aristocracy to serve as patrons of poetry. However, its modern roots can be traced to the nineteenth century when it was revived again, this time mainly under the auspices of various London

Welsh literary societies. Another feature, which has become a salient characteristic of the contemporary National Eisteddfod, was added in the early part of the nineteenth century – the Gorsedd of Bards introduced in 1819. The Gorsedd (meaning throne) was the creation of the stonemason and antiquarian Iolo Morgannwg, who developed the idea that the Welsh bards were the inheritors of the ancient Druidic tradition and proceeded to create various rituals for them. The first meeting of the Gorsedd was in London in 1792. It caught the imagination of both the London Welsh and others in Wales, and provincial *gorseddau* were established, as well as the national one, which in the course of the century became a part of the National Eisteddfod. The formal and colourful rituals, including processions of robed poets and others honoured by the Gorsedd (see Figure 7.1), solemn ceremonies at which the victorious poets are crowned or chaired, and quasi-religious services carried out in stone circles with the archdruid speaking from the logan stone (*maen llog*), added to over the decades but all built on the imaginings of Iolo Morgannwg, have become intimately associated with the contemporary National Eisteddfod and are among the most commonly presented images of it.

The National Eisteddfod lasts eight days spanning the first week in August and is held at different sites, alternating between north and south Wales; thus particular *eisteddfodau* become known by their locations: the 1995 National Eisteddfod was Eisteddfod Bro Colwyn, the Colwyn Bay area; in 1996 it was Eisteddfod Bro Dinefwr, encompassing Llandeilo and vicinity. At the centre of the Eisteddfod field is a large pavilion seating over 3,000, where the main ceremonies and competitions are held. The central ceremonies are those in which the winners of the two main poetry competitions are announced: the crowning and chairing ceremonies. The chair is awarded for a long poetic composition in the traditional strict metres, the crown for free verse. The former is required to use the complex forms of internal alliteration and rhyming that developed over many centuries in Welsh poetry. Other competitions for various ages go on all day in the main pavilion (except for breaks for the various formal ceremonies). These include both group and individual competitions in a large variety of the performing arts, such as *cerdd dant*,[1] folk singing, recitation, folk dancing, choral singing and so on. This pavilion provides the spatial and conceptual centre of the Eisteddfod. However, it by no means exhausts the content of the event, either formal or informal. Scattered around the Eisteddfod field are other large tents designated for particular purposes: the literature tent (*y babell len*) houses various literary events, such as *ymryson y beirdd*, a competition in spontaneous poetry composition between teams of bards; the societies' tent (*pabell y cymdeithasau*) is the site of numerous lectures, usually on social issues, as well as a location where the numerous Welsh special societies may hold annual meetings; there is a young people's tent where a variety of popular music events are held – this usually has to be located towards the peripheries of the

Figure 7.1 The *gorsedd* of bards on parade through Builth Wells, 1982

field so the loud rock music frequently emanating from it does not interfere with the strains of the harp in the competitions more typical of the main pavilion; the arts tent (*pabell y celfyddydau*) houses an art exhibition, which has also been judged and various prizes awarded. Besides these special-purpose tents for particular types of activity, the field is surrounded by smaller tents which house exhibitions, from that of the Welsh Office to various charitable societies, environmental groups, and groups which campaign for the Welsh language, such as Cymdeithas yr Iaith Gymraeg (the Welsh Language Society) and Mudiad Ysgolion Meithrin (the Welsh Nursery Schools Movement); other tents contain craft shops, souvenir shops and bookshops. The sale of books on the Eisteddfod field is substantial and many publishers schedule the release of new publications during the week of the National. There are also activities that take place off the Eisteddfod field entirely, some of which are officially linked to the Eisteddfod, such as dramas and concerts, others of which have no formal links, such as *nosweithiau llawen* (literally, 'happy nights') that have long been a feature of late night entertainment and, more recently, rock concerts that are staged virtually every evening of the week.

Approximately 150,000 attend the week-long activities, about 20,000 per day. The way the Eisteddfod is experienced by those attending varies greatly. Some come for the week or a portion of it – there are official caravan and camping fields in the vicinity – others for a day. Some people are very involved in the competitive performances and may book a seat in the main pavilion for the week, bringing sandwiches, seat cushions and other paraphernalia. Others may never go into the main pavilion or do so only briefly.[2] Although most people who come to the Eisteddfod undoubtedly come onto the Eisteddfod field at some time, walking around and meeting friends and acquaintances, there are some, certainly, who participate mainly in the unofficial activities off the Eisteddfod field.

MEDIA REPRESENTATIONS

The National Eisteddfod has always been a performance directed not only to audiences actually present in the space that it annually constructs for itself but also, through media representations, to audiences both real and imagined elsewhere. In the nineteenth century, as will be discussed below, this absent and partly imagined audience was primarily English and there was great concern as to how the Eisteddfod was depicted in the English press. With the advent of radio and television in the twentieth century and the gradual shift in focus to a Welsh audience, the nature of media representations and their effects on the festival changed. The establishment of a Welsh region of the British Broadcasting Corporation (BBC) in 1937 meant that the Eisteddfod was given more extensive coverage than previously, rising from five to eight hours over three years to the accompaniment of criticisms in the press that the broadcasts were adversely affecting the festival's character, in particular its spontaneity (Davies 1994: 113). Television coverage was similarly expanded when the fourth television channel was secured for a Welsh-language service in Wales in the early 1980s. By the mid-1990s television programming during the week of the Eisteddfod could be characterized as follows. Typically there are one-and-a-half to two hours of live broadcast from the Eisteddfod field during the day, providing coverage of the main ceremonial events as they occur as well as some of the competitions and other less formal activities. There is a nightly prime-time programme showing highlights of the day's events. There are occasional special-interest programmes covering particular topics such as the visual arts or drama. Both

Welsh- and English-medium news programmes carry items from the Eisteddfod, such as the winners of the main poetry, drama and other literary competitions, sound bites from the speeches made by those honoured by invitations to preside over the festival for that day, reports of any political protests, or simply human interest stories. In addition, the English-medium regional services, both BBC Wales and the commercial service, normally broadcast one or two programmes on the Eisteddfod during the week, either a selection of highlights or one with a special-interest focus.

The coverage tends to emphasize more structured and formal activities over the informal and unscheduled performances of those attending. However, some media devices are employed in an attempt to redress this balance and to provide more of the flavour of the festival; for example, reporters move around the Eisteddfod field and conduct impromptu interviews, and increasingly media attention is given to activities outside the main pavilion and even off the Eisteddfod field. During the 1995 National Eisteddfod I conducted a more systematic analysis of television representations of the Eisteddfod, recording this output and subsequently viewing and selecting images to suggest the range of performative activities being disseminated to Welsh audiences. The selection was not intended to be statistically representative, although in its weighting of types of performance it was approximately so. What follows is an attempt to provide a verbal description of the impressions created by the approximately seven minutes of video tape I distilled from this week's recording of Eisteddfod media representations.

The first item on the tape records the most dramatic moments of what is often regarded as the high point of the week's activities, the chairing of the victorious poet. For this ceremony the main pavilion is full and on the stage are the members of the Gorsedd in full druidic costume. Entries for all the literary competitions are submitted under pseudonyms, and in the earlier part of the ceremony, one of the judges delivers a detailed critique of all the submissions, ending with the winning work, all still identified only by their bardic pseudonyms. The tape begins, immediately after this lengthy adjudication, with the archdruid extending an invitation for the winning poet, 'Porthor' (caretaker), to stand. Heraldic trumpets are sounded, and in the darkened pavilion spotlights play over the crowd, until they find and focus on a single young man. The television commentator notes that there is 'a cry of joy, of great joy'. As the winning poet is met by a party from the platform who place a robe around his shoulders and then escort him to the platform, the organ plays 'Men of Harlech' and the commentator informs the television audience that the poet will be named by the archdruid, as is traditional, but adds that 'he knows him well'. In fact, he is the archdruid's son, a result made even more unusual as well as moving by the fact that the archdruid, in his last year in that office, only two days earlier had presented the Eisteddfod crown for free verse to his brother in a similar ceremony. With the victorious bard standing before his chair, a sword held over his head is unsheathed as the archdruid proclaims 'Y gwir yn erbyn y byd. A oes heddwch?' ('The truth against the world. Is there peace?'), to which the audience responds 'Heddwch' ('Peace') and the sword is returned to its sheath. 'Let the poet be seated in his chair.'

The ceremony continues but my tape moves to the second item, which illustrates one of the musical forms, *cerdd dant*, considered most characteristic of traditional Welsh culture. Initally, with the camera focused on the hands of a harpist, we hear a single melody, joined after a traditionally specified number of measures by two young women singing, in two-part harmony, a second melody which blends with that played by the harp. The camera moves to the singers' faces, then out to show the group of three on the huge stage.

The third item is a brief excerpt from the winner of one of the recitation competitions; her presentation involves a lot of facial animation as well as vocal agility. An interview backstage with her father reveals that he too has been very successful in recitation in the past and coached his daughter.

The fourth item begins with the winner of the solo *cerdd dant* for those under 16 years of age, singing to harp accompaniment. This is followed by a brief interview with the winner and her father on the Eisteddfod field. As a product of Welsh-medium schools, she is interviewed in Welsh. Her father then says in English that 'coming from an English part of Wales and we haven't spoken Welsh for a couple of generations, it's fantastic that she can speak Welsh first of all and second that she can come here and win the National first time'.

The fifth item changes both atmosphere and location, shifting to one of the performers at a rock concert off the Eisteddfod field; Meic Stevens, who has been on the Welsh pop scene since the late 1960s, appears with dark glasses, long grey hair in a ponytail and guitar, singing about 'bwrw cwrw yn y dre' ('raining beer in town').

The sixth item returns to the main pavilion for a montage from one of the more recently introduced competitions, disco dancing, showing both individual competitors and group routines.

The final item is from one of the raves held on nearby campsites. There are multicoloured lights flashing, music blaring and young people jumping in front of the camera to give brief shouted commentaries on the scene: 'It's just young people can just have a brilliant time. And older people can't understand it.'[3] 'Blydi amazin!' 'When you go out to a night club, you see English people, you come here, meet Welsh people, cool!'[4]

As the tape suggests, television representations of the Eisteddfod, in both the distribution of activities selected for broadcast and the weighting of programmes, tend to reinforce the more traditional images and performances from the Eisteddfod. However, as the final three items illustrate, television also disseminates a range of other images at variance with these stereotypical expectations. In so doing, it informs those who attend (and who very often subsequently view televised versions of what they experienced directly) as well as a broader Welsh public about the multivocal and polysemic nature of the festival. Furthermore, such televised representations validate these various activities as all part of the Eisteddfod, encompassed in the spectacle and hence contributing to its meanings, not simply occurring coincidentally with it.

I return below to a fuller consideration of how, as Wales's major public spectacle, the Eisteddfod may include and project various and often competing versions of Welsh identity, and the role of the media, television especially, in this process. But first I want to consider briefly an alternative interpretation which regards traditional *eisteddfodic* performance as hegemonic for Welsh identity.

PERFORMING WELSHNESS?

In a recent anthropological treatment of the subject, *eisteddfodau* are used as the primary basis for an analysis of Welsh identity and Welsh concepts of self (Trosset 1993). In particular, the National Eisteddfod is taken to be the main arena in which Welshness is defined. Trosset suggests that 'the National Eisteddfod is the central cultural performance of Welsh-Wales. . . . [It] is felt to be an enactment of fundamental elements of Welsh culture' (1993: 42). Thus she uses a performance idiom in developing her discussion of the nature of Welshness, identifying a particular Welsh performance style associated with *eisteddfodau*:

> The feature I found the most noticeable, and the one most frequently commented on by Welsh speakers, is an animated facial expression, which is accompanied by a bodily alertness showing a total awareness of the performance situation. . . . The animated face is only seen during moments of actual performance, that is, while words are being produced. Here we encounter the second salient feature of Welsh performance style: the way it is turned on and off. Rather than framing a performance by formalizing entrances and exits, . . . Welsh stage presence leaves these moments unregulated but formalizes the moments of sound production themselves. Most performers of all ages wander onto the stage and rush off. Before starting to sing or speak, or even between the verses of a song during the instrumental interlude, the performer's face remains, or returns to being, absolutely deadpan.
>
> (Trosset 1993: 144)

This performance convention is then generalized to describe what she regards as a fundamental feature of the Welsh self, that of a supposed sharp distinction between being on stage and off, between public and private. Trosset says that she observed the same kind of animated face during brief social encounters followed by the sudden complete blankness on parting, 'leaving no indication that either person is still thinking about the encounter' (1993: 144–5). She links this turning on and off of facial animation with another aspect of Welsh cultural expectations of selfhood, that of emotionalism, which leads to performances that display emotion in culturally expected forms which again are learned in *eisteddfod* performances. 'Emotional style is standardized to a large extent by eisteddfod competition and training, which marks certain ways of acting as emotionally and aesthetically effective' (1993: 167). As this suggests, Trosset believes that Welsh children are socialized into a performance idiom. She argues that the conventions of *eisteddfod* performance are important in children's early socialization both at home and in school, and further contends that this experience of performance and competition is so widespread as to be a significant basis of Welsh personhood and, through that, of Welsh identity.

Although Trosset disavows the definition of identity in terms of a set of essences, she argues that Welsh people view Welshness in this way, as composed of a number of qualities, the most important of which is the Welsh language. Since only 20 per cent of the people of Wales are Welsh speakers, this definition of Welshness clearly makes some more Welsh than others. Additional related features of this Welshness are those that are enshrined in the tradition of *eisteddfodau* and in particular in the National Eisteddfod. Trosset argues that even those who might disagree with this version of Welshness are entrapped in this particular vision of it in that they must locate themselves with respect to this discourse:

> When individuals in Wales think about society in terms of the theory of degrees of Welshness, they feel pride or shame, affinity or alienation, based on where they are able to locate themselves in relation both to the center and to the hierarchy of Welshness. . . . Though not everyone agrees with the dominant definition, its frame of reference is always present in public discourse, such that it can never be ignored. All Welsh people in some way use it to think with, or at least have to deal with its assumptions in others' responses to them.
>
> (Trosset 1993: 55)

While Trosset's analysis of this performance idiom is insightful regarding some aspects of Welsh personhood and their expression in social relationships, its utility as an explanation of Welsh identity is more problematic. Her discussion of Welshness, in fact, appears to deal with only one segment of Welsh society, whose cultural expression and sense of Welshness are particularly closely linked with *eisteddfodau*; but there is less support for her view that this segment is hegemonic in defining Welshness in terms of their relationship to the Welsh language, *eisteddfodau*, cultural and (usually) political nationalism.

This particular segment of Welsh society is recognized among Welsh speakers as those who are active in and have a love for '*y pethe*' (the things).

These 'things' are the types of performance and activity that traditionally are central to *eisteddfodau* – singing, both individual and choral, and especially *cerdd dant*; recitation, again both individual and group; harp playing; and less prestigious, but still highly valued, various sorts of group dramatic activity, most typical being the *can actol* in which a short presentation involving both singing and acting depicts some set theme. There is often a high degree of family continuity among those whose lives are wrapped up in *y pethe*, with parents who have themselves competed successfully coaching their children (as was observed in one instance on the video tape described above); indeed the '*eisteddfod* mam' who sits in the front row mouthing words and making facial expressions as her offspring perform on stage is one of the comic stereotypes of this collectivity. However, numerous experiences from my own fieldwork lead me to question the ideological hegemony accorded them in things Welsh by Trosset.

The *eisteddfodau* at which children primarily compete are run under the auspices of Urdd Gobaith Cymru, a Welsh youth organization. They are organized in a hierarchy from local to regional and finally to the Urdd National Eisteddfod, a scaled-down version of the Welsh National Eisteddfod which takes place in early June. At each level, there are trials to select the best three in each competition, who then compete again on the main stage, with the winner at that level moving on to the next in a fortnight's time. These local and regional *eisteddfodau* have none of the peripheral activities of the two Nationals. Thus attending a local *eisteddfod* means listening to large numbers of individual children reciting or singing the same piece time and again. Not surprisingly, there is a great deal of fairly good-natured grumbling among parents – especially among those who do not themselves speak Welsh, but by no means restricted to them. One parent described it as the Welsh form of self-torture. This individual was not someone who felt his Welshness was at all threatened by his lack of inclusion in 'the things'. He was himself a Welsh speaker, both his work and family life were carried on mainly in Welsh, he was involved in Welsh education for adults and was an active campaigner for Welsh-medium education. At one local *eisteddfod*, I met another parent, a Welsh speaker and an active political nationalist, who expressed his dismay that his son had just been placed in the recitation preliminaries, an outcome which was totally unexpected by both of them and which meant they would have to remain there for several more hours so the boy could compete again on stage. Certainly there are numerous examples of Welsh people whose Welshness is quite secure on most of Trosset's criteria, yet whose interest in 'the things' is perfunctory at best. On the other hand, those who are devoted to 'the things' are not necessarily archetypically Welsh in other respects, as the following example illustrates. In a village school *eisteddfod* in North Wales, the 4- and 5-year-olds were preparing to compete in the solo singing. Just before the start of the competition the great-grandmother of one of the youngsters seated on the stage waiting to perform stepped out into the aisle of the crowded school auditorium and loudly instructed the accompanist as to the key in which 4-year-old Rhianwen was to sing. This was the family tradition of devotion to 'the things' in action; both Rhianwen's mother and grandmother also sang, played the harp and piano and competed regularly as well as teaching others.

But what of the complex of attitudes, including nationalist sympathies, that make up Trosset's idea of Welshness? The village where Rhianwen's parents owned a house was in an area that at that time was experiencing an influx of English immigrants who were considered to be undermining the vitality of the Welsh language there. Welsh political nationalists and language activists were voicing great concern and attempting to find ways of regulating both the migration and its effects. However, Rhianwen's parents, who were trying to sell their house in order to move to a larger one in the same area, seemed unconcerned; her mother confided that they hoped to find some English people to buy the house since they knew no local people could afford it. In her case the links between the continuation of 'the things' to which she was totally committed and other aspects of the nature of Welshness and its obligations to the group, as Trosset depicts it, appear to be non-existent.

Thus I argue that Trosset's view of Welshness as emanating from what is even a relatively small segment of Welsh-speaking society, let alone Welsh society as a whole, is ultimately unconvincing, although the question she raises regarding the relationship between *eisteddfod* performance and Welsh identity is clearly an important one. As the major public spectacle in Welsh society for over a century, the National Eisteddfod should provide insight into Welsh cultural meanings and identity. However, to encompass the variety of ways of performing Welshness requires a more catholic approach to *eisteddfod* performances, one in which the activities outside the main pavilion, with all the conflicts and contradictions they entail, are at least as important as the competitions within; and one in which a variety of audiences both participate in and affect the performances and their meanings.

PERFORMING WELSHNESSES

I argue that the National Eisteddfod is used for performances not of a single homogeneous and hegemonic Welshness but rather of alternative and often competing Welshnesses. Boissevain (1992), commenting on the growth in European rituals since World War II, noted a shift away from outsiders as the principal audience and the increasing importance of celebrations by and for the permanent residents of communities, often taking place outside the tourist season. It appears that a similar shift has occurred in the audience towards which the Welsh National Eisteddfod primarily directs its perform-ances. In the nineteenth century, the primary audience for the National Eisteddfod was, in fact, not the people of Wales but English society, with the Gorsedd displaying a vision of a romantic Celtic past to appeal to English imaginations. A major additional stimulus for this orientation towards England was the desire to disprove the extremely negative picture of Welsh culture drawn by the Government's 1847 *Report on Education in Wales* (the 'Blue Books' Report). This report portrayed the Welsh as illiterate, uncouth and immoral and blamed their condition primarily on the continued existence of the Welsh language. The attempt to use the National Eisteddfod to respond to these accusations was to shape the nature of the festival well into the first half of the twentieth century. Basically the National Eisteddfod became a platform for projecting a Welshness that would find favour among the English.

What did this entail? The first response was to curtail the use of Welsh in performances and administration. This was clearly a somewhat delicate undertaking for a festival whose core ceremonies were intended to celebrate and develop Welsh poetry. However, one device was the establishment, in 1862, of a Social Science Section which sponsored annual lectures, virtually all of which were given in English, on topics of contemporary social concern albeit with a view to promoting the progress of the Welsh nation. Another way in which the role of the Welsh language in the festival was de-emphasized was by giving greater importance to musical competitions. The principal historian of the National Eisteddfod noted: 'Before the end of the [eighteen-]sixties the Welsh discovered that they could sing. Even worse, they discovered that the English were willing to recognise their talent. They have been singing ever since.... From 1863 onwards the cultural condition of Wales was more and more to be decided by the number, size and success of her choirs' (Edwards 1976: 70–1, my translation; also see Edwards 1980, 1990). After victories in the Crystal Palace in 1872 and 1873 of one of the major Welsh choirs, most of whose members were from coal-mining and iron-working communities, the Welsh journal *Y Cerddor Cymreig* (*The Welsh Musician*) commented:

> The national body of the English have become accustomed to think ill and speak contemptuously of the Welsh. They have taken for granted that there is no work or knowledge or imagination in Wales, any more than in the grave. This choir proved that there is life here, there is ability here, there is value here; and the Welsh in Wales are not to be scorned henceforth.
>
> (quoted in Edwards 1976: 71, my translation)

Thus the modern National Eisteddfod in its origins was a ritual directed primarily at an audience outside Wales. The editor of the Welsh journal *Y Faner* commented that at least three-quarters if not nine-tenths of the speech at the 1873 Eisteddfod had been in English, and opined that this would 'create amongst the English correct views and a fair judgement about the true nature and high principles of the Eisteddfod as a national institution of the Welsh' (quoted in Edwards 1976: 79–80, my translation).

Naturally there were those who resisted this orientation towards English society and opinion. As early as 1866 there was an attempt to hold an alternative *eisteddfod* (Eisteddfod y Cymry – the Welsh people's Eisteddfod) where such pessimism about the future of the Welsh language would not be heard. However, it was not widely supported and proved a financial disaster (Edwards 1976: 67–8). It was not until 1950 that the performative focus of the National Eisteddfod was clearly shifted to a Welsh audience by the enactment of the Welsh Rule, which allows only Welsh from the Eisteddfod platform as well as making it the language of the ruling Eisteddfod Council and promoting its use in all displays and activities on the Eisteddfod field. This rule represents the culmination of attempts to shift the performative focus of the Welsh National Eisteddfod onto a Welsh audience and away from its former concern with English opinion. However, it has not meant a shift to an exclusively Welsh-speaking audience. This is made clear at the most obvious level by the simultaneous translation equipment available for the performances in the main pavilion, although not normally available for other activities. Of greater significance is the broadening of participation through expansion of available competitions to include many that do not require Welsh-language ability: brass bands and folk dancing have long been points of entry for non-Welsh speakers; and art and craft competitions have more recently gained in importance and salience in the festival. While television has not been primarily responsible for the introduction of these non-traditional competitions, it has played an important part in increasing their visibility and prestige.

Furthermore, television has exercised a more direct influence on the development of one of the most popular of the newer competitions, namely that for the Welsh learner of the year (*dysgwr y flwyddyn*). This particular competition selects one individual, from the winners of similar competitions in each of the Welsh counties, for her or his success in acquiring fluency in Welsh as displayed by a portfolio of submissions as well as in interviews with the judges. This competition has aroused a great deal of interest and in recent years has been the subject of a television programme with brief film presentations about all the contestants, how they learned Welsh and how they use it in their everyday lives, as well as excerpts from their interviews. Many of the past winners have been English incomers to Wales, making the National Eisteddfod instrumental in the campaign to protect the Welsh language in the face of continuing immigration of non-Welsh speakers to Welsh communities, but also involving it in support for a different, non-traditional way of becoming Welsh.

Another example of the complexity of the versions of Welshness now supported and performed in the context of the National Eisteddfod comes from one of the recent medal winners in the arts competition. Tim Davies has had installations awarded the silver medal in two recent National Eisteddfodau: *Waliau Du Du* (*Black, Black Walls*) which took the silver medal in 1994 was a response to the government's announcement that it was to close the last remaining coal-mines in Wales (see Figure 7.2); his second successive silver medal, in 1995, was for *Wal Wedi Llosgi (Burnt Wall)* – a wall of matches which had been set alight. This work also nearly won the People's Choice prize, determined by popular vote, and was in response to immigration and the problems it has created for Welsh communities (Tomos 1996). In their explicitly political content, such as the implied reference of the second work to burning holiday homes in protest against the effects of such properties on Welsh communities, these works both challenge the more accommodating version of Welshness projected by many among the Welsh elite and appear to have struck a responsive chord among those attending the

Figure 7.2 Waliau Du Du (Black, Black Walls) by Tim Davies

Eisteddfod. They provide yet another example of the contemporary festival being used for performances of alternative versions of Welshness, significantly as well, in this case, by an artist who is not a Welsh speaker.

There are in addition many less formal performances of different kinds of Welshness which take place during the National Eisteddfod. Among them are the political protests, especially those of Cymdeithas yr Iaith Gymraeg (the Welsh Language Society), which have been a feature of virtually every Eisteddfod since the Society's inception in 1963. Perhaps one of the most memorable and controversial of the Society's protests occurred in 1969, the year of the investiture of the Prince of Wales, during the Urdd National Eisteddfod, rather than the National Eisteddfod. When Prince Charles was being brought to the stage to address the audience in the main pavilion, about a hundred protestors displaying anti-investiture slogans walked out. Among them was Dafydd Iwan, then chair of Cymdeithas yr Iaith, who had already greatly upset some of the Welsh establishment with his pop song 'Carlo', which made fun of the prince. He was booed and cheered by different sections of the audience when he performed at a *noson lawen* later that evening; ironically, and again indicative of the tensions in the meanings of Welshness projected in the National Eisteddfodau, he included in his performance some lines from that year's winning poem by Gerallt Lloyd Owen about the last Prince of Wales, who was killed in 1282 (Iwan 1981: 45–6). The poem bemoans the lukewarm patriotism of Welsh people with lines that begin:

Wylit, wylit Lywelyn
Wylit waed pe gwelit hyn.
Ein calon gan estron wr,
Ein coron gan goncwerwr.
    (Owen 1972: 24)

[You would weep, weep, Llywelyn
You would weep blood to see this.
Our heart with a foreigner,
Our crown with a conqueror.]
    (my translation)

More typical of Cymdeithas protests over the years have been invasions of one of the tents of an establishment organization – the Welsh Office is a common target – in which the display is wrecked, usually by painting slogans over everything. In the 1995 Eisteddfod, Cymdeithas activists, attempting to draw attention to their campaign to establish a democratic body to take control of education away from the Welsh Office, were accused, under the banner headline 'Yob fury at Eisteddfod', of mobbing Welsh Education Minister Rod Richards (Dube 1995).

A final example of the different and often contradictory versions of Welshness being performed, and taken as characteristic of the National

Eisteddfod, concerns the role of alcohol in the festival. The Eisteddfod officially has been a bastion of sobriety for most of this century; alcohol is not permitted on the Eisteddfod field. There has been a controversy raging about the decision to allow alcohol in the 1997 Eisteddfod at events for young people held in the evening on the Eisteddfod field. On the one hand, there are those who object to what they see as a lowering of moral standards; on the other, there are those who object to the availability of alcohol being limited to young people's events. Certainly the informal performances during Eisteddfod week have for decades included a great deal of very public consumption of alcohol, not to mention considerable drunkenness. One individual who attended the National regularly in the 1960s and 1970s said:

> I remember driving into Bala at the start of the week [in 1967]. The place was heaving with people out on the streets from pubs that were overflowing. So I thought this is going to be a good Eisteddfod. That year the archdruid was so disturbed by the excessive public drinking that he spoke against it from the *maen llog*.

This sort of fringe *eisteddfodic* performance was memorialized in 'The Cross Foxes' by poet Harri Webb, about the 1961 Eisteddfod Dyffryn Maelor near Rhosllanerchrugog, where 'we drank the pub dry' (Stephens 1995: 47–8):

> The National Eisteddfod was on Ponciau flat
> But Undeb y Tancwyr[5] saw little of that.
> They slept all the day and they drank all the night
> The gin, rum and whisky, the dark and the light.
>
> . . .
>
> The Gorsedd were marching with nightshirts so clean,
> The sexiest sight that Rhos ever had seen,
> Said Cynan[6] – I think we're a wonderful lot
> But next to a woman I do like a pint pot
>
> The landlord he gave on the pump a last pull,
> His cellar was empty, his till it was full,
> The barmaid was fainting, the potman was weak –
> Thank God the Eisteddfod's not here every week!

A final aspect of this view of the Eisteddfod as encompassing a variety of performances representing a range of Welshnesses concerns the role of the media, particularly television. Whereas superficially television might appear to support the more traditional *eisteddfodic* performances, its overall effect is to legitimate alternative performances as also being part of the Eisteddfod and hence of any Welsh identity it might project. To take but one example, the activities of young people in pubs and campsites, as just noted, have long been a part of the festival week but could be viewed by those primarily concerned with the main ceremonial and competitive events as little more than a by-product of the festivities. However, once television begins to broadcast from the campsite raves, as part of its Eisteddfod coverage, they then become both more visible than formerly to all Eisteddfod audiences (those physically present as well as home viewers) and a more legitimate part of the festival and the Welsh identities it projects. One indication of this has been the recent controversy sparked by some of the Welsh rock bands electing to perform in English as well as Welsh at gigs held off the Eisteddfod field during the week.

'A OES HEDDWCH?'

The main pavilion is always at capacity for the ceremonies in which the winning poets in each of the two main competitions are announced. After a lengthy adjudication discussing the merits and demerits of other entries as well as that of the winning work, the bardic name of the winner is announced. In one of the highlights of the subsequent ceremony, as described above, a sword held over the bard's head is unsheathed as the archdruid proclaims, 'A oes heddwch?' ('Is there peace?'), to which the audience responds, 'Heddwch' ('Peace'), and the sword is returned to its sheath. This is repeated three times. Certainly this performance suggests and seems to promote a symbolic unity among those observing and participating in the spectacle. And the National Eisteddfod is commonly viewed as bringing together and somehow succeeding in uniting the Welsh community. On the other hand, I have argued that the Eisteddfod is in fact composed of different and often conflicting performances, and that the activities in the main pavilion are only one aspect of a very heterogeneous festival. Thus it is worth asking whether this spectacle can in any way also be a display of collective meanings and identity, can indeed create 'communitas'.

Turner (1987) has suggested that 'communitas' is only expressed through performance, giving it a dynamic nature that means it is never fully realizable. Thus in the spectacle of Carnaval, he describes 'communitas' as 'shared flow' resulting from 'the holistic sensation when we act with total involvement, when action and awareness are one' (1987: 133). However, to enable these performances which make up the flow of 'communitas', some structure must be available. In a sense the spectacle provides the boundaries within which 'communitas' may be sought and approximated, but never totally created. In a similar analysis of the Palio festival of Siena in central Italy, Handelman (1990) describes such structure as a 'model that transforms the *comune* by taking it apart and putting it back together – thereby yearly regenerating the *comune* as a holistic urban entity' (1990: 116). This view of spectacle, as a structure, a vehicle or model, which provides occasion and symbolism for performances that do not create a single collective identity but instead promote 'communitas' through the act of performing different identities within its context, accords well with the nature of the Welsh National Eisteddfod. As one commentator on youth culture in Wales observed:

> Like a dinosaur in DM's, the festival is as old and as ludicrously traditional as its coloured sheets and slowly fading no-alcohol policy, but there is always much more to it than meets the eye. It's the festival we love to hate, but every year hundreds of young people join the annual pilgrimage to the stone circle, the pavilion and the rock tent. . . . Once a year druids, poets, ravers, Welsh speakers, non-Welsh speakers, academics, pop stars and people in sandals co-exist quite happily, and then go their separate ways.
>
> (Brown 1996: 12)

They go their separate ways having performed their various Welshnesses in a context that both allows difference and still encourages a sense of commonality in creating the spectacle that depends on the variety of their performances to qualify as spectacle; further, it will be re-enacted in another year, the same vessel containing varying performances and dynamic meanings. This combination of continuity in form and fluidity in content provides the basis for the claim of spectacle to express collective identity.

NOTES

1 *Cerdd dant* is a unique Welsh musical form in which voice and harp perform different harmonizing melodies. There is an annual festival devoted entirely to *cerdd dant*.
2 There are two categories of tickets on entry to the Eisteddfod field, one for the field only, the other, more expensive, for the pavilion as well.
3 'Mae jyst pobl ifainc yn jyst yn gallu cael amser brilliant. A dyw pobl hyn ddim yn gallu deall y peth.'
4 'Pan ych chi'n mynd allan i neit clyb, chi'n gweld Saeson, chi'n dod yma, cyfarfod Cymry, cwl!'
5 The Drinkers' Union.
6 The archdruid at that Eisteddfod.

REFERENCES

Baumann, G. (1992) 'Ritual implicates "others": rereading Durkheim in a plural society', in D. de Coppet (ed.) *Understanding Rituals*, London: Routledge.
Beeman, W.O. (1993) 'The anthropology of theater and spectacle', *Annual Review of Anthropology*, 22: 369–93.
Boissevain, J. (1992) 'Introduction', in J. Boissevain (ed.) *Revitalizing European Rituals*, London: Routledge.
Cohen, A. (1993) *Masquerade Politics: Explorations in the Structure of Urban Cultural Movements*, Berkeley CA: University of California Press.
DaMatta, R. (1984) 'On Carnaval, informality and magic: a point of view from Brazil', in E.M. Bruner (ed.) *Text, Play, and Story: The Construction and Reconstruction of Self and Society*, Prospect Heights IL: Waveland Press.

Davies, J. (1994) *Broadcasting and the BBC in Wales*, Cardiff: University of Wales Press.

Edwards, H.T. (1976) *Yr Eisteddfod: cyfrol ddathlu wythganmlwyddiant yr Eisteddfod, 1176–1976*, Llandysul: Gwasg Gomer.

—— (1980) *Gwyl Gwalia: yr Eisteddfod Genedlaethol yn oes aur Victoria 1858–1868*, Llandysul: Gwasg Gomer.

—— (1990) *The Eisteddfod*, Cardiff: University of Wales Press.

Handelman, D. (1990) *Models and Mirrors: Towards an Anthropology of Public Events*, Cambridge: Cambridge University Press.

Iwan, D. (1981) *Dafydd Iwan*, Caernarfon: Gwasg Gwynedd.

Leach, E. (1984) 'Conclusion: further thoughts on the realm of folly', in E.M. Bruner (ed.) *Text, Play, and Story: The Construction and Reconstruction of Self and Society*, Prospect Heights IL: Waveland Press.

Morgan, P. (1983) 'From a death to a view: the hunt for the Welsh past in the romantic period', in E. Hobsbawm and T. Ranger (eds) *The Invention of Tradition*, Cambridge: Cambridge University Press.

Owen, G.Ll. (1972) *Cerddi'r cywilydd*, Caernarfon: Gwasg Gwynedd.

Schechner, R. (1988) *Performance Theory*, London: Routledge.

—— (1993) *The Future of Ritual: Writings on Culture and Performance*, London: Routledge.

Stephens, M. (ed.) (1995) *Harri Webb: Collected Poems*, Llandysul: Gomer.

Trosset, C. (1993) *Welshness Performed: Welsh Concepts of Person and Society*, Tucson AZ: University of Arizona Press.

Turner, V. (1969) *The Ritual Process: Structure and Anti-Structure*, Ithaca NY: Cornell University Press.

—— (1987) *The Anthropology of Performance*, New York: PAJ Publications.

Newspapers and periodicals

Brown, B. (1996) 'A youth culture that's for all of us', *Western Mail*, 6 March: 12.

Dube, S. (1995) 'Yob fury at Eisteddfod', *Western Mail*, 8 August: 1.

Tomos, R. (1996) 'Codi pwnc llosg', *Golwg*, 22 February: 17.

Chapter 8

Macedonian culture and its audiences
An analysis of *Before the Rain*
Keith Brown

This chapter discusses *Before the Rain*, a feature film in which images that were displayed and understood as Macedonian were placed on view before a worldwide audience. It seeks to explore the ways in which studying such a site can contribute to understanding the relationship between representation and realism in the context of national culture. The particular focus of the chapter is to try to theorize the different modes of interaction that were set up between different audiences and the cinematic images, at a time when the republic with which the film was associated had yet to establish itself as a stable political entity.

Anthropology's distinctive methodology and mission are perhaps summed up in the title of a recent introduction to the discipline, *Small Places, Large Issues* (Eriksen 1995). The discipline's claim to a particular authority continues to rest on this combination of an empirical pointillism and theoretical broad sweep, which separates its practitioners from travel writers and local correspondents on the one hand, and armchair pundits of humanity on the other. The salience of the disciplinary self-perception can be glimpsed in the continuing prominence of fieldwork and its paradoxical cornerstone, participant observation.

Yet the curious location of anthropological knowledge, betwixt and between, is precarious in a world where information and images of the faraway seem to circulate far beyond their origins. Indeed, the very use of the notion of origin, where past borrowing and imposition are so thoroughly woven into the perceived present, is tantamount to declaring a commitment to an ever-receding ideal – the anthropologist as Tantalus craning after the fact. In recognition of the global interconnectedness of this modern world, the language of anthropology has stretched to try to do justice to the cultural forms implicated in these realities. From 'culture contact' and 'plural society', through more recent forays into the 'world system' and 'Creolization', the technical language of anthropology now deals in terms that blur the edges of accessibility; 'diaspora' and 'ethnoscape', 'transnation' and 'hybridity'. By such means, the sovereignty of the discipline is preserved, in a closed world of theoretical exchange.

Where anthropologists do still attend to local specificities, and seek to incorporate indigenous understandings of culture and society, they tend to employ terms that are part of ordinary language; 'identity', 'ethnicity', 'nation' and 'home'. In situations where tensions already exist they increasingly find that without the protective shading of language their work, intended to stand outside local disputes, can be recycled selectively as local knowledge. Thus, for example, a scholar's careful account of the processes of nation building in northern Greece, in which existing loyalties are reconfigured as either neatly subordinate or potentially threatening to a state project, can be itself read as an ongoing part of the debate about a state's legitimacy. In the adversarial politics of identity, the ethnographer finds her or his work put to work on one side or the other of questions whose validity she or he may not recognize (Karakasidou 1997).[1]

The division within anthropology between ethnology and ethnography is not, of course, a new one. But the demand now placed upon anthropologists, to write simultaneously for a hitherto unimagined range of audiences, cuts away at the space in which the two could coexist, however uneasily. And for those whose interest lies in the formation and maintenance of collectivities – in whatever form they are willed or imagined by their members – the problem is peculiarly acute.

One innovative response to the challenge is that set out by Arjun Appadurai and other scholars in what could be termed the *public culture* circle. They locate the terrain of anthropological study in what Appadurai terms the 'historical present' and take seriously the notion of '-scapes' as sites of study.[2] This chapter seeks to engage with Appadurai's assertion that what must characterize ethnography in the 1990s and beyond is not a preoccupation with 'thickness' of description, which could be argued to represent little but the reinflection of locally discovered data. Instead, he argues, 'where lives are being imagined partly in and through "realisms" that must be in one way or another official or large scale in their inspiration, then the ethnographer needs to find new ways to represent the links between the imagination and social life' (Appadurai 1991: 199). This chapter examines the connection between a set of 'realisms' and the representations that can be taken simultaneously to constitute them, arise from them and depict them. It seeks in particular to engage with the notion of 'frames of belief' (cf. Wulff, this volume) as a heuristic to explicate different modes of viewing and interpreting cinematic images, and to demonstrate that such modes constitute the stuff of human cultural life.

RITUAL AND AUDIENCE

Milton Singer's (1972) definition of 'cultural performances' as sites of anthropological study remains influential today. Much work on ritual, in particular, retains this focus on the notion that within such discrete units of observation key cultural and social meanings are encoded. The perspective has been applied to ritualized aspects of the domain of national sentiment, notably by Kapferer (1988), Handler (1988) and Herzfeld (1992). In each case, following Durkheim, they are concerned with the presentation to an audience of a set of values with which that audience may identify. Such approaches emphasize what Turner (1986) considered as the reflexive as well as the reflective qualities of ritual performance. The implied focus is on rituals that affirm the existence of a community of which those performing and those watching are all members. Such rituals are in one sense or another held 'at home,' and 'outsiders' are not customarily invited to peer at them.

In a recent overview of ritual theory, Catherine Bell considers the manner in which performance 'distils' culture in a different context. Her example is an audience not of 'natives' but of reflective intellectuals who cast themselves as eavesdroppers on the culture of others:

> If culture is the giving of performances, then culture is that which is given to an 'audience' or the outside theorist who has joined it. Researchers and theorists [are] repositioned in performance theory: no longer peering in through the window, they are now comfortably seated as members of the audience for whom the performance is being presented.
>
> (Bell 1992: 39)

These two contrasting constructions of performance as cultural distillation – from one view reinvigorating its context, from the other serving as digestible synecdoche – point to the key dynamic in performance theory, which is the audience's conceptualization of the relationship between performer, performance and the context of which it is a part. In particular, they raise the question of the status of the audience and the frames of belief that inform their spectatorship.

As scholars in various disciplines have noted, performance is never oblivious to its audience. Meaning is not simply present, and detachable, waiting to be found, but is rather constructed out of the interaction between the viewing subjects and their imagined object. John MacAloon, explicitly acknowledging Turner's work, draws attention to the roles that spectators of the Olympic Games play in establishing the genre of particular performances, whether as spectacle, festival, ritual or game (1984: 258). He focuses in particular on framing and spectator position, as well as the international and political dimensions of the Games. In cinema studies, Rey Chow has sought to theorize a position for the 'ethnic spectator' as active participant in the construction of meaning, when confronted with media representations of himself or herself or of his or her culture (Chow 1991).

These approaches demonstrate the complexity of cultural interaction and belonging in contexts where performances serve as the points at which difference is maximally apparent. At the Olympic Games, host countries in one way or another leave their particular imprint on festivities which bring countries together as competitors; Chow's study of *The Last Emperor* demonstrated a case where an Italian director marshalled a mainly Chinese cast to recount an episode from Chinese history. Such performances have worldwide, international audiences, for whom they may stand as emblematic of that which they depict, or of the creative qualities of their producer. But they also reach audiences who may consider the images presented as representing them, and who may embrace or reject what they see. Audiences may also align themselves with the producer or performer, and thus interact differently again with the mode of the representation.

In each case, it can be argued that the interaction between viewer and image is mediated by what will be called here 'frames of belief'. These frames are conceptualized as constituting the mode in which spectators take an active role, rather than being merely passive receptors. In the realm of cinema, such frames might include listening to a narrative, watching a director's craft, learning information, or indulging in nostalgia. In any and all such inter-actions, the frame can be argued to undergo some sort of re-evaluation by the viewer in light of the image. This evaluation may constitute straightforward reaffirmation of the frame's efficacy, or, under the impact of images, it may lead to some shift in the ongoing nature of that frame.

It might appear that the term 'frame of belief' here represents little more than an attempt to render 'culture' in a scientist vein. It might also appear that the individual viewer is privileged not only as interpreter, but as self-conscious creator or selector of such frames. The point of the formulation is not, though, to relocate the creation of meaning to the moment of its reception. If agency appears to be highlighted, it is because the goal is to illustrate that the impact of media texts cannot be understood without paying attention to the distinctive and persisting differences between modes of imagining that an audience may undertake.

THE EXAMPLE OF *BEFORE THE RAIN*

The script of *Before the Rain* was written by its director, Milcho Manchevski, in 1991, after a visit home to Macedonia from the USA. British Screen picked up the script for development in 1993. The film's production was orchestrated by companies in London and Paris, and it received backing from British, French and Macedonian sources. It was shot with a budget of under US$3 million in Macedonia for seven weeks and London for three. The crew and actors were drawn from more than half-a-dozen countries, including France, Britain, South Africa and Bulgaria (Pall 1995). This multinational ensemble of money and labour created a film which shared the Golden Lion of Venice in 1994, and collected a score or so of other awards from film festivals. Its crowning achievement was a 1995 Oscar nomination for best foreign-language film.[3]

The central story follows a photographer who returns to Macedonia after a successful career in the west, and gets involved in the ongoing conflicts of his homeland. This narrative unfolds in a non-linear fashion, through an episodic structure. The film has three parts, entitled 'Words', 'Faces' and 'Pictures'.

In 'Words', a frightened Albanian girl is hidden by a young Macedonian monk. A group of armed Macedonian villagers interrupt a church service, looking for an Albanian girl who has killed their leader's brother. The monastery is searched, but they do not find the girl; the monastery officials do, and send her away with the young monk. The couple are met by a group of armed Albanians, led by her grandfather. They send the monk away: when she follows him, her brother kills her.

In 'Faces', a Macedonian photo-journalist, tired of covering wars around the world, returns to London from Bosnia. He tells his British lover that he plans to return to the peace of Macedonia. She refuses his invitation to go with him, and instead seeks a reconciliation with her estranged husband. In the restaurant where they meet for dinner a quarrel begins between a waiter and a stranger, conducted in a Balkan language. The quarrel escalates, shooting begins, and the husband is killed by stray shots.

In 'Pictures', the narrative refocuses on the photo-journalist as he returns home to his native village. His visit to a former sweetheart, an Albanian widow, only reveals the hostility between Macedonians and Albanians. His cousin is knifed in unknown circumstances, and a local group of Macedonians capture the young Albanian girl who they believe killed him. She is the daughter of the photographer's sweetheart; he rescues her, is killed by another cousin, and she runs away to the monastery. The film thus, as it were, begins again.

THE VIEW FROM OUTSIDE

The film's three-part structure defies straightforward chronology; a photograph is examined before it could have been taken, and a phone call is received before it could have been made. Two dream sequences foretell events which immediately come to pass. These moments of rupture, and of apparent repetition, occur within a whole that sharply juxtaposes disparate locations and characters and also includes a series of apparently traditional rituals.

At any other time, such stylish aesthetic elements might have occupied the central attention of reviewers. Some did allude to the paradoxes in the time line, and drew comparisons with Quentin Tarantino's *Pulp Fiction*. However, the principal points of interest among the first wave of American reviewers were the visual impact of *Before the Rain* and its main subject matter; Balkan violence. In the *International Herald Tribune*, on 25 January 1995, under a headline which declared 'Macedonia movie confronts Balkan hatreds', the film was summarized as 'a story of ethnic conflict set in London and

Macedonia' (Pall 1995). In the *New York Times* on the same day, it was 'a wrenching tale of ethnic hatreds with a love story that has its own mysterious power' (Maslin 1995). On 21 February 1995, Richard Woodward wrote in the *Village Voice* that 'Its three interrelated stories, built around the tale of a disillusioned war photographer returning to his native village in Macedonia, are concerned with ethnic hatred in the region' (Woodward 1995).

In a longer piece in *Newsday*, on 24 February, Jack Mathews used the phrase 'ethnic hatred' three times, while calling the film a 'parable' (Mathews 1995). On the same day, the *Los Angeles Times*, ringing the changes on the theme of ethnic hatred, called it a tale of 'fratricidal horror' (Rainer 1995). The *Christian Science Monitor* on 1 March told the reader that in the film's third part, in Macedonia 'ethnic strife leads to a tragic climax' (Sterritt 1995).

The *San Diego Union–Tribune* of 9 March reintroduced the romantic element, reporting that 'in the film love keeps being routed by political, ethnic and religious tensions' (Elliott 1995), while the *BPI Entertainment Newswire* called *Before the Rain* 'a three-part story of ethnic conflict and romance set in Macedonia and London' (Ryan 1995). By the time the film reached Ohio in June love had disappeared again, and the film critic of the *Columbus Dispatch* wrote '*Before the Rain* is most effective in conveying the extreme hatred between ethnic factions' (Gabrenya 1995).

The dominating impression here is of ethnic hatred, violence and strife as the principal impact of the film. That impact, clearly, fits into certain ideas that people in the USA had of Yugoslavia. Reporting on the Yugoslav War in the period of 1991–3 followed a similar pattern – irrational as it seemed, said a majority of reporters, Serbs, Croats and Muslims had returned to fighting, after the 'unnatural' peaceful interlude of Yugoslavia. A further dimension to the reporting was an emphasis on the messiness of the fighting that resulted, as populations were so integrated. Indeed, in the coverage of the break-up of Yugoslavia it could be said that chaos and disorder were organizing tropes. This is perhaps true of war in general: the coverage of the Yugoslav War was striking in that chaos and disorder were presented at every level. Cease fires, front lines, refugee routes; all were disputed. Disorderliness extended to the men depicted as doing the fighting; paramilitaries, volunteers, irregulars, militias, all were in action. More often than not the images presented in the west were of scruffiness and improvisation.

The authenticity of the movie as Macedonian for a non-Macedonian audience appears to be lodged primarily in the correspondence between the images depicted and other more familiar impressions. Manchevski's Macedonian villagers, seen in both the first and third sections, are an odd group, heavily armed with automatic weapons, yet dressed in a motley collection of clothes. Where the leader appeals to sartorial conventions of the past, others in his entourage pay homage to global fashion, whether with baseball caps or sneakers, or with the Beastie Boys on a Walkman. Their appearance and demeanour correspond with pictures from the Yugoslav War that appeared either on television or in the printed media in the early 1990s. The sentiments that these characters expressed also resonated with a prevalent idea that Yugoslavia was riddled with age-old hatreds, influentially promulgated in Robert Kaplan's best-selling *Balkan Ghosts* (1993).[4]

The authenticity of these characters appears to be reinforced by the other single quality of the film on which most foreign reviewers agreed: the visual impact of the landscape in which the action is set. Indeed, the scenery is for some western reviewers the main attraction of the film. Whether they focus on 'spectacular Macedonian hillsides' (Woodward 1995, in the *Village Voice*) or the 'glowing Balkan countryside' (Billson 1995, in the *Daily Telegraph*), the 'hard tan hills of Macedonia, the cobbled stone houses of the village' (Johnson 1995, in *Maclean's Magazine*) or 'the limitless vistas and star-clustered night skies' (McKenna 1995, in the *Los Angeles Times*), reviewers were drawn to compete in their descriptions of Manchevski's images. Some made more explicit their recognition that the aesthetic element lay not in the landscape, but in the film's cinematography, and transferred their adjectives of approbation to the apparatus. The *Village Voice* also applauded the 'wondrous shots of the forbidding landscape' (Woodward 1995) and *The Times* in England commented that 'the camera feasts on the rolling Macedonian hills' (Brown 1995).

Despite this recognition of Manchevski's creative input, the various reviewers nevertheless all appear to have fallen under the spell of the landscape as a site of authenticity, which further contributed to the realism of the events that unfold within it. In this respect, viewers harnessed that landscape to their interpretation and stance. Where *Maclean's Magazine*, for example, described the 'fierce poetry to his images, but also a strong sense of authenticity' (Johnson 1995), the reviewer's phrasing echoed theoretical writing on cinematography. In 1960, Maya Deren described the manner in which 'an artifice borrows reality from the reality of the scene' and 'natural phenomena [can] be incorporated into our own creativity, to yield an image where the reality of a tree confers its truth upon the events we cause to transpire beneath it' (1992 [1960]: 64). The actuality of the landscape thus confers *actualité* on events.

THE FRAMING OF MACEDONIA

Reviewers, then, did not doubt the beauty or authenticity of the images. Indeed, at times they appear to wallow in the tragic paradox that was created; that such violence could exist in a landscape so beautiful. In *Maclean's Magazine*, again, the film was seen as an unveiling of some essential truth, 'as if the director is revealing his homeland to the world for the first time in all its beauty and pain' (Johnson 1995). In the words of another critic who was particularly transported, 'the scenes near an Orthodox monastery could have been painted by Mantegna or Bellini, with stacked puddles of limestone and stubborn ascetics doing penance under a moth moon' (Woodward 1995, in the *Village Voice*).

In such reviews, nature's beauty, comprising the primitive and unspoiled, stands against the neo-primitivism of the people of the landscape. The contrast with and distance from the non-Balkan reviewer's home is absolute. For this audience, Manchevski's representation of Macedonia thus combines elements of otherness and distance: it is magnificent and unmodernized, and yet threatened by the forces of barbarism and backwardness. Running through the assemblage of North American and British reviews of the film are these two dimensions of the film as a whole, which are seen to encapsulate its message. Macedonia is a beautiful country, spoiled by those that inhabit it.

This impression, derived here from reviews, is confirmed by the immediate reaction that various amateur audiences in Europe and the USA had. Audiences there appeared to consider they were seeing the landscape of Macedonia, and the people of Macedonia. Jonathan Schwartz recalls that in discussion with Dutch university students, he had to convince them that the film was 'not an actual documentary but a dystopian nightmare' (Schwartz n.d.). For a range of audiences outside Macedonia, then, the film documented recent Yugoslav history, and made contemporary Macedonia a part of that history. The Republic is thus implicitly put into a celluloid realm – the same one inhabited, to all intents and purposes, by the rest of Yugoslavia. And the events of Yugoslavia hover in the background to such viewing as a road of destiny for the Republic. The effect is to suggest that violence must and will spiral out of control in reality, as it appears bound to in the film. In subscribing to such impressions, reviewers cast themselves as documentary watchers, privy to an insider's snapshot, of Balkan brigands in a Balkan landscape.

In terms of work on cinema spectatorship, which resonates with that of Bell with regard to theorists, the audience, in this mode, interacts as controlling spectators of a distant object.[5] From such a viewpoint, *Before the Rain* is framed as a spectacle: the events depicted are thus cast as maximally distant and irrelevant to that viewer, an object of study or curiosity rather than engagement. Yet the mode is simultaneously that of documentary realism, whereby the screen images are taken to correspond to actual events in the Balkans. Here it could be said that a second dimension of a previously constructed frame intervenes, to equate a set of cinematic images with those seen elsewhere as documentary reportage.

The potential slippage between these frames could be argued to find its mediation in the central place of a western-trained photo-journalist in the film. The character offers non-Macedonian reviewers and audiences a point of reference within the film to cast Macedonia as passive object of observation, in front of the lens. They concentrate attention on the locations and characters that the photo-journalist encountered on his return. The country is thus simultaneously conceptualized as a place to which a spectator – in this case, the character of the photo-journalist – travels from afar. Non-Macedonian viewers thus 'gaze' at a distant object along with the camera and director, and label that object as 'Macedonia'.

BEYOND THE FRAME

Two ironies underpin this particular mode of imagining, in which realist qualities are ascribed to the film. In the first place, as Manchevski pointed out to some interviewers, Macedonia is the one Republic that has *not* yet seen ethnic conflict of the order of the other constituent parts of the former Yugoslavia. The Yugoslav Army withdrew peacefully from their Skopje barracks in early 1992, and a coalition government managed to restrain the extremists on both sides of the principal ethnic divide, between Macedonians and Albanians. The government has also welcomed the presence both of UNPROFOR, the United Nations Protection Force, and, after 1993, of US ground troops in the Republic.

The second irony is that the landscape that Manchevski depicts does not exist on the ground, but was produced in the making of the film. This was noted by some reviews; stressing the arduousness of the shoot, the *International Herald Tribune* reported: 'Occasionally, the crew had to build its own roads. Manchevski would sometimes shoot a single scene in places miles apart, then splice the footage together. Kiril's mountaintop monastery, for example, is a composite of four different monasteries' (Pall 1995). The creation of a single monastery, seen on film as comprising church, sleeping quarters, walled compound and vegetable garden, brings together a set of different places that are cherished as treasures of Macedonian culture. The exterior of the church is Sveti Jovan Kaneo, on the shores of Lake Ohrid in the Republic: the interior, however, is either a church in Skopje, the capital, or at the monastery of Sveti Jovan Bigorski, in the hills of north-western Macedonia.[6]

More reviewers latched onto the road building of the crew, in part because Manchevski drew attention to it. In an interview reported by the *Seattle Times*, he said 'In general, the less accessible, the better the locations look' (Hartl 1995). Taken with the revelation about the roads being built, we discover then that the landscape we see on screen is not just a product of putting together images of different locations: to create the sweeping landscapes we see, the real landscape has been literally scarred.

MACEDONIAN VISIONS

Manchevski creates an image of Macedonia: he does not recreate Macedonia. Much of the film is shot in sites that are spread across the Republic and constitute the historical legacy of Macedonia – a legacy that most of its inhabitants recognize. But although there can be no forgetting that those sites exist, a Macedonian audience is also aware that they are taken out of their context and relocated in close proximity to one another. This is not to suggest that people continuously monitor what they are watching and compare it with some pristine 'reality'. But only an audience without experience or knowledge of the Macedonian landscape could read the film as documentation of an existing locality.

Similarly, Macedonian audiences in 1994, at least, when the film opened, knew that armed bands of this kind were not operating in their own country. They knew, as did the western viewers, that violence had occurred in Bosnia – but they were also aware that by that time, Bosnia and Macedonia were no longer part of the same country, and that internal conditions in the two were very different. They were aware that they were watching a potential future, rather than an account of what was happening. Thus, when asked about Macedonian reactions in an interview in February 1995, Manchevski was able to give the following answer: 'I was concerned that people would be upset with me . . . Some people said, "We don't all live in run-down villages, we also drive Mercedes cars. Why didn't you show that?" But most of them read the film just as I wanted them to, which is as a warning' (Woodward 1995, in the *Village Voice*).

Macedonian reviewers and audiences could not straightforwardly connect Manchevski's images to their own experiences. For the place depicted, although comprised of locations that were recognizable, was not as a whole familiar to them. As a consequence of this, the frames within which they read the film as Macedonian were thus strikingly different from those of their counterparts outside the Republic. Instead of viewing as Macedonian the object of the camera's gaze and the photo-journalist's encounter, they focus instead on the character who undertakes a journey to a war, and becomes enmeshed in the quarrels of those he once lived among.

Aleks, the photo-journalist, is a cipher for the director and author himself – in some sense Manchevski is documenting his own return to Macedonia from New York in 1991. The character is played by a famous actor from the Yugoslav period, Rade Sherbedzija. According to a variety of sources, his was one of the best-known faces in Yugoslavia, from stage and screen. The double impact of seeing such an actor lends additional textures to a Macedonian audience's reception, which are unnoted by foreign reviewers. In the final part of the film there is a short scene in which Aleks wakes up from a bad dream in the house he has inherited from his parents, and looks for a cigarette. The *Los Angeles Times* reviewer reduced the scene to a heavy-handed director's point, that by smoking, Aleks is returning to his 'Balkan' roots. In so doing, she takes smoking to be a sign of Balkan identity. A few months earlier, though, an essayist in a Skopje weekly, Mirko Kostovik, reacted differently to this same scene:

Sherbedzija opens a suitcase. In it is an issue of 'Nova Makedonija' [the daily Macedonian newspaper] from the past, and one unsmoked cigarette. On the cover page Josip Broz Tito, and in the cigarette opium of past happy days. Rade smokes the cigarette in the role of Aleksander, Tito is still proud and happy in that picture, and in the darkness of the night the music of the Sarajevo band 'Indexi' and Pimperkov's voice with the song 'Sonuvam' [I'm dreaming].

(Kostovik 1994: 56–7)

Kostovik here indicates how much is going on in this depiction of one of the most personal rituals of all. For what Manchevski presents here is a multilayered evocation of the past, and simultaneously an image of what has come to be an increasingly familiar refrain from artists from the former Yugoslavia – a kind of 'Yugo-nostalgia'. The scene with the opened suitcase is a return not to Balkan roots, but to a very different mode of life, in which Sarajevo stood as a symbol of co-operation between today's divided ethnic groups; and the soft music from the Yugoslav period tells the story of the actor as well as the character. Sherbedzija still considers himself 'Serbo-Croatian'; he, as well as Aleksander within the film, has found himself without a place he can call home.

The grounds for such an interpretation are further strengthened by the nature of the music in this scene. Although it is extra-diegetic, the beginning of the song is preceded and accompanied by the rhythmic scratching that would be heard on an old gramophone recording. The foregrounding of the obsolescence of the reproductive medium complements the nostalgia encoded in the music itself – by a band from a country and a city whose meanings have radically changed.[7]

This emphasis by a 'native' interpreter, on the complex relationship between Macedonia and the federal country of which it was once a part, is one that one would not expect from a western audience for whom Yugoslavia, Tito, Sarajevo, Macedonia and the actor Rade Sherbedzija are not related in the way that they are for any Macedonian in their late twenties or older.[8] In this vision, Macedonia is not straightforwardly categorized as a site of the same violence that has overtaken the country of which it was once a part. Instead, it could be argued that Macedonia is located in the person of Rade the actor, Aleks the character, and the engaged audience, confronting a scenario where bitter confrontation has replaced former coexistence.

FILM AND POLITICAL CONTEXT

Manchevski's vision puts on offer a set of objects to the Yugoslav Macedonian viewer that compel a far more complex and interactive mode of imagining the connections between image and reality than that of non-Macedonian reviewers. The film does not simply reflect realism, nor is it some buttress to national ideas of authenticity. In evoking Yugoslavia and Macedonia alongside the forces that continue to play a part in their futures – local activism and global voyeurism – he reminds us that there are other ways to organize life, outside the contemporary idiom of nationalism that has forced people to locate themselves in ways that they have not chosen. This the film accomplished not just in the dynamics of internal interaction but in its life as an artefact of culture.

When the film opened in Skopje in 1994, after its triumph in Venice, it reportedly outgrossed the Hollywood blockbuster *The Fugitive*, released at the same time (Woodward 1995). After the première at the beginning of October 1994, the Macedonian press described *Before the Rain* as the most distinguished Macedonian film ever. The film's director was purportedly the second most popular public figure in the Republic – after the president, Kire Gligorov (ibid.).

The film thus came to be identified, both from within and without, as Macedonian, in the same time frame in which a state of that name sought international recognition. Indeed, the film brought the Republic publicity – according to some interviews, a reason for its popularity within the Republic. In a conversation with Roger Ebert, Manchevski stated of Macedonia, 'It's a country where, even in volleyball, the national team cannot be called the Macedonian National Team. Suddenly a Macedonian film does well. People respond to that' (Ebert 1995, in the *Chicago Sun–Times*). The identification of the film as Macedonian, in this vision, was connected to the legitimacy of the country of the same name. What is striking in this formulation is that the film's identification as Macedonian, in the international sphere, preceded or anticipated that of the country. In some sense it could be argued to occupy an active role in the transition of the Republic, from part of Yugoslavia to a sovereign state.

DIRECTOR AND NATIONAL IDENTITY

In a parallel mode, the identification of the director himself followed a similar path, in the course of which the ontological status of Macedonian national identity was highlighted. Manchevski's identity as 'hybrid' was the subject of several of the reviews in the USA in late 1994 and early 1995. Writers picked on the juxtapositions in his own life and work – from Skopje to Carbondale, and art film to music video – to identify him and his work as bicultural (Mathews 1995, Pall 1995, Woodward 1995).[9] In this mode, his own location was separated from that of the filmic images taken to embody Macedonian identity. Manchevski was cast as some kind of intermediary – giving outsiders a glimpse of Balkan life. By this mode of presentation, Manchevski's own connection with Macedonia is diluted. Indeed, it is only by dissociating Manchevski as creative artist from Macedonia that the latter can be imagined as object of the gaze of others. Manchevski's own relocation to a position behind the camera is implicitly considered as equivalent to losing his connection with Macedonia. It is also assumed that his critical perspective is a product of that very distance.

Macedonian visions of the director are very different. As stated above, he was considered the second most popular figure in Macedonia, and his featuring in such a poll demonstrates the extent to which he was regarded as an insider. As one Macedonian reviewer picked out as significant not the images of violence, but a quiet moment which indexed a complex web of temporal and geographical connections, so in a similar vein Macedonian audiences embraced the film not as a depiction of Macedonian life, but as an expression of Macedonian artistry. Where foreign reviewers saw the film as capturing Macedonian authenticity from the outside, and thereby cast the director as an outsider, Macedonian audiences were more likely to include the director and his image in a single sphere, the whole of which – both creative and created – was Macedonian.

MACEDONIA AND THE WORLD STAGE

This was, however, not the limit of what the *Before the Rain* offered to the Macedonian imagination of cultural identity. The film was screened in Skopje only after sharing the Golden Lion in Venice. It acquired status, then, in the sense that it had already occupied a stage of international attention. Macedonian audiences in 1994–5 were thus watching something that had been watched (and deemed worth watching) in the wider world. They were enjoying not simply a film, but also the fact that the film had been watched, or would be watched, by many others, elsewhere. Even those Macedonians who criticized the film did so with this international audience in mind. The limits of the 'imagined community' (Anderson 1983) of any particular film audience, then, do not lie at the edges of any nation state. To watch any film on general release is to partake of 'world culture'; when the film watched is connected to a small country, viewers in that country can imagine themselves as equal citizens in the film world.

The award of the Golden Lion was the beginning of the film's public life as Macedonian. Its final flourish came on the eve of the Academy Awards ceremony in March 1995, when *Before the Rain* was one of five films nominated for the award of best foreign-language picture. Along with others involved with the production of the film, Manchevski threatened to boycott the ceremony because the Academy were planning to refer to its country of origin not as Macedonia, but as the Former Yugoslav Republic of Macedonia (O'Steen 1995). Manchevski rejected the emendation and thereby signalled a call for a decisive separation, in the world imagination, of Macedonia from Yugoslavia. The terms in which he did so, as reported by the journalist, put the relationship of Macedonia with Yugoslavia as rhetorically equivalent to that between the USA and Britain: '"In the larger picture, the name is a small thing" said Director Manchevski, "But it would be like calling the U.S. 'the former British colony of America.' It's an insult to the people back there in Macedonia."' (O'Steen 1995). In this moment, it could be argued, on the eve of its final international recognition as national, the transition of the film itself, and of its director, was complete. From being a process of co-operation in production, overseen by a bicultural hybrid, it became a product of a single nation and a director from that nation. It did so in the forum of the Oscars, in which a country's entry confers status on the nation as a cultural producer, equal in ontological status to all others.

CONCLUSION

This chapter has sought to trace the parallel biographies of a film, its director, and the country which both came to represent in the course of 1995, when the images of *Before the Rain* travelled an international circuit. I have tried to demonstrate the utility of a notion of 'frames of belief' in the analysis of the different interpretations of the film and its relationship to the recent realities of Yugoslav history. Simply put, the central goal is to show *how* different understandings of that history impact upon practices as seemingly apolitical as watching a feature film, or describing a director's background.

At times it may appear that the result of the analysis is to put in place a binary distinction between 'non-Macedonian' and 'Macedonian' readings of the film, and to suggest that the former are untrue while the latter are true. The principal point of comparison, though, is not in terms of any correspondence with any single 'reality'. Rather, the aim is to illuminate the existence of different modes of imagining by which realisms are constituted.

Arjun Appadurai notes that in comparison to commercial cinema, 'Art cinema . . . is spread both more broadly and more thinly across the world' and constitutes a realm of its own (1995: 218). At the same time, the artefacts of this realm may, as in the case of *Before the Rain*, retain or acquire particular significance for specific agents or groups. So too their creators may lead double lives, like Milcho Manchevski, and be characterized as being at home in different localities. To consider the global interconnections and implications of local cultural phenomena, and vice versa, it appears that some notion of 'framing' may be useful. The appeal of such an approach is precisely that it allows an analytical demarcation between interpretive realms, while acknowledging that frames may coexist and blur into one another.

The recognition of the expressive and artistic complexity of *Before the Rain* yields one further result. Anthropologists and others who are engaged in the debates over the legitimacy of the new Macedonian nation state are frequently asked to classify and identify practices, customs, beliefs or norms that are characteristic of and unique to Macedonian culture. If they claim to do so, they find themselves cast as overengaged Macedonian nationalists: if they challenge the validity of the classification project, in the language of cultural flows or globalization, they are likely to be dismissed as irrelevant obscurantists. It is perhaps too glib a response for an anthropologist to respond to the challenge simply by pointing to *Before the Rain*. None the less, to encourage focus on a site which demonstrates the different modes in which imagining, viewing and reviewing constitute a range of realisms could be a further step towards understanding the interconnections of cultural practice and political consequence.

NOTES

1 The focus of Anastasia Karakasidou's work has been the Hellenization of the northern region of what became part of the Greek state in 1912. In the course of her research she has found herself caught up in rhetorics of continuity, ethnic identity and loyalty, as well as debates over academic freedom and publishing policies (Doyle 1996).

2 *Public Culture's* contributors include prominent members of the school of subaltern history, such as Partha Chatterjee and Ranajit Guha, and other scholars of the post-colonial moment, including Pierre Balibar and Nicholas Dirks.

3 Of the film's funding, 65 per cent came from British Screen (including 20 per cent originally provided by Channel 4, which was then withdrawn); 25 per cent from Noe Prods, a unit of PolyGram France; and the balance of around 10 per cent from the Macedonian Ministry of Culture (West 1995).

4 The prevalent ideas here described briefly are analysed in greater detail by Todorova (1994), who claims that they constitute a discourse of 'Balkanism'.

5 This section draws on Laura Mulvey's pioneering work (1992 [1975]), which argues that the effect of this alignment of the 'gaze' of audience and apparatus is masculinizing, and serves simultaneously to feminize the object displayed for the audience's pleasure. Her argument stands at the beginning of an extended debate over relations of gender and power implicit in the gaze, and established the importance of making analytical distinctions between the multiple modes in which audiences can engage with images on screen.

6 Non-Macedonian reviewers frequently misidentified specific locations, and drew false inferences from the term 'Macedonia'. Among the misrepresentations were that the action took place in a Russian monastery, or in northern Greece. One reviewer presented a bizarre vision by placing the church scenes in the landlocked Former Yugoslav Republic of Macedonia at the seaside.

7 This foregrounding of the reproductive medium, in music which is on the sound track rather than occurring in the scene, serves to blur the line between extra-diegetic and diegetic. By creating the impression that what we are hearing as audience is what the character is hearing inside his head, the director can be seen again playing with the boundary between the world and the world of the film.

8 See further Thiessen (n.d.). Sherbedzija became famous for playing Hamlet in Dubrovnik in 1974. Tito died in 1981, and his death is as mythological within Yugoslavia and Macedonia as that of John F. Kennedy in North America: most people claim to remember where they were when they heard the news. Sarajevo was the spiritual home of much of the best Yugoslav rock music of the 1970s and 1980s, including the most famous of the bands, Belo Dugme. It was also host to the Winter Olympics in 1984. A significant dimension of the shock felt in Macedonia when fighting began in Bosnia was the inability to locate ethnic hatreds in a city that had become synonymous with an easy urban cosmopolitanism.

9 Manchevski himself referred to feeling 'culturally schizophrenic – and glad about it' (Woodward 1995).

REFERENCES

Anderson, B. (1983) *Imagined Communities: Reflections on the Origin and Spread of Nationalism*, London and New York: Verso.

Appadurai, Arjun (1991) 'Global ethnoscapes: notes and queries for a transnational anthropology', in Richard Fox (ed.) *Recapturing Anthropology: Working in the Present*, Santa Fe NM: School for American Research Advanced Seminar Series.

—— (1995) 'The production of locality', in Richard Fardon (ed.) *Counterworks: Managing the Diversity of Knowledge*, London: Routledge.

Bell, Catherine (1992) *Ritual Theory, Ritual Practice*, Oxford: Oxford University Press.

Chow, Rey (1991) *Woman and Chinese Modernity: The Politics of Reading Between East and West*, Minnesota and Oxford: University of Minnesota Press.

Deren, Maya (1992 [1960]) 'Cinematography: the creative use of reality', in Gerald Mast, Marshall Cohen and Leo Braudy (eds) *Film Theory and Criticism*, Oxford: Oxford University Press.

Eriksen, Thomas Hylland (1995) *Small Places, Large Issues: An Introduction to Social and Cultural Anthropology*, London and East Haven CT: Pluto Press.

Handler, Richard (1988) *Nationalism and the Politics of Culture in Quebec*, Madison WI: University of Wisconsin.

Herzfeld, Michael (1992) *The Social Production of Indifference: Exploring the Symbolic Roots of Western Bureaucracy*, Chicago: University of Chicago Press.

Kapferer, Bruce (1988) *Legends of People, Myths of State*, Washington DC: Smithsonian Institute Press.

Kaplan, Robert (1993) *Balkan Ghosts: A Journey Through History*, New York: St Martin's Press.

Karakasidou, Anastasia (1997) *Fields of Wheat, Hills of Blood: Passages to Nationhood in Greek Macedonia 1870–1990*, Chicago: University of Chicago Press.

MacAloon, J.J. (ed.) (1984) *Rite, Drama, Festival, Spectacle: Rehearsals Towards a Theory of Cultural Performance*, Philadelphia: ISHI.

Mulvey, Laura (1992 [1975]) 'Narrative cinema and visual pleasure', in Gerald Mast, Marshall Cohen and Leo Braudy (eds) *Film Theory and Criticism*, Oxford: Oxford University Press.

Schwartz, Jonathan Matthew (n.d.) 'Civil society and ethnic conflict in the Republic of Macedonia', unpublished paper.

Singer, Milton (1972) *When a Great Tradition Modernizes*, New York: Praeger.

Thiessen, Ilka (n.d.) 'Mapping of urban identity', unpublished paper.

Todorova, Maria (1994) 'The Balkans: from discovery to invention', *Slavic Review*, 53 (2): 453–82.

Turner, Victor (1986) *The Anthropology of Performance*, New York: PAJ Publishing.

Newspapers and periodicals

Billson, Anne (1995) 'Very watery, but by no means a wash-out', *Daily Telegraph*, 14 August: 7.

Brown, Geoff (1995) 'Waterbaby's damp squib', *The Times*, 10 August.

Doyle, Leonard (1996) 'Academic uproar at banned book', *Guardian*, 2 February.

Ebert, Roger (1995) 'The "Rain" maker: from Macedonia to Carbondale to Hollywood', *Chicago Sun–Times*, 5 March: 7.

Elliott, David (1995) '"Rain" drenched in agony, ecstasy', *San Diego Union–Tribune*, Night and Day, 9 March: 21.

Gabrenya, Frank (1995) '"Rain" evokes despair as ominous clouds gather over Macedonia', *Columbus Dispatch*, 9 June: 12E.

Hartl, John (1995) 'Award-winning film comes from Macedonia, with love', *Seattle Times*, 5 March: M8.

Johnson, Brian D. (1995) 'Forbidden affection', *Maclean's Magazine*, 27 February: 69.

Kostovik, Mirko (1994) 'Dushata, nashata bleskava kometa', *Puls*, 7 October: 56–7.

Maslin, Janet (1995) 'Innocence departs as show biz finds its way to Sundance', *New York Times*, 25 January: C13.

Mathews, Jack (1995) 'Within the circle of Balkan grief', *Newsday*, 24 February: B2.

McKenna, Kristine (1995) 'From the ashes of a ravaged land', *Los Angeles Times*, Calender Section, 26 February: 26.

O'Steen, Kathleen (1995) 'Macedonia flap hits Academy', *Daily Variety*, 27 March: 1

Pall, Ellen (1995) 'Macedonia movie confronts Balkan hatreds', *International Herald Tribune*, 25 January.

Rainer, Peter (1995) 'Shining a harsh light on Balkans war', *Los Angeles Times*, 24 February (Calender Section): F1.

Ryan, James (1995) '"Before the Rain" director takes a new look at his homeland', *BPI Entertainment Newswire*, 3 March.

Sterritt, David (1995) 'Powerful portrayals of human struggle', *Christian Science Monitor*, 1 March: 12.

West, Stephen (1995) 'Panel probes Byzantine art of Euro financing', *Variety*, 20–6 February: 11.

Woodward, Richard B. (1995) 'Slav of New York', *Village Voice*, 21 February: 50.

Chapter 9

Hard sell

Commercial performance and the narration of the self

Nigel Rapport

ACT ONE

The postcard came in the morning mail, personally addressed: "N Rapport, 5 Stratford Av, Manchester, M20 8LZ". "SCRATCH AND WIN", it suggested. "Simply scratch off the coating from the box overleaf. Three crosses in a row and you have won: **either** a new Austin Metro, **or** a wide-screen colour television set, **or** a karaoke set. Three noughts in a row and you have won: **either** a VW Dormobile, **or** a personal computer, **or** £500 in cash."

I scratched off the plastic while I was making my breakfast: I had a row of three crosses . . . I read the rules again to make sure, but it seemed certain: I had won something!

I wasn't too excited by the idea of a karaoke set, but a new car or TV sounded great. There must be strings attached but, reading the Conditions of Eligibility for Receiving Prizes on the back of the postcard, they did not seem too onerous. And the fact that there were conditions cited, and that I seemed to pass them, convinced me further that I might have won something. The Conditions read that I had to be over 25 years of age, earning more than £12,000 a year, not connected personally or through my family with the "giveaway program", and if I was married or part of a couple, then my partner should accompany me to the prize-giving ceremony because I had to be able to make a financial decision there and then.

The prize-giving ceremony would take place, I read next, at the (plush-sounding) offices of Infostar, on Oxford Street, in the centre of Manchester. In order to receive my prize, I had to telephone the offices and book an appointment one afternoon that week; before the presentation, Infostar kindly requested two hours of my time to show me some products of theirs in which they were sure I would be interested. However, there would be no obligation to buy, rent or join anything, and I should merely bring along my postcard with its computerized number-identification as proof of my identity and the key to which prize I had won. I read the card over a few times as I ate breakfast. And I couldn't see the catch. I had a row of three crosses on my postcard which translated (without any subjunctive clauses) into a car, a TV or a karaoke set. And there was mention of a prize-giving presentation too; I foresaw handshakes, photographs and flashcubes. All I seemed to need to do was give up a couple of hours of my time.

I noted that the postcard had been mailed in Malaysia; no stamp, just a "Postage Paid" sticker. How did anyone in Kuala Lumpur know my name and address? Why choose me as a possible winner? I knew that banks checked potential customers' credit ratings through some computerized database of names, so maybe I was on one of those? A list of reasonably well-off, upwardly mobile professionals who, it was felt, might have some money to put down on the table or invest in some new product or venture? I realized I would feel quite chuffed to be regarded as such; it had been leaked to a company of foreign investors trying to win friends or secure a toe-hold for their product or name in Britain that Nigel Rapport might be amongst those they could influence and would be well worth influencing – even at the cost of a new Austin Metro.

"Call Now To Confirm A Win: 061–8397000", the postcard said, and when I had finished my breakfast, I did. "I think I have won something", I excitedly told the woman who answered the phone, "I have a row of crosses." But she didn't sound surprised; more perfunctory. 'When could I come down to the offices to collect the prize? Thursday afternoon? Fine.'

INTERLUDE: AGREEING TERMS

In Bauman's concise formulation (1978: 48), 'performance' is a nexus of tradition, practice and emergence; performative practice mediates between the traditions of performance and what emerges from particular ones. But what emerges? For Giddens and neo-Durkheimian action-theorists (Giddens 1976, Garfinkel 1967, Bourdieu 1977, et al.), performative practice produces action. This is a socio-cultural force distinct from the meanings and intentions of participating individual actors – since their awareness of the consequences of their performances and the skills which they involve may be minimal – a force which effects, instead, a continuing structuration of society. As recently formulated for anthropology by Hastrup (1995; cf. her chapter, this volume), the acting body of the individual is the locus of cultural agency; what is stored in individual bodies, made manifest and transferred in individual performances, is social practices. Indeed, agency is inconceivable outside the continuing conversation of a socio-cultural community: "[t]o be a competent human agent is to exist in a space defined by [a community's] distinctions of worth" (Hastrup 1995: 106). So that a collective habitus serves as "the basis for [an] intentionless convention of regulated improvisation" which gives onto the social-structural coherence of the world (1995: 42). In short, what emerges from performance for the above commentators is social structure. Social structure is both a condition and a con-

sequence of performance. Hence, performance is ripe for 'institutional analysis' (Giddens 1976: 156–60).

Alternatively, however, what emerges from performance is the self; what action produces is selves. That is, in more existential vein (Cohen 1975, Kleinman 1988, Jackson 1989, et al.), performative practice translates as performances of individual selves in variable alignment one with another: as the self is embodied in performance so any performance is an embodiment of selves. The observable and concrete event thus becomes what Fernandez terms a metaphor for the expression and conveyance of what is unobservable and inchoate: psychological experiences (1971: 58). Put more starkly still, if there is a duality inherent in performance, then it pertains not, à la Giddens et al., to its overdetermination by social structure – its being simultaneously structured and structurating – but to a (Simmelian) distinction between form and meaning (cf. Rapport 1990). In the form of traditional public perform-ance, in the guise of social performance, takes place the meaningful emergence, the emergence to meaning, of the individual self. The public and observable is an occasion whose purpose and meaning are rather located in the expression of what is otherwise individual and hidden.

Of such performative duality, Steiner has written long and convincingly. Every language-act, he explains, has a dual phenomenology: a "common surface and a private base" (1975: 173). The base is the element of individual specificity – the irreducible singularity of personal remembrance, the unique-ness of the "association-net" of personal consciousness, the personal lexicon – in which public language is rooted. It is this too which gives linguistic performance its "duplicity": outward speech as against a concur-rent flow of articulate consciousness within it (1975: 46). And Steiner concludes, provocatively, that internal linguistic performance, speaking to oneself (with variable coherency) before, during or after a voiced, social encounter with another, may represent "the major portion of all 'locutionary motions'" and take primacy (1978: 62ff).

Certainly, I have wished to allude to this existentialist duality, if not demonstrate it, in my own work (e.g. Rapport 1986); also to explore the variety of personal fulfilments that might accrue to the individual speaker in his or her 'external' performance of (voiced animation of) the linguistic forms of a speech-community (Rapport 1993: 173–92). What I would emphasize here is the importance for the maintenance of this duality of performance per se. *Not only does the individual performance of conventional (linguistic) forms keep them 'alive', current and contemporary, but their performance (voiced and unvoiced) is the currency of ongoing individual consciousness. In brief, performance is the activity of individual consciousness, the means and the medium of consciousness: individuals come to consciousness (of themselves, of others) through voiced and unvoiced performance.*

And what they come to perform is personal narratives. 'Narrative' may be defined as: "the telling (in whatever medium, though especially language)

*of a series of temporal events so that a meaningful sequence is portrayed –
the story or plot of the narrative" (Kerby 1991: 39). Narrative is also the
"form" of consciousness, the form of our experience through time (Crites
1971: 291–7); there is a human "predisposition to organize experience into
a narrative form" in the process of constructing orderly and coherent worlds
(Bruner 1990: 45). We are, Barthes concludes, "narrating animals" (1982:
251). We are also, I would stress here, performers of narratives. What is basic
to the 'humanity' of our narratives is our performing of them. It is through
narrational performance that we maintain conscious selves; through the
performance of narratives, we continue to write and rewrite the story of our
selves.*

*The story of this chapter intends to be one such performance. Recounting
personal experiences of an aggressive hard-sell campaign, and taking the
form of an extended autobiographical narrative of self-conscious interiority,
the chapter explores the ritual practices and power of current commercial
exchange amid the performative practices of the self-conscious self.*

*If power, après Foucault (après Nietzsche), is properly devolved to
the micro-socialities of every exchange in every relationship, then contra
Foucault, I argue that such power cannot be understood without the
interpreting person: without those individuals who partake of the relationship and perform the exchange. I contend that it is a personal exchange
into which the ritualized performance is ever translated so as to have an
effect. Furthermore, the experiencing of the exchange as a personal affront
elucidates the process by which its institutional implications can come to be
rejected. However seemingly totalizing and totalitarian, commercial performance is found to be a surface beneath which are persons able, through
narrative, to maintain and control senses of self; through the performance of
personal narratives (part voiced, part unvoiced) individuals create spaces
for themselves beyond the public surfaces of the exchange, affected by it to
varying extents but in no measure the effect of it.*

*Finally, then, when Turner writes that "one learns through performing"
(1982: 94), achieving wisdom "not by abstract solitary thought, but by
participating, immediately or vicariously, in the performative genres of socio-
cultural dramas" (1986: 84), I would concur, while adding that what such
participating and performing inexorably give onto is narratives of personal
interpretation (cf. Coleman and Elsner, this volume). Indeed, there is no real
binary distinction between solitary experience and socio-cultural drama or
ritual, because the heightened sensorium of the latter is a paraphrase for the
imaginative potential of the former. The social is at base personal.*

ACT TWO

Walking into the marbled foyer of the Infostar office block, I was surprised
to find myself looking for the lift to the second floor in the company of a

couple who were also clutching a postcard. "It looks like they'll be giving away a few cars this afternoon, then!", I joked as we went up in the lift together. They didn't answer, simply looked at me suspiciously. I felt suddenly in competition with them; maybe the cars were going to be in short supply.

I made sure I was out of the lift and at the entrance to Infostar before them. The glass door was opened by a security guard – who appeared to be armed. I must have looked worried by the time I had passed through the guard's anteroom into a secretarial office and reached one of the women sitting behind desks in a uniform blue suit, because after she had taken my postcard from me, she told me: "Smile!" I smiled weakly.

I was ushered into another room and was again surprised to find others waiting: some twenty to thirty people seated on plastic chairs in four or five rows, facing a partition wall with closed doors. I was stared at as I came in and I quickly found an empty chair on the front row. We seemed a motley crew and an uncertain audience: a mixture of economic classes, dress styles and ethnicities. What did it mean that I had been selected for a prize alongside this group of people?

There was not a long wait, however, before one of the doors in the wall opened and a man entered holding a clipboard. "Mr and Mrs Singh?", he read out from it; a Pakistani couple got up from their seats. "Would you like to come with me please." It all appeared so organized and knowledgeable, and I felt so off-balance, so much a cog in a larger process which somehow expected me to be there, that I was pleased that before Mr and Mrs Singh had reached their man-with-a-clipboard (official? bureaucrat? manager? controller?), another man had come through the same door and called out, looking up from his pad of paper, "Mr Rapport?" He had trouble pronouncing my name, he had a foreign accent, and I liked him less than the first man who had called the Singhs (I wished I could have gone with him instead). But then the postcard had arrived from Malaysia and maybe the (white) security guard and secretaries were merely fronting an organization of foreign businessmen . . .

ACT THREE

"My name is Fahwaz Mahmoud. But whenever I tell people that they say 'What!? Fah-who?? Sounds like Fuzzy-Wuzzy or something! Come again?!' So why not just call me 'F.M.'? Okay? And I'll call you 'Nigel'. All right?" My interlocutor smiled. We faced each other across a small table in a cavernous room. The room was abustle with activity: men and women officials, dressed in suits and ties, walking around the room, seated singly on small tables in deep conversation with a couple or a family seated opposite them, and other besuited men and women in seeming conference with one another huddled around notice-boards, photographs, and what appeared to be a ship's bell hung on the wall. The officials all seemed busy and all smiled: they were happy to be busy, they were knowledgeable, and they seemed to be trafficking profitable secrets between themselves around the room. Above it all was music, loud and with a disco beat: it added to the sensation of a happy club, eagerly engaged in the business of getting on, doing and becoming.

But Fahwaz's introduction came out too pat. It was a patter he had practised many times before and he was too unskilled or too bored already with our exchange to make it quite sound new or authentic. I could feel sympathy for what I could imagine to be the circumstances that had led him to introduce himself like this – hadn't I recoiled from his tripping over my own surname? – but I resented him not giving me a chance to get his name right and set our exchange on an individual and personal course. I was already being categorized by him as part of a stereotypical group of people whose characteristics I found demeaning: parochial, racist, stupid. I bristled, and gave him a somewhat supercilious glare. I waited slightly before replying, and then said in a reserved and slightly bored voice which I hoped would convey my hurt at his tired categorizing: "Hello Fahwaz."

"Did you park okay?" Fahwaz carried on regardless. "Oh, you came by bike!", he seemed a little surprised, and a string of other questions followed. "Where do you live, Nigel?", "And what job do you do?", "So, are you self-employed?" . . . But why did my answers make no impression on him? Because this was all just part of a dull, routine introduction? Because Fahwaz knew it all anyway? His organization had sent me a postcard to my home in the first place: knew my name, knew my likely income bracket. If this exchange was a charade then were members of his organization even now burgling my home? (They knew I was not at home, and they knew I lived alone.) I felt at Fahwaz's mercy. I didn't want to jeopardize my chances of winning a car, but what would I have to do to get it?

Before I could reflect further, a bell rang in the room and Fahwaz fell silent. The whole room went quiet. I looked round to see what was going on, and there was a woman official standing by the side wall with the ship's bell-rope in her hand. When she had the room's attention, she said: "Operators. Please be advised that Week 7 has already gone to Mr and Mrs Chandler! Congratulations." Fahwaz started clapping and all the other officials around the room did too – even more excitedly. Some of them 'whooped' and punched the air. There were a few cries of "Yeah!", and "All right!" I watched a few of the officials and followed their gaze to one of the tables in the middle of the room, where an 'operator' sat with a broad smile on his face and the couple facing him wore a sheepish grin, accepting the accolades of the room. Did they know why, I wondered, because I certainly didn't. What had gone in Week 7? Was it something I might have got if I had been working well enough or fast enough with Fahwaz? I did not know whether to laugh at what I had just heard and seen as being something ridiculous, or to feel embarrassed for the officials and their display, embarrassed for myself for feeling so removed from it, or embarrassed for the couple who had just 'got Week 7' for being so deeply and gullibly immersed in it.

Without meeting my eye, Fahwaz got back to work again on our conversation (his interrogation) with a new impatience and determination. "So: do you own your house, Nigel?" I nodded. "Yes you do. And why do you own your own house and not rent it? Because it makes economic sense; you're right to. If you can afford it, it's more sensible to own than to rent. Anyone will tell you. Well I'm going to tell you about something that makes equal sense, that anybody can see makes sense. And you'll be kicking yourself at the end, when I've finished telling you, because you didn't know about it sooner and saved all the money you might have."

Fahwaz shifted in his seat and geared himself up. "What sort of holidays do you like, Nigel?" I wondered what to say. 'Holidays' were not a category of experience that I had considered as such for a number of years, not since 'family holidays' as a child. These days it was more a matter of tagging on a few days somewhere at the end of a conference abroad, or dropping into a travel agent, last minute, to book an available city break or week in the sun somewhere. But I could see what sort of answer Fahwaz was fishing for: package tours, Club Med, adventure safaris, etc. Nevertheless, I still wanted to distance myself from his stereotypical assumptions about me. "No particular sort", I replied, "all sorts." "Okay, where did you last go on holiday, Nigel?" "Uh . . . Budapest." Fahwaz looked a bit wary, but tried not to seem nonplussed. "Okay, and how much did that cost you?" "Uh, about £250, for five days." Fahwaz was taken aback. "That's pretty cheap! What did the hotel cost?" "About £80. It was at the end of a conference, and the hotel price was part of an arrangement with the conference organization I went with."

Fahwaz took a deep breath. "OK, Nigel, but how much did your last proper holiday cost?" I tried to think back to the last time I had been on something which Fahwaz would recognize as a proper holiday. "Oh I don't know, Fahwaz", I countered eventually, "I went to Paris for four nights for £135." "Flight included?", Fahwaz asked, clutching at a faint hope. "Yes, flight included. It was a special deal with Airtours, from Manchester via Beauvais . . . But anyway, Fahwaz, I get your drift. So these are cheap holidays I go on. But tell me what you want to say", I concluded, seeing that I needed to concede something to Fahwaz for him to move along with the next part of his patter. He was looking at me quizzically enough as it was, trying to picture just what sort of holidays this latter-day hippy-type was satisfied with.

"OK, Nigel. Well, let's say that normally a holiday is going to cost you £1,000. Maybe a bit more, maybe a bit less. But let's say £1,000 as a ballpark figure." The figure seemed astonishing to me, but Fahwaz seemed back on track. I was not sure of the consequences of allowing myself to go further down the road of being seen as someone who might normally spend £1,000 on a holiday, but it seemed better than stalling matters further. So I nodded, in a way which I hoped was recognizably 'semi-non-committally', 'just-for-argument's-sake'. "Okay", Fahwaz steamed on, "now I'm going to tell you how to get a week's holiday, anywhere in the world, every year, for just £155 . . ." Fahwaz sat back to let the figure sink in – and looked quite pleased with himself. He leaned forward on the table again. "That's right. £155! Now, it's not a time-share, it's actually buying a property abroad for a week per year. You buy a week – say in Lanzarote – and you need never go there at all. That week is like your key to a week's holiday anywhere in the world. Now how does that sound, Nigel! Good?" Fahwaz brought out a pen and began sketching on the pad of paper between us: a house shape, subdivided into numerous little boxes. "Look, here are 52 squares for 52 weeks in the year. We divide up the cost of the property – to build and maintain – by 52."

I tried to sound uncommitted and unimpressed while still 'uh-huh'-ing in the affirmative as Fahwaz went into the details of the operation: how once I owned my week, then it was mine in perpetuity, like any other possession, and I could sell it, rent it, gift it, exchange it, will it, exactly as I saw fit . . . How the company owned 7,000 units in thirty countries spread all round the world in every holiday destination I could imagine . . . How they built in places where property was cheap – such as Lanzarote ('Had I been there? Beautiful!') – and how they made sure no more planning permissions would be forthcoming for anyone else. How I would be met at the airport by a company coach, fully air-conditioned, and taken directly to the holiday resort and the apartment.

In the middle of his stream of explanation, the bell sounded again, the woman announcing again to the silent room that Mr and Mrs So-and-So had bought week such-and-such; there was more applause, whooping and back-slapping. Afterwards, Fahwaz returned to his exposition at the precise point he had left off without overtly even recognizing the interruption. Obviously we were to treat it simply as an intermittent punctuation of our exchange: too noisy actually to speak through, but still not to be 'noticed'. I hoped this was because Fahwaz was now treating me as more of an 'adult' – able to see through the charade, even if not to talk through it. But then was it my imagination that as more bells sounded, Fahwaz's anxiety and his speed of delivery gradually increased? As though the bells were timed 'rounds' of our conversation, and something had to be won before the final one.

The problem was that as I tried to sound *au fait* but also non-committal, Fahwaz took my distance to be a lack of understanding. And so he would repeat the details and their logic. Only when I then sounded convinced, and admitted that here was 'a great idea', would he proceed with the next part of his explanation. "Name somewhere, anywhere, you would like to go for a holiday, Nigel", he suggested at one point. "Russia", I answered, trying once more to steer the conversation into more individual waters. "Russia!"

Fahwaz actually grinned. "Naughty boy, Nigel! But ask me again, next year about there and I might just say 'Yes'." 'Naughty boy'! I didn't quite know what to make of that. Fahwaz was playing with me again, playfully castigating me for not properly playing my part in our conversation and giving 'reasonable' answers – and I was put back on my guard. If he was admitting that the whole conversation was a game we were engaged in, and he expected me to be recognizing the parts we were playing – then what was the real purpose of my being here? Quickly I added, "France". "Okay, Nigel. We have units on the Riviera, in the Alps, in Paris".

"But look," Fahwaz finally concluded, "I've been talking enough. It's boring if I just do the talking all the time" – so it was some kind of game of repartee we were playing together? – "I've explained the set-up to you, you say you understand it, and you agree it's a good idea. Now, is there anything else about it you wish to ask me? Ask me some questions." Suddenly it was like being at an interview, where having nothing to say shows a distinct lack of motivation or creativity. And I really did want to find out more about Fahwaz – whom I kept feeling I could quite like if I could get him to eschew the bureau-speak and come out from behind the Organization. So I asked him about the latter first. And he explained readily enough (if a bit bored): 'the organization was international . . . The postcard I received was sent from Malaysia because a special price had been arranged by The Company with the Malaysian government, making it cheaper than the British GPO!' Fahwaz tapped the side of his nose and looked at me conspiratorially. And I understood: his company knew all the canny business tricks. This bit of his company's 'game', too, Fahwaz was prepared to share with me, so confident was he in The Company's power. Was I really going to miss the opportunity of being on the same team!?

As Fahwaz's revelations continued, so my confidence in 'reading' our exchange decreased. 'Every recipient of a postcard was a winner', he admitted next, 'while the gifts cost his company nothing because they were all promotions.' But how, I wondered, was Fahwaz able to tell me all this? What was his relationship to his patter, and what did he expect mine to be? At one point in my questioning Fahwaz had exclaimed: "Good question, Nigel!", which pleased me because of how animated and entertained Fahwaz had momentarily become, and worried me because of what it implied about my becoming part of Fahwaz's category of 'conventional members of the public and their mindset'. In some desperation, I asked him about himself. He again looked bored, but he humoured me. 'He had been a solicitor, originally, with his own company, but he gave it up to take on this job. And now he earned far more and was very happy. He had two brothers living in Canada. He owned a Holiday Week of his own in Puerto Rico, but through it he'd had holidays all over the world'.

Eventually I ran out of ideas, and Fahwaz ran out of patience. I still didn't know if our conversation was going to plan or not. Was I passing? Would my performance affect my prize? 'Well', Fahwaz concluded, 'if there was absolutely nothing else he could explain to me about the workings of the Holiday Concept, that was the end of his part of the afternoon.' And he repeated one last time: "So you understand everything I've told you, Nigel, and you agree it's a very good idea? Good. I'll bring my boss over to talk to you now about the financial side of things. I don't do that. My job is just to explain the workings to you and then I hand you over to him for a chat."

ACT FOUR

As it happened, the boss was busy at another table and so, as a time-filler, Fahwaz led me first to view the photographs dotting the walls of the room. They all showed happy smiling faces, and tanned bodies in swimsuits, and then more formally dressed smiling faces around a bar later that night. Also there were framed endorsements from happy customers: "Never had it so good", "Best decision I ever made". Fahwaz escorted me past the photos as if he were showing off his family: I should feel not a little privileged to see these photographed people feeling so relaxed and at home. So, as we toured the walls, I tried to make impressed and grateful sounds.

All the time of my exchange with Fahwaz to date, however, I had been nursing an increasingly full bladder. There simply had not seemed an apposite moment in our conversation to break off and 'ask to be excused'. It would have felt too much like seeking a favour from Fahwaz, and demeaning myself by revealing a lack of bodily control. But now I broached the subject with my guide and Fahwaz said "Fine".

After some one-and-three-quarter hours of verbal sparring, it was an enormous relief to be alone in the toilet, and I took advantage of the comparative privacy to say aloud "Hell's bells" and "Thank God" a few times, exorcizing the sense of being unable to say what I wanted, to fill the public air with verbalizations I actually felt.

ACT FIVE

I found Fahwaz waiting for me again at the table. Shortly afterwards, the boss arrived; Fahwaz stood up for him and moved his own chair around the table slightly, so that when they sat down they were both facing me. Fahwaz introduced me, and his boss extended his hand.

The boss seemed busy – just off a plane, on a tight schedule, able to settle a few deals and extend a few benefits, before jetting off again. Fahwaz seemed in some awe of him. He got straight down to business: "So Fahwaz has explained the workings to you, Mr Rapport, 'Nigel', and there is nothing you do not understand: you agree it's a great idea?" I nodded, still hopefully non-committally. The boss and Fahwaz looked at each other. "Good." I wished that Fahwaz were not there. It was not just that the two of them at the table with me seemed unfair odds. It was also that it seemed I would in the end be reneging on an arrangement with Fahwaz if I did not sign up with the boss – and I wished Fahwaz were not present to witness that. But I did not see how I could do otherwise. Because I was telling the truth: I did understand what Fahwaz had told me, I did think that for some people, in some circumstances, it might be a good idea, but no one had then asked me if I thought it was a good idea for me. It was as if there was only one logic – the logic of what people conventionally wished to get out of a holiday, the logic of financial sense – and that since this logic had been explained to me and I had claimed to have understood it, therefore there was no way out of my taking the next step of signing up to The Idea myself.

Now the boss got out a pad of paper and began scribbling figures onto it, talking through his calculations with professional ease: "One week's apartment ownership in Lanzarote, freehold: that's £8,200 at cost; less this month's special reduction of £1,200; less £1,850 deposit payable today; which would leave you owing £5,000 odd; and with interest-free credit, I could get that for you, Nigel, at just £26 per week." He finished writing and handed the pad over for me to see. "Now, how does that look, Mr Rapport? Doesn't that look a good deal!" I pretended to read the page in front of me – studying the scribbled figures studiously, and knowing I was blushing – before deciding there was nothing to do but admit that: 'Yes, it did seem like a good deal'. "Welcome to the club, Nigel!" The boss's hand shot out towards mine and he beamed a smile . . . So this was the moment of truth. And somehow because it was a matter of a physical not verbal exchange which was now being demanded of me, I felt more able to take a stand against it. There was no way I was going to shake the hand extended towards me, and there was no way that this spare, white-shirt-and-tied, young and pushy operator could make me. I would refuse to be further part of the farcical rigmarole of this afternoon's interaction. I sat and glowered at the hand extended towards me, adamantly refusing the gesture, feeling flushed, until the hand was withdrawn. The boss looked at Fahwaz and then back at me:

"I don't understand, Nigel. I thought you said the deal was a good one?"

"I did. But it's not for me. I'm not going to join anything. It's a good deal but I don't want it. Certainly not in Lanzarote."

"I don't understand. Fahwaz told me you understood what he told you, and you agreed it was a good idea, but now you say you don't want to sign up for it. Why not?"

"I'm sorry. Fahwaz did explain it all very well, but I just don't want it. I'm not a joiner. I don't want that sort of holiday."

"Well, I don't understand. Do you, Fahwaz?"

"No. I don't understand. Nigel told me he understood and he said it was a good idea. That was why I brought you over, boss. I wouldn't have bothered you if I knew Nigel thought this."

"Look, it's not Fahwaz's fault. It's just that I don't go in for this sort of thing. The deal seems a good one, and I can think about it – but I don't think it's for me. I'm certainly not signing anything here and now. OK?"

The boss and Fahwaz looked at each other again, quizzically. Finally, the boss said:

"Well, there's nothing more I can say. Maybe I should go and leave you two to have another chat."
"Sure, boss. I'm sorry. I don't know what happened."

The boss rose and left me alone again with a very embarrassed-seeming Fahwaz. I did not want to meet his eye. I felt as though I was about to be told off, like a naughty child, and that I had deserved whatever I got because I had let Fahwaz down. "I'm sorry Fahwaz", I began, "you explained yourself very well but it's just not for me." He looked hurt: "You made me seem a fool, Nigel. You said you understood."

I felt so bad at this point, and so foolish – about getting myself into this situation, about getting Fahwaz into some sort of trouble – that it almost seemed better to sign. If I did sign, if I spent some £5,000, £8,000, it wouldn't break me financially (my family and friends would always help out money-wise if the worst came to the worst), and I would be away from this interaction, this room, this afternoon – and Fahwaz's displeasure, dislike, vengeance. However, Fahwaz stayed silent for a few seconds more, wondering how now to proceed with me, and that breathing space gave me a moment mentally to regroup. I would simply leave. Now. Prize or no prize.

I told Fahwaz. He looked resigned. "Look: I don't care if you sign or not, Nigel; it's just my job. It's just that I thought you said it was a good deal . . . Okay. I'll just go out and arrange your prize."

ACT SIX

As the minutes of Fahwaz's absence mounted and I was left to be stared at like a pariah and a failure (clutching my coat and bicycle pump), my worries returned. How long did it take to 'arrange my prize'? What needed to be 'arranged' anyway? A 'welcoming committee' of some sort on the other side of the door?

At last, Fahwaz re-emerged and, without fully meeting my gaze, motioned me to follow him out. As I did I considered the fact that of the people who had arrived with me at 2.30, I was the first to leave; it was now after 4.30, but there were Mr and Mrs Singh still deep in conversation with their operator. Fahwaz held the door open for me; it was clear that he was now in a hurry to see me off. "This is where we say 'Goodbye', Nigel." That sounded ominous. Why the rush? I wanted us to part friends. I extended my hand to Fahwaz and he shook it, but only grudgingly. "No hard feelings,

Fahwaz? Thanks. You were very good." I tried my best to draw out our farewell, in order to calm myself, but Fahwaz withdrew his hand and closed the door behind him.

In the secretaries' office, I was beckoned to the desk of the woman who had first told me to 'Smile'. En route, I noticed that the security guard was standing by the door and appeared to be fingering a holster at his belt. "Postcard number 572835", the uniformed woman said. "That means you win a wide-screen colour television set." Not bad, I thought; at least better than a karaoke set. But then the woman continued: "Unfortunately, the batch we ordered has proved to be below British standard. So, like it says on the back of your postcard, we are replacing it with goods of equal value." She held up a small padded case for me to see: "These two gold watches, gent's and lady's, will be sent you in a few weeks." She finished the sentence and looked down, returning to her papers. I was left standing by the desk.

It all seemed so sudden, such an anti-climax, that for a second I didn't react. What could I do or say to show my disappointment, to protest? I took a step forward, to make a token gesture at inspecting the watches and checking their worth against my time and discomfort; they were not going to be rid of me in complete silence. As I did so, the security guard took a step forward too and bristled, his hands at his belt. "Can I see?" I asked weakly, and the woman looked up, scowled, and grudgingly handed me the box of watches. They were both of some yellow metal, but I could see they did not form a matched set. "You can't take these away with you", she said. "Yours will be sent you in ten days or two weeks." I was clearly being fobbed off with nothing, but as far as they were concerned the exchange was over. I felt spineless, but I did not know what further I could do or say. I returned the watches to the secretary and mumbled "Right" as rudely as I could; the security guard escorted me out of the office.

The letters I received in the mail the following week, trusting my time spent with Infostar had been "both entertaining and informative", and inviting me to send £29.95 in order to 'redeem' my 'award' of "His and Hers Pair of Designer Watches", only added to my sense of injustice. Only by writing my own narrative of the encounter have I been able to overcome my feelings of foolishness and powerlessness.

POSTSCRIPT: DISAGREEING CONCLUSIONS

The 'commercial performance' which my narrative describes combines features of monetary exchange and bureaucratic process which, respectively, Simmel and Weber would see as archetypal forms of a 'modern' social condition, of the institutionalization of modernity. The 'ritual' of such commercial performance embodies – at the same time dramatizes, re-constitutes and institutionalizes – the essence of modernity and produces the modern consciousness. What modernity is said to entail is a globalism and universalism which would do away with all intermediary social formations between individual and (super)state, while at the same time framing the individual in a set of rigid and iconic categories which stereotypically define the proper form of his or her belonging: as customer, as citizen.

For further glossing of the exchange, one might turn to Goffman – not to mention Garfinkel, Bernstein or Foucault. Here (après *Goffman 1961:* passim) *is a quasi-'total institution' inculcating me into its encompassing, bureaucratic control, through an initiation process designed to 'disculturate' – to break down my confidence and mortify my conception of self (violate the erstwhile territory of the self through an invasive public knowing of what was once private) – and so programme me for a new moral career in a new world. Fahwaz and his company and boss intend my complete resocialization, and I am 'naughty' if I refuse to toe the line. Here* (à la *Garfinkel 1968:* passim) *is a 'status degradation ceremony' in which a social group employs certain organizational and communicational strategies so as to cause shame in one or more of its members or neo-members and transform their public identity into a lower type, for the purpose of effecting a certain group function, such as eschewing eccentricity and rebelliousness; I am shamed into accepting the definition of others in the room concerning the worth of what they propose, and feeling that my own lack of loyalty (to Fahwaz and The Company) is a failing in me. Here* (à la *Bernstein 1972:* passim) *is a 'restricted code' of limited verbal resources and conversational manœuvre which holds me in thrall for the benefits of social solidarity; I find no way to counteract or reroute the course of my exchange with Fahwaz, no way to elaborate on its relations in more personal directions, and must abide by its formal terms or cause rupture and fear violence. And here* (à la *Foucault 1972:* passim) *is a 'discourse' at once verbal and behavioural, collective and coercive, which inhabits my body and habituates my mind. The discourse of organized capital and commerce devolves into the micro-social power of the salesperson over the potential consumer, whereby the pressure to buy and partake translates into all manner of sensate, psycho-social and mental pressures and reactions. I feel it is almost better to part with my money than to disappoint and distance Fahwaz and his boss, and hence undergo further discomforts, corporeal and conscientious.*

'Almost better to part with my money' . . . but not quite, and the difference is surely crucial. I did not sign, I did not become embroiled, I did walk away. No great victory perhaps, but a significant enough one for my purposes here. For what I would emphasize in the encounter and in my narrating of it are the interruptions, the puncturings, the aporias, which cause the process of the encounter (the ritual, the code and the discourse) to be suspended and, however marginally, undermined. For these bring to light the persons behind the role players (the ritual officiants, the speakers of code and the discursive sites), persons who cannot help themselves from periodically standing back from the social routines in which they are engaged. They reflect on them,

make sense of them, in ways which subvert the totalizing effects of those routines, and ways which reveal those persons to be able consciously to adopt cognitive positions beyond the domain and determinism of those routines. Every routine (however technologized and efficient) will have its gaps – and have its determination of reality thereby undermined (cf. Brown, this volume). Whatever the order and sense propounded by the logic of the routines, therefore, the persons taking part are ever able to look askance and say: 'Here I am partaking of a scripted encounter (a language-game, a ritual, a code, a discourse).' They are able to write their own sense. It is they, after all, who animate the routines by their mental and bodily, verbal and behavioural, presence in them, engaged in the process of composing their own personal narratives of life.

Of course, to theorists of social determinism such as those alluded to above, this sort of cognitive move is not possible. 'There is no metalanguage', Lacan would exhort; and Derrida: 'There is no outside-text.' All that is possible, Foucault would explain, is a move from one discourse to another. Since there is always power (in every exchange in every relationship), there is always entrapment, always a coming to consciousness in terms of a particular system of social signification, a particular discourse or other. Hence there are always and only bodies totally 'imprinted by history', and no authenticity beyond conventional performance. The only transcendence is a playing off of discourses against one another, a subverting of one power relationship in terms of others.

Notwithstanding, it seems to me that what the above narrative elicits is an account of the interpreting person: the individual who stands beyond the discourse. For Fahwaz, then, there were moments when it seemed clear that he was aware of the playing out of a language-game: a commercial game he learnt and was paid to play, but nevertheless a game of his own instigation, a game from which he intermittently stood back, a game he at some times played better than others, a game which he was able to treat more or less lightly. Hence: "Naughty boy, Nigel", as I enquire about holidays in Russia; his taking a deep breath and then: "but how much did your last proper holiday cost?" as I prevaricate with accounts of cheap conference breaks; and his embarrassed reticence surrounding the episodic ringing of the ship's bell and the ceremonial announcements. Were I to know him better, I might discover whether the 'concurrent flow of consciousness' (Steiner) which emerged within his performance of the language-game articulated irony, humour or fear.

Moreover, if my account of Fahwaz's being affected by our language-game is only ever an interpretation, an empathetic account of what, to me, Fahwaz's behaviour seemed to say, I know what I thought and felt; and, of course, it is of this that the above narrative largely treats. What I have tried to show is that there was no moment at which I did not experience the mixed emotions of both recognizing what the language-game expected of me, and knowing precisely where I stood – actually, personally – in relation to it. It was not always so easy a matter to decide how to reconcile these positions – what to say, how to act, how to seem – and it was by no means an easy matter to decide where my interlocutors, the chief perpetrators, stood in relation to their language-game, but it was never hard to see myself both present and absent: a conscious player in the game (however reluctant) but never unconsciously played by it. In the ritual of commercial performance, in short, I constructed my own terms of membership, and on this basis would claim Fahwaz to be doing likewise.

The determinist theorists, of course, have one last string to their bow. This is the argument that I no more know my own mind than I know Fahwaz's; because both are the playthings of unconscious urges which are closed to conscious retrieval and reflection (Freud, Lacan), or, alternatively, because the 'interiority' of our minds is a mere fiction constituted through public and shared systems of signs (Foucault, Lévi-Strauss). Either way, my mind and Fahwaz's are equally open to being read through exterior procedures of interpretation (Goffman, Garfinkel). Moreover, since presence is no guarantee of authenticity (Derrida), our being there – seeing, thinking, imagining, feeling, intuiting – provides no claim to any knowledge that is not the property of the language-game that is being played out. The language-game knows its speakers but they do not know it: the 'first-person point of view' is overdetermined.

Against this final ploy, this last play, there is no response. For this is the point where, to adapt Victor Turner (1983: 191), teleological and tautological mystifications would obscure the fact that, "we human beings are all and always sophisticated, conscious, capable of laughter at our own institutions" (cited in Ashley 1990: xix). In ending this brief (voiced) postscript, therefore, I simply say that I would hope the above narrational exposition of anxious (unvoiced) interiority is able to speak for me.

REFERENCES

Ashley, K. (1990) 'Introduction', in K. Ashley (ed.) *Victor Turner and the Construction of Cultural Criticism*, Bloomington: Indiana University Press.

Barthes, R. (1982) *A Barthes Reader*, London: Cape.

Bauman, R. (1978) *Verbal Art as Performance*, Rowley: Newbury House.

Bernstein, B. (1972) 'A sociolinguistic approach to socialization', in J. Gumperz and D. Hymes (eds) *Directions in Sociolinguistics*, New York: Holt-Rinehart-Winston.

Bourdieu, P. (1977) *Outline of a Theory of Practice*, Cambridge: Cambridge University Press.

Bruner, J. (1990) *Acts of Meaning*, Cambridge MA: Harvard University Press.

Cohen, A.P. (1975) *The Management of Myths*, Manchester: Manchester University Press.

Crites, S. (1971) 'The narrative quality of experience', *Journal of the American Academy of Religion*, XXXIX: 291–311.

Fernandez, J. (1971) 'Persuasions and performances: of the beast in every body . . .

and the metaphors of Everyman', in C. Geertz (ed.) *Myth, Symbol and Culture*, New York: Norton.

Foucault, M. (1972) *The Archaeology of Knowledge*, London: Tavistock Press.

Garfinkel, H. (1967) *Studies in Ethnomethodology*, Englewood Cliffs NJ: Prentice-Hall.

—— (1968) 'Conditions of successful status-degradation ceremonies', in J. Manis and B. Meltzer (eds) *Symbolic Interaction*, Boston: Allyn-Bacon.

Giddens, A. (1976) *New Rules of Sociological Method*, London: Hutchinson.

Goffman, E. (1961) *Asylums*, Harmondsworth: Penguin.

Hastrup, K. (1995) *A Passage to Anthropology: Between Experience and Theory*, London: Routledge.

Jackson, M. (1989) *Paths Toward a Clearing*, Bloomington: Indiana University Press.

Kerby, A. (1991) *Narrative and the Self*, Bloomington: Indiana University Press.

Kleinman, A. (1988) *The Illness Narratives*, New York: Basic Books.

Rapport, N.J. (1986) 'Cedar High Farm: ambiguous symbolic boundary. An essay in anthropological intuition', in A.P. Cohen (ed.) *Symbolising Boundaries*, Manchester: Manchester University Press.

—— (1990) 'Ritual conversation in a Canadian suburb: anthropology and the problem of generalization', *Human Relations*, 43 (9): 849–64.

—— (1993) *Diverse World-Views in an English Village*, Edinburgh: Edinburgh University Press.

Steiner, G. (1975) *After Babel*, London: Oxford University Press.

—— (1978) *On Difficulty, and Other Essays*, Oxford: Oxford University Press.

Turner, V. (1982) *From Ritual to Theatre: The Human Seriousness of Play*, New York: PAJ Publications.

—— (1983) 'The spirit of celebration', in F. Manning (ed.) *The Celebration of Society*, Bowling Green: Popular Press.

—— (1986) *The Anthropology of Performance*, New York: PAJ Publications.

Chapter 10

Problematizing performance

Edward L. Schieffelin

INTRODUCTION

In the last ten or fifteen years anthropologists interested in cultural performances (religious rituals, political pageants, folk entertainments, curing ceremonies, spirit seances and so on) have moved increasingly away from
studying them as systems of representations (symbolic transformations,
cultural texts) to looking at them as processes of practice and performance.
In part this reflects a growing dissatisfaction with purely symbolic approaches
to understanding material like rituals, which seem to be curiously robbed of
life and power when distanced in discussions concerned largely with meaning. 'Performance' deals with actions more than text: with habits of the body
more than structures of symbols, with illocutionary rather than propositional
force, with the social construction of reality rather than its representation.
Performance is also concerned with something that anthropologists have
always found hard to characterize theoretically: the creation of presence.
Performances, whether ritual or dramatic, create and make present realities
vivid enough to beguile, amuse or terrify. And through these presences, they
alter moods, social relations, bodily dispositions and states of mind.

As is not unusual with a new direction in anthropology, there is a tendency
for us to head enthusiastically in pursuit without carefully considering
fundamental epistemological issues. What precisely (if that is possible) do
we mean by 'performance', where does the concept come from, and what
baggage – as well as benefit – does its usage bring to the discipline?

'PERFORMANCE' IN SOCIAL SCIENCE

The notion of 'performance' has been used in essentially two ways in social
science. The first refers to particular 'symbolic' or 'aesthetic' activities, such
as ritual or theatrical and folk artistic activities, which are enacted as
intentional expressive productions in established local genres. 'Performance'
in this usage refers to bounded, intentionally produced enactments which are
(usually) marked and set off from ordinary activities, and which call attention

to themselves as particular productions with special purposes or qualities for the people who observe or perform them.)

Following this view, (Bauman (1986) characterizes performance as a display of expressive competence or virtuosity by one or more performers addressed to an audience. Such performances aim to evoke an imaginative reality or an intensification of experience among the spectators, and bring about an altered awareness of their situation and/or a sense of emotional release. 'Performance' in this usage refers to the particular kind of performative event treated as an aesthetic whole in a larger social context. Studies of this focus on the structure of such events, the means by which they are carried out (or have their effect), and their relation to social context.)

(The second usage of 'performance' in social science is associated with the work of Erving Goffman (Goffman 1959) and the symbolic interactionist school. The focus here is not on a type of event but rather on performativity itself: the expressive processes of strategic impression management and structured improvisation through which human beings normally articulate their purposes, situations and relationships in everyday social life. Here the notion of performance converges with implications of theories of practice, a topic we will return to in due course. The point to be made here is that both of these anthropological usages of 'performance' (or 'performativity') draw their inspiration and conceptual terminology from the western notions of theatrical performance: either specific cultural genres such as rituals are seen as analogous to theatrical performances, or everyday activities can be seen as brought off through expressive processes analogous to those by which imaginative realities are produced on the stage.)

Before exploring the limitations of extending such theatrical concepts into anthropology, it is useful to expand a bit on what I see as the value, indeed the enormous power and potential, of the notion of 'performance' in our discipline. I believe there is something fundamentally performative about human being-in-the-world. As Goffman has suggested (1959), human intentionality, culture and social reality are fundamentally articulated in the world through performative activity. When human beings come into the presence of one another, they do so expressively, establishing consensus on who they are and what their situation is about through voice, gesture, facial expression, bodily posture and action. Common values or at least working agreements about social identity and purpose are established between people not so much through rational discourse as through complex and subtle expressive manœuvres that create an atmosphere of trust and a sense of mutual expectations.

Carried to the extreme, it would not be too much to say that without living human bodily expressivity, conversation and social presence, there would be no culture and no society. The ponderous social institutions and mighty political and economic forces of late capitalism which weigh so heavily upon us are, like illusions of maya, without any reality except in so far as they or their effects are actually and continually engaged and emergent in human discourse, practice and activity in the world: generated in what human beings say and do. It is because human sociality continues in moment-by-moment existence only as human purposes and practices are performatively articulated in the world that performance is (or should be) of fundamental interest to anthropology.

PERFORMANCE AS CONTINGENT PROCESS

Performance (of either kind above) is often thought of as characterized by conscious intent. In a recent work Humphrey and Laidlaw (1994) differentiate between 'ritualization' and performance as distinct modalities of action on this basis. 'Ritualization' in their formulation refers not to a type of event but to the attitude of consciousness with which it is carried out. In particular the 'ritual' attitude refers to a mode of consciousness in which 'acts are felt by those who perform them to be external to their intention': a person submits to ritual activity in such a way as to 'remove the sovereignty of herself as agent', (1994: 96), experiencing herself or himself rather in the manner of the object or the vehicle of the pre-ordained acts she or he performs. The person carries out (or rather undergoes) her or his own enactments in the mode of automatic habitual practice with little ego-involvement.

Humphrey and Laidlaw explicitly exclude 'performance' from their discussion of 'ritualization', considering it to be quintessentially an activity involving conscious purposiveness and self-direction (1994: 10). In so doing, they exclude perhaps three-quarters of those activities that anthropologists have traditionally considered as rituals (1994: 10).[1] Susanna Rostas (this volume) seeks a middle ground by attempting to co-ordinate a notion of performance with Humphrey and Laidlaw's 'ritualization'. She associates performance (or performativity) with the 'extra energy' or expressivity one puts into an act to raise its meaning to something more than its ordinary significance in everyday practice – giving it a non-conventional, 'creative' edge, and enhancing (or changing) its significance or using it as a vehicle for meaning. As with Humphrey and Laidlaw, performativity essentially entails intention: 'the deployment of consciously formulated strategies. It implies individuality . . . [and] it can be seen as creative' (Rostas, this volume).

I should mention, at this point, that I am uneasy with both of these formulations. In the first place I am uneasy with a differentiation of human activity that turns primarily on privileging the performers' internal state of mind or mode of consciousness (ego-involvement or personal intention) and downplays their interaction with others. This is not to say that a person's internal attitude is not important (indeed it can largely determine the meaning of the interaction), but as Rostas notes, it is almost impossible, in practice, to separate ritualized from performative aspects of human action on this basis. Moreover, while the role personal intentions play in performative action can be highly important, it is by no means clear that it ultimately differentiates 'performance' from 'ritualized' action (as formulated above). Indeed one can question whether 'performance' or 'performative' action necessarily entails conscious intention at all. This may be clarified through one of Rostas's examples:

> Take washing up: this is precisely the kind of action that is done ritual-istically; it is done frequently, usually in the same way, with attention but not conscious intention, other than that of getting the dishes clean, which has become an embodied, habitual activity. If someone carries out this action rather more dramatically . . . with expansive movements and rather amusingly or angrily, for example, then we might want to classify this as 'performance', and look more closely at the performativity, the non-conventionality of the act.
>
> (Rostas, this volume)

Now it may be that the furrowed brow and/or the clattering and banging of the dishes in the sink constitute a conscious and intentional display of emotion by the dish washer, but is there really a necessity for this? It may simply be that he or she is upset or elated and this is the way the washing gets done when the washer is in-the-world-feeling fully, without entailing any expressive intent or even awareness of self-revelatory behaviour. If this is the case, it cannot be 'performance' (by the criteria of intention). But neither would it seem to be 'ritualization' (though Humphrey and Laidlaw do not really deal with the question of the status of a ritualized act that might be performed unwillingly or exuberantly by the actor whose actions it authors). However, the expressed emotion in the washing up is tangible and readily analysable in performative terms (a Goffman-type exercise), as Rostas points out. What this example really reveals, I would suggest, is the expressivity (and hence performativity) inherent in any human activity in everyday life, which renders our actions communicative and effective to others in our situations whether we mean them to be or not. We are, in effect, more performative than we intend, and we are in good measure 'submitted to' our performativity as part of our active being-in-the-world.[2]

Every act has an expressive dimension: it reveals something (and accom-plishes something) about the actor and the situation. It is 'read' by other participants. We act both for ourselves and in the eyes of our beholders. The issue here is not that our expressivity is not entirely under our control, but rather that it (also) belongs to the situation. If we strive for expressive control in everyday life and in special 'performance' situations, this is *ipso facto* part of our act of participation in the situation and our contribution to its determination, process and outcome – whether or not what others see us to be doing (or revealing) is what we intend them to see.

It follows from this that any performance (indeed any performative activity) is inherently a contingent process. In some part this resides in the socio-historical circumstances in which it takes place and to which it relates. But, for the participants and their observers, a great deal of contingency resides in whether the performance itself is 'properly carried out', whether it 'works'. Everything (in ritual no less than theatre), from the observance of the correct procedures to the resonance of the symbolism, the heightening of emotion, the sense of transformation, all depend on whether the performers and other participants can 'bring it off'. It is always possible the performance may fail. Thus 'performance' is always inherently *interactive*, and fundamentally *risky*.[3] Amongst the various people involved (who often have different agendas) there is always something aesthetically and/or practically at stake, and something can always go wrong (Schieffelin 1995).

The burden of success or failure in a cultural performance is usually laid on the central actors, but the real location of this problem (and of the meaning of the terms 'actor', 'spectator', 'participant') is the *relationship* between the central performers and others in the situation. In western theatrical performance, this is the relationship between actors and audience. We will return to this important issue shortly.

Finally, a performance is always something accomplished: it is an achievement in the world. This is reflected in the borrowing of the term in sports or business discourse, such as, 'Jones performed well in sales this month'[4] or 'Smith's poor performance cost Enfield the game.' Here the connotations of 'performance' move somewhat beyond the domain of expressive culture, but preserve its presentational resonances by carrying a connotation of 'making a showing' which is accountable to the evaluation of others. We are talking here not only about the achievement in bringing such a performance off successfully, but also about the accomplishment of the work it was meant to do.

PERFORMANCE AND TEXT

The character of performance as accomplishment, together with its interactive quality and element of risk, make it easy to differentiate it from the notion of 'text'. Although some scholars have written as though performance could be treated as a form of text, in my view performance can never be text, and its unique strategic properties are destroyed when it is considered as, or reduced to, text. To be sure, performances share some qualities with texts. They have beginnings, middles and ends, they have internal structure, may refer to themselves, etc. But it is precisely the performativity of performance for which there is no analogue in text. Unlike text, performances are ephemeral. They create their effects and then are gone – leaving their reverberations (fresh insights, reconstituted selves, new statuses, altered realities) behind them. Performances are a living social activity, by necessity assertive, strategic and not fully predictable. While they refer to the past and plunge towards the future, they exist only in the present. Texts are changeless and enduring. One may return to the same text for a new reading, but a performance which one goes to see again is not the same as yesterday's. While texts and performances may be produced out of one another, this is very different from saying they are reducible to one another. Text can never be 'duplicated' in performance, and performance is not reducible to text (whether script, directors' notes or ethnographic description). Still, ethnographic accounts can usefully attend to (and meditate upon) those particular properties of performances through which they produce their various modes of social reality and articulate the human world.

PERFORMANCE AND PRACTICE

Much of what we have just said about performances has been said by anthropologists of 'practices' – and the relationship is a close one. The term 'practice' focuses on that aspect of human life and activity which is structured largely through unquestioned, unthought habit, through which human beings normally carry out the business of living both in everyday life and in important strategic situations. Practices have an internal 'logic' of their own, which provides the strategic rationality or purposive orderliness of 'the way things are done' in most ordinary cultural activity. Collectively, practices form the shape of the unthought behavioural regularities of a cultural world, which Bourdieu has called the habitus (Bourdieu 1977). Practices can be said to emerge from this ground of habitude in the form of structured or 'regulated' improvisations when people deal with the situations in which they are involved in customary practical ways. Practices always emerge as improvisations because situations and the people that participate in them are always only analogous to each other; they are never exactly the same (Bourdieu 1977: 83).

The relation between performance and practice turns on this moment of improvisation: performance embodies the *expressive dimension of the strategic articulation of practice*. The italicized expression here could stand as our definition of performativity itself. It is manifest in the expressive aspect of the 'way' something is done on a particular occasion: the particular orchestration of the pacing, tension, evocation, emphasis, mode of participation, etc., in the way a practice (at that moment) is 'practised', that is, 'brought off'. It gives the particular improvisation of a practice in a particular situation its particular turn of significance and efficacy for oneself and others at the time – in the moment where habitude becomes action. Thus performativity is located at the creative, *improvisatory* edge of practice in the moment it is carried out – though everything that comes across is not necessarily consciously intended.

We could go on – but it should again be clear that the concepts 'performance'/'performativity' have the potential to open a considerable domain for anthropological exploration of the way that cultures actively construct their realities. It should also be clear that whether regarded as contingent self-presentation or expressive edge of practice, the process of performance, the power of performativity, turns crucially on its *inter*active edge, and hence on the nature of the relationship between 'performers' and others in the situation to whom the performance is directed, or (in the west) 'the audience'. And here, at least in conventional anthropology, we encounter a significant epistemological stumbling block: the popular western notion of theatre.

THE THEATRICAL RELATION BETWEEN PERFORMER AND SPECTATOR IN SOCIAL SCIENCE

For most middle-class western academics with average experience of attending theatrical performances, the notion of live performance conjures up an image of actors on a stage. Fundamental to this image is the division between (relatively active) performers and (relatively passive, but emotionally responsive) audience. In Euro-American (basically Aristotelian) tradition this divide is also a metaphysical, even ontological, one between a world of spectators which is real and a world conjured up by performers which is not, or more precisely, which has another kind of reality: a virtual or imaginary one. Schechner summarizes the basic idea with his remark: 'acting means make-believe, illusion, lying . . . In America we say someone's "only acting" when we detect the seams between the performance and the non-acting surround' (Schechner 1982: 63). Although we appreciate the power and message of performance illusion, and admire the skill with which it is done, it necessarily remains for us a simulacrum.

While this traditional western concept of the performance–audience relationship can easily be shown to vary across cultures, theatre traditions and historical time, and while both the western mainstream and avant-garde theatres have consistently experimented with different ways of constructing and deconstructing the relationship, this conventional notion of the theatrical relationship between 'performers' and 'audience' is still with us. What I am concerned with here is that this set of ideas about the relationships entailed in performance carries hidden moral and epistemological judgements, when transported into anthropology, that tend to undermine our ethnographic intent.

According to the popular conception, the acceptance of theatrical illusion is enjoyable in the way it enthrals an audience or takes them out of their everyday lives. But this also makes it fundamentally unsettling. Actors may be brilliant virtuosos, capable of astonishing or moving us profoundly; but in their very virtuosity they are weavers of illusion and deceit. Thus, in a philosophical tradition like the Euro-American which is deeply concerned with locating and establishing truth, and in a religious tradition which is concerned with individual moral integrity and empowerment in relation to an invisible sacred reality, the status and efficacy of these illusory productions are unavoidably problematic. Laurel Kendall (1995: 19) outlines the moral and epistemological dilemma that western theatrical convention lays upon the study of performative ethnographic materials as follows:

> Our students inevitably ask us if we 'believe' in the powers of the shamans we have studied, or if the spirits are 'really' there. The question discomforts insofar as it implies, on the one hand, that the ethnographer [might] follow Castaneda's (1968) leap beyond the pale of professional credulity, or on the other, that acknowledgments of simulation make charlatans of one's informants.

Such a question (and also the dilemma posed in answering it) is a product of, and is driven by, western assumptions about theatre as illusion and acting as a form of inauthenticity. Kendall does not attempt to resolve this dilemma, and I will only pose it here.

Beyond these problems of truth status, and what to believe about the 'presences' emergent in performance, lie the issues of manipulation and vulnerability, knowledge and power. Conventional experience in a western theatre would suggest that performers and audience must maintain quite different modes of consciousness for the performance to work. Actors in a western theatrical event must never lose sight of the broader theatrical context of the event. They are conscious not only of what they are doing in relation to each other, but also that they are performing before an audience. The audience's awareness (if all goes well) narrows its focus to the imagined situation presented, excluding awareness that the characters are performers, and/or of itself as an audience. It is this forgetfulness of the context, partly voluntary on the part of the audience, but in good part compelled by the quality of the performance, that constitutes so-called 'suspension of disbelief' and enables the activity of the players to assert itself as an emergent reality, vivid and alive. This vividness is emergent from the interaction between performers and audience and (as every performer knows) is fraught with risk. And it is the product of a profound manipulation. The performers, being professionals (or virtuosos), know what they are doing. The manipulation is rationally conceived, intentional and carefully prepared. The audience (by convention) opens itself to being led by the performance and is drawn in and beguiled. To the extent that this beguilement is play and entertainment the situation is benign. But it need not be so. Where the audience is hoodwinked and betrayed, or aroused to political consciousness and action by a perform-ance, the issues of the power of illusion, of truth and deception, become increasingly urgent. There is a dormant unease about the potential for this kind of performative manipulation embedded in the conventional western notion about the relationship between performers and audience, and it is hard to still. It drives Laurel Kendall's students' questions: 'do the spirits really appear at shaman's performances?'

It is also endemic to Goffman's theoretical extension of theatrical models into social science (Goffman 1959, 1967). Goffman often writes as if the whole process of impression management in social interaction is a matter of rational calculation and individuals consciously manipulating their situations. All social life, by this implication, becomes a matter of performative illusions and strategic manipulations. Or at least it is easy for people steeped in popular conceptions of theatrical performance to read his theatrical terminology and discussion in this way. Goffman rarely carries his analysis forward to deal with the more philosophical question anthropology is ultimately concerned with here: what the relationship is between strategic impression management and the social construction of reality. Rather, the built-in issues of truth and deceit, reality vs imaginary, become the epistemological blocks on which theory couched in these sorts of theatrical metaphor stumbles.[5]

My point is that these popular assumptions about the nature of the relationship between theatre audience and performers in conventional western theatre form probably the most problematic part of the extension of theatre metaphors and performative ways of thinking into social science theory. Is social life merely a tissue of illusions skilfully woven by us all? Where are the truth and efficacy in ritual located? The fact of the matter is that these issues are in large part an artefact of the way the relation between performers and audience is conventionally (if naively) conceived. As such they have become problematic issues that plague not only western epistemologies but ethnographic understanding. It is fundamental that we find a way to resolve them if we are to come to some understanding of the role performativity plays in the social construction of human reality.

Theatre people, to their credit, (and for their own reasons), have problematized and creatively experimented with this relationship for some time. Brecht encouraged actors to avoid enthralling their audiences in an imaginative reality, but to display or demonstrate what they were doing in a didactic mode so that the audience remained at an intellectual distance from the action, never forgetting they were watching a performance and able to focus on the message it modelled. At the opposite extreme, Schechner in his production of *Dionysis in 69* worked for a collapse of aesthetic distance to the point of encouraging a degree of sexual participation between audience and performers.

The simplest lesson for anthropology is that the exact nature of the performative relationship between the central performers and the other participants (including spectators) in a cultural event cannot be assumed analytically, but must be investigated ethnographically. In Papua New Guinea, where I have done my fieldwork, the relationship between dancers and spectators in the Gisalo ceremony of the Kaluli people was not at all like that between audience and performers in a western theatre. In Gisalo, the dancers sing nostalgic songs about the lands and rivers of their audience's community. Members of the audience are moved so deeply they burst into tears and then, becoming enraged, they leap up and burn the dancers on the shoulder blades with the resin torches used to light the performance (Schieffelin 1976: 21–5). Indeed, this remarkable response could be interpreted as virtually necessary to the performance, since if the audience is not moved and the tension between performers and audience does not rise to the pitch of violence, the ceremony falls apart and is abandoned in the middle of the night. In any case, after a successful performance, the dancers pay compensation to those whom they made weep. I should point out that the spectators' response is not a Durkheimian 'conventional display of ritually appropriate sentiment'. It is real grief and rage that are evoked. The ceremony is taken by the participants more in the manner of a deliberate provocation than of a moving performance in the western sense. The performers are held accountable for the painful emotions they evoke – and the retaliation upon them (and the compensation they must pay) return that account – as well as those emotions being an indication of the beauty and effectiveness of the performance. The dancers and song composers, for their part, certainly see it that way and are extremely pleased if they have managed to provoke numbers of the spectators to tears, despite the consequences to themselves. It is not unusual for aesthetically provoked emotion in New Guinea to be taken as deserving compensation whether or not those who provoke it are conceived to be deliberately and calculatedly causing the feelings evoked.[6]

Another kind of 'audience–performer' relationship is visible in spirit seances. Kaluli spirit seances in Papua New Guinea were highly entertaining, even thrilling events, but they could only ethnocentrically be called performances in a western sense (see Schieffelin 1985, 1996). This is because, in seance, the issue is not performative illusion but the exact opposite: it is the presence of spirits. If anything, it is the spirits themselves who perform.

Kaluli spectators know very well that spirit seances can be faked and keep a sharp eye for signs of 'performing' or, as they see it, deception. Spirits in seance cured illness and revealed the identity of witches, both of which were activities of considerable (even life-and-death) social and political consequence, and people did not fool around with them. It was essential that the characters who spoke through the medium were really spirits and not the performance tricks of someone who was trying to con his listeners. A 'performance' in the western sense was precisely what speaking with the spirits through a medium was not and could not be. It had more of the character of a telephone conversation. Kaluli themselves likened it to speaking with someone over two-way radio. To describe the Kaluli seance as a performance in the popular western sense would be to violate its ethnographic nature.

Closer to western experience, the members of the Word of Life Movement, a Protestant evangelical sect studied by Simon Coleman (1996), base their practice of worship on the belief that sacred language (the words of scripture or speaking in tongues) contains concrete sacred power. They see the visual and physical changes in the world effected by these words as a testament to the presence of God. Sacred words act as autonomous physical sources of power. Speaking such words is an illocutionary act that creates what it pronounces. Before building their temple, members of the sect held a service in which they walked over the building site speaking tongues into the ground to saturate it with divine power. The subsequent rise of the building could be seen as a concrete manifestation of the power of this sacred language. The point here is this dramatic service at the site could not be seen as a performance in a western sense either: the performative action of speaking the power into the ground is misunderstood if it is taken as metaphorical or symbolic action. Rather the force is illocutionary and instrumental. To the members of the sect, this act of saturating the ground with the divine word was more akin to spreading fertilizer to render a field productive than to laying a cornerstone to inaugurate a construction.

Clearly there are significant problems with extending the conventional western conception of the relation between performers and audience into anthropological discussions of rituals and other cultural performances. Yet understanding the precise nature of this relationship in a performance event is fundamental to understanding the structure and character of the event itself. Where western assumptions align the relation between performer and spectator with relations like signifier/signified, text/reader, illusion/reality, deceit/authenticity, activity/passivity, manipulative/straightforward, they conceal important moral and epistemological judgements that undermine anthropological discussion which makes use of western performance ideas in an unexamined way. It is for this reason that it is important to make the relationship between the participants and others in performative events a central subject of ethnographic investigation.

PERFORMANCE AND THE SOCIAL CONSTRUCTION OF REALITY

It is not only for the sake of ethnographic accuracy that it is important to problematize the relationship between performers and participants. More importantly for anthropology, these relationships need careful investigation – both in formal performances and in everyday life – because it is within these relationships that the fundamental epistemological and ontological relations of any society are likely to be implicated and worked out: because this is the creative edge where reality is socially constructed. If this is so, we may entertain the hypothesis that just as western notions about the relationship between performer and spectator convey fundamental (western) assumptions about the nature of action in ordinary situations, so the same may be true for people of other cultures (or historical epochs; cf. Foucault 1973), though their assumptions and the implications that flow from them may be quite different.

We may return to the Kaluli Gisalo ceremony to illustrate. When Kaluli are moved by a performance to the point of becoming enraged and attacking the dancer, they are not confusing performative evocation with reality but rather taking it as provocation. That is, they privilege the actual psychological and social effects of the poetic act over its purely aesthetic and representational qualities, and the process of social reciprocation over (what we would call) the suspension of disbelief. In this way poetic evocation (an act of aesthetic performance) is held to be morally consequential and the performers are held accountable.[7] For traditional Kaluli, playing with these volatile edges was the 'stuff of theatre': what their performances were all about. At the same time it had important implications for understanding their everyday modes of moral determination, which was grounded in a sense of reciprocal practice rather than a sense of good and evil or a set of sacredly given rules or norms. In short, investigation of the structure of the performer–participant relationship in Kaluli ceremonies reveals a particular structure in the way their cultural values are aligned within their performative processes, and suggests interesting lines of further enquiry into their mode of socially constructing their reality.

CONCLUSIONS

The fundamental assertion underlying this chapter is that any ethnography of performance is inherently addressing the issue of the social construction of reality, and that, in fact, performativity is not only endemic to human being-in-the-world but fundamental to the process of constructing a human reality. However, the nature of the relationship – both moral and epistemological – between performers and participants is not specified prior to this process, but rather constituted within it (as experimental theatre people have known all along).

The central issue of performativity, whether in ritual performance, theatrical entertainment or the social articulation of ordinary human situations, is the imaginative creation of a human world. The creation of human realities entails ontological issues, and these need to be explored ethnographically rather than a priori assumed. It is time for anthropologists to include this task once again in greater depth if they are to elucidate more clearly the processes entailed when human beings construct a human world.

NOTES

1 Humphrey and Laidlaw characterize these sorts of ritual as 'ritualized religious performances of a quasi-theatrical kind' (1994: 10), adding 'whose success and failure is of the essence' (1994: 10). They thus appreciate the contingent and risky nature of performance. 'Ritualization' is in theory free of contingency, since it is simply the doing of the act (or the act doing itself through the person) rather than its manner of conduct, outcome or result that is important.

2 This would be true even of the most routine activity. What the performance of

ordinary, mindless washing-up activity expresses is an ongoingness in life, the low-profile, apparent performative neutrality of familiar convention which forms the background of any situation. Depending on what is happening in the lives of the participants, it may also constitute an 'escape' from the complexities of the rest of the situation, or an abdication of responsibility in an apparent fulfilment of it. Conversely such activity may represent the numbing of self in a stifled life, or a refuge in familiar activity, or many other things. But such activity is always placed in some context – though perhaps in very low performative profile – in relation to the ongoing situation.

3 See Wulff, this volume, for a comparable point.
4 Cf. also Rapport this volume, on the performance of 'selling'.
5 Indeed one might observe that the western theatre convention stands in a sort of convenient analogy to fieldwork. Rituals and other cultural activities are easy to see as akin to theatre not only in their substantive resemblances to theatrical performances, but in the way anthropologists usually find themselves positioned in relation to such events in an audience-like observer role.
6 For an early observation that aesthetically provoked emotionality is due compensation in Papua New Guinea, see Read (1955). For a detailed discussion of the emotional economy of Gisalo performance, see Schieffelin (1976). For an exegesis of the aesthetics of Kaluli music and poetic evocation, see Feld (1990).
7 The situation is in some ways analogous to an occasion when a national state arrests (or shuts down) a theatre troupe for 'subversive' or 'politically provocative' or 'immoral' performances. For the powers that be, the effects of such theatre are socially real and powerful enough for the performance to be taken as political action rather than entertainment.

REFERENCES

Bauman, Richard (1986) *Story, Performance, Event*, Cambridge: Cambridge University Press.
Bourdieu, Pierre (1977) *Outline of a Theory of Practice*, New York: Cambridge University Press.
Castaneda, Carlos (1968) *The Teachings of Don Juan: A Yaqui Way of Knowledge*, Berkeley CA: University of California Press.
Coleman, Simon (1996) 'Words as things: language, ritual and aesthetics in Christian evangelism', paper presented to social anthropology seminar, University College London.
Feld, Steven (1990) *Sound and Sentiment: Birds, Weeping, Poetics and Song in Kaluli Expression*, Philadelphia: University of Pennsylvania Press.
Foucault, Michel (1973) *The Order of Things*, New York: Vintage Books.
Goffman, Erving (1959) *The Presentation of Self in Everyday Life*, Garden City NY: Doubleday Anchor.
—— (1967) *Interaction Ritual*, New York: Doubleday Anchor.
Humphrey, C. and Laidlaw, J. (1994) *The Archetypal Actions of Ritual*, Oxford: Clarendon Press.
Kendall, Laurel (1995) 'Initiating performance: the story of Chini, a Korean shaman', in C. Laderman and M. Roseman (eds) *The Performance of Healing*, London: Routledge.
Read, Kenneth (1955) 'Morality and the concept of the person among the Gahuku-Gama', *Oceania*, 25: 233–82.
Schechner, Richard (1982) 'Collective reflexivity: restoration of behavior', in J. Ruby

(ed.) *The Crack in the Mirror: Reflexive Perspectives in Anthropology*, Philadelphia: University of Pennsylvania Press.

Schieffelin, E.L. (1976) *The Sorrow of the Lonely and the Burning of the Dancers*, New York: St Martin's Press.

—— (1985) 'Performance and the cultural construction of reality', *American Ethnologist*, 12 (4): 707–24.

—— (1995) 'On failure and performance', in C. Laderman and M. Roseman (eds) *The Performance of Healing*, London: Routledge.

—— (1996) 'Evil spirit sickness, the Christian disease', *Culture, Medicine and Psychiatry*, 20: 1–39.

Chapter 11

Bound and unbound entities

Reflections on the ethnographic perspectives of anthropology vis-à-vis media and cultural studies

Eric Hirsch

The argument of this chapter pursues three related themes. The first theme draws on examples from a north London middle-class family and from Papuan highland society:[1] in their different ways each exemplifies a concern with the ability to achieve specific forms of visibility. By 'visibility' I refer to the ways in which a person or persons appear efficacious in specific cultural contexts of 'audienceship'; moreover, in contexts involving historically particular forms of standardization. By 'standardization' I refer to the attempt to render such entities as knowledge, objects, persons and even 'society' into forms that correspond to an explicit model, where the overt goal is the possibility of replication regardless of context. This is a process that is often associated with the pursuit of objectivity in the natural sciences but has also been increasingly evident in the shaping of modern social and political domains over the last two centuries (see Porter 1994).

The second theme is concerned with how the specific examples (from north London and Papua) are organized and presented through ethnographic description and interpretation; an enterprise recently seen as a standardizing process (that is, how pre-formed categories of analysis dictate a particular reporting of 'data').

The third theme is drawn out from the other two: the visibility performed in contexts of particular standardization, and the organizational features of the text whereby this is recorded, are both specific instances of the rendering of bounded entities (units). A strand running through each of these themes, then, concerns the attributes of bounded entities deployed in specific contexts.

In elaborating on these themes I will be drawing on a contrast first proposed by Strathern (1988) between cultural contexts predicated on differing forms of bounded entities: one pertaining to the western context and one pertaining to the Melanesian. My intention in highlighting this contrast is to suggest that Melanesian cultural practices allow us to discern our own western cultural practices in a sharper and less taken-for-granted manner. In the western context there is a preponderance of standardized (pre-formed) units of which the commodity, and a range of commodity metaphors, are most significant.

In this context, there is a conceptualization of persons as unitary selves having a proprietorial relationship to unitary objects fashioned either by themselves or by largely anonymous others. One set of bounded entities (unitary selves) relates to another set of bounded entities (unitary objects) as a product either of the self or of some other. In this context, 'Persons "are" what they "have" or "do"' (Strathern 1988: 158).

The Melanesian context corresponds to a cultural context predicated on a 'gifting' basis and conceptualized through the interrelationships of persons and objects; the distinction between persons and objects, so significant in the west, is of less significance. In this Melanesian context, persons and objects are composed of a matrix of relationships, and bounded entities (units)[2] are created through unifying particular relationships; that is, by submerging the heterogeneity or hybridity generally present, to produce unitary person(s) or object(s). This process of creating bounded entities occurs in contexts where persons and objects are objectified by the subjective regard of others, and this is always a reciprocal act (for example, a unified collective of dancers is brought forth by a unified collective of inviting hosts).

In the western context persons work at creating relationships between a plurality of bounded entities (such as individuals and society, individuals and individuals, individual and mass produced goods and images) in order to demonstrate capacities (such as the ability to hold together work and family). In the Melanesian context, persons work at eclipsing relationships in order to create bounded entities through which they reveal their capacities as persons (for example, men detaching themselves from the domestic context of women to create a ritual unity of 'maleness'). More generally, westerners resist to greater or lesser degrees attempts to objectify them as persons, as it is seen as a denial of their agency and capacities (their individuality); Melanesians, in a sense, actively seek objectification in order to reveal their capacities. In the western context the forces of objectification are largely anonymous and part and parcel of the standardizing processes bound up with domains such as the state, the market or broadcasting. In the Melanesian context, objectification, as noted, is a reciprocal process and sustained in contexts where both sides are mutually implicated.

Intrinsic to the above contrast are two forms of performance. One is predicated on rearranging relationships to create bounded entities; to eclipse a multiplicity of relationships and reveal capacities, often in ritual; in other words, where the emphasis is on the process of unit formation. The second is predicated on the process of relating bounded entities together as a demonstration of one's skill at 'modern' living; or often, in a sense, to subvert their boundedness (to make them more 'personal', less anonymous). In the first, visibility is construed in the context of eliciting others; in the second, visibility is construed largely as a process of self-creation, of being the producers of meaning instead of just a 'passive' consumer (the archetypal 'couch potato').

Performances (whether those generally pertaining to the Melanesian or western) are context-dependent and specific to local spatio-temporal settings. Standardized units such as a televisual unit (a programme), units of weights and measures, or unitized time (such as time zones) are produced and distributed so as to be ideally context-free and generally replicable wherever the standardized units are conventionally accepted. If anything, it is only since the early nineteenth century that such 'objective', standardized units came to be generally pervasive throughout Euro-America (cf. Mitchell 1988: 18–21).

The argument of the chapter suggests that the ethnographic perspectives of anthropology and media and cultural studies, in their distinctive but increasingly related ways, have cause to be clear about the centrality of bounded entities in their disciplinary enterprises: both in the way social and cultural life is performed and organized (as this is participant-observed) and in the arrangment and presentation of this in textual form (as ethnography). The ethnographic perspectives of anthropology and media and cultural studies need to converge around the comparative study of local bounded entities, or units, as these are rendered performatively, increasingly in the historically specific contexts of standardization. I will pursue this argument in relation to both western and Melanesian cultural materials.

MIDDLE-CLASS VISIBILITY

Mr and Mrs Simon of north London were ambivalent about television and its viewing. They saw it as a potentially passive form of behaviour and were concerned, in particular, that their children should only watch it minimally. In many respects Mr and Mrs Simon articulated a sort of folk model of the Frankfurt School regarding the mass media: that it rendered one potentially passive, and if anything, one needed to deobjectify oneself in relation to it. The Simons live in two adjoining terraced houses. The family comprises Mr and Mrs Simon, their three sons and two daughters. The girls are adopted and each has a black parentage origin. The parents are in their early forties and the children range in age from 8 to 16. The father, Charles, describes himself as a technologist. The mother, Natalie, is a primary school teacher. The children all attend state schools (see Hirsch 1992 for more details).

In addition to their London residence the family also possesses a cottage and a sailing boat in the West Country. The cottage is inaccessible by road and the family spend six weeks every summer sailing around the south coast. During the remainder of the year the family visit their cottage about every six weeks and/or during half-term holidays. The details of the cottage and sailing boat in the West Country are not of incidental interest but form part of the more general processes intrinsic to the ethnography of this family and its relationship with television. In brief, these processes can be characterized as an open, public form of sociability associated with life in London and a closed, private sociability associated with life in the West Country;[3] each is conceptualized by Mr and Mrs Simon as providing sustenance or support for the continuity of the other. As I shall argue in a later section, this 'classic' English opposition between the country and the city is the widest spatial and temporal context through which the Simons make visible their ability to relate a range and diversity of bounded entities.

It is of note that Mr and Mrs Simon's negative attitude about television is tempered by the family's own appearance on the medium; the parents through their active involvement in local or national issues and the children through theatrical and acting opportunities encouraged by their parents. I got to know the Simons during the late 1980s and earlier 1990s (the 'ethnographic present') and made numerous lengthy visits to their home during this period. The passive viewing of television was a concern of Mr and Mrs Simon but a more active relationship with the medium, as evidenced through their appearance on it, was seen as appropriate and even valued. In short, Mr and Mrs Simon were concerned about television use because, among other factors, it mirrored to them their concerns about their own efficacy and social visibility (as active, caring parents and citizens leading what they imagined as a noteworthy family life to be appreciated by other like-minded persons). The screen brought into focus the possibilities and problems of achieving their particular middle-class project of explicit self-creation.

These different attitudes about contrasting relationships with television exemplified by the Simon family raise an important issue, highlighted in media and cultural studies (see Morley 1992: 265–6). On the one hand there are objects and experiences in the world which are produced through a system of standardization predicated on standardized ideas of space and time. There is a history to this standardization process which is peculiar to western European and American societies and is linked to the emergence of their 'modern-ness' (cf. Porter 1994).[4]

Television technology and the programme content of television are units produced according to spatio-temporal standards. Television and its texts are obviously more than just a set of units based on standardized notions of space and time (it could be said that television programmes and programming attempt to construe specific performative aspects of social life, as in programme genres, through editing and timing, within a standardized framework). None the less, intrinsic to television and its texts, so to speak, is the bottom line of these standardized aspects. Television technology and its content are a powerful example of this standardized template through the processes of production and transmission. Part of Mr and Mrs Simon's apprehension about the passivity sustained by television is linked to the manner in which it captures spatial and temporal horizons through a standardized format produced by others; where one's own agency and performative skills are curtailed and thus potentially not visible (that is, one becomes objectified).

On the other hand, and as part and parcel of their logic of production, these standardized units form part of performative processes predicated on particular quotidian ideas of space and time: thus in particular contexts the standardized units are 'unbounded'. This has been a growing theme in media and cultural studies, where television programmes are seen as consumed and consumers do the conceptual work of transforming them within particular limits (see Morley 1992: 210–12). The Simon family provides an illustration of this relationship between the standardized and the performative, again around the use of television technology, but are able to take it much further than simply actively consuming. In this instance it is a video recorder and Mr and Mrs Simon's reluctance to purchase this technology, that are at issue as they fear it will lead to ever greater use of television and thus passivity. As they put it:

CHARLES: I thought on some occasions it is too late for them to watch, I would love to have recorded it. It was probably my decision not to get one.

NATALIE: I knew we would watch a lot more television and I thought that the children would be tempted to. They do an awful lot of other things than television which I think is very valuable to them. I think . . . television is always going to be there but perhaps the opportunities to do these other things might not be.

It was then asked whether the children desired a video, but the discussion swiftly moved on to the idea of a video camera:

CHARLES: A video camera, that would be the thing for the children . . . they would be 'making' . . . not just sitting there watching *Neighbours*!

NATALIE: I would encourage them . . . if they came up with that bright idea I would seriously consider getting a video camera for them . . . if one of them really wanted to.

CHARLES: So anytime they make their own videos they can watch them; if they make their own videos they can watch them anytime.

NATALIE: They will be getting pleasure from it and learning at the same time.

The only way they imagine such a technology would be appropriate in their home is if it were accompanied by a video camera and the children were actively able to perform and create their own video recordings; their own bounded entity (recording), where it was they who were visible and the producers. This example illustrates in microcosm a more general form of self-creation that the Simon parents strive towards for themselves as a family, to which we will return.

PASSIVE VS ACTIVE: A CORE THEME IN MEDIA AND CULTURAL STUDIES

Part of the history of media and cultural studies could be written as an attempt to understand the relationships people sustain with the bounded entities of the mass media and with mass consumption more generally. The early part of this history would focus on the efforts of the Frankfurt School and their attempts to theorize and document what they saw as the negative, ideological structuring effects of standardized units on those experiencing the media through everyday use. What came to be known as the 'hypodermic' model of media impact stressed the power of the media to 'inject' its repressive message almost directly into the unsuspecting viewer. Throughout the 1950s, 1960s and 1970s, communication studies, media studies and what came to be known as cultural studies debated the merits of this legacy and refined alternative models to account for the performative powers of the viewer vis-à-vis the structuring power of the programme text.

Since the 1980s the emphasis has shifted in a marked direction, as what is known as an ethnographic perspective has emerged in media and cultural studies. Television and its texts are acknowledged to be negotiated within the everyday contexts of domestic and family life, and ethnography has emerged as the appropriate method for describing and interpreting this complex milieu. The use of ethnography in media and cultural studies attempts to document the ways in which media products are domesticated into the routines of everyday social life. If anything, the trend has shifted in almost a polar direction, as what is now called the 'active audience' (Ang 1996: 9) is seen as largely discrediting the legacy of the Frankfurt School and its account of the media as a mass victimization process. The bounded entities of the media are routinely shown to be 'unbound' (for instance, read and/or used in unintended ways by the activities of the viewers in their daily lives).

ETHNOGRAPHIC PERSPECTIVES

Note should be taken, however, of the manner in which the notion of ethnography has been deployed by media and cultural studies. Ethnographies are not produced; rather, ethnography is used as a method of data collection; ethnography in this context is synonymous with a form of qualitative research most often based on interview. This narrow conception of ethnography which has been appropriated within media and cultural studies has not passed without comment in the discipline itself. As Radway (1988: 367, quoted in Morley 1992: 196) has noted:

> Those of us who have turned to the ethnographic method to understand how specific social subjects interact with cultural forms have none the less always begun with a radically circumscribed site . . . cordoned off by our preoccupation with a single medium or genre . . . Consequently

we have often reified, or ignored totally, other cultural determinants besides the one specifically highlighted.

Radway is highlighting the problem that a focus on, for example, television creates when it is the appropriation of television and its texts that one is trying to understand; ethnography as a form of qualitative data collection is seen as the means whereby a fine-grained description of this appropriation can be explored. However, what the anthropologist conventionally understands as ethnography – the attempt to provide a persuasive description and interpretation of a particular socio-cultural context (that is, an ethnography) – has been reformulated: instead of the endeavour to draw out from a particular field-site a set of unifying themes and perspectives, ethnography is now commonly used to refer to a particular mode of securing and presenting data (cf. Van Maanen 1988).

It is somewhat ironic that at the very time that Radway was sounding the call for media and cultural studies to become more explicitly anthropological in the way they approached ethnography, anthropologists were arguing about the contrived nature of ethnography. Thornton (1988), for example, argued that the holistic authority presented in anthropological ethnographies was more rhetorical than substantial. He refers to this as the rhetoric of ethnographic holism:

> One of the problems that emerges is how are the descriptive or experiential 'items' of behaviour and thought to be recognised or defined. For our consideration of ethnographic rhetoric, the nature of the units of description determines the ways in which the descriptive text is able to relate the microcosmic level – the 'items' of the field notebook, and the 'evidence' of the ethnographic presentation such as a person met, a mark seen and sketched, a ritual attended – to the macrocosm of economy, culture, society or cosmos.
>
> (Thornton 1988: 296)

Social life is continuous, and ethnography through its form of rhetorical holism introduces discontinuity where it would otherwise not exist: 'we might ask if there are "units" (experiential or descriptive quanta) at all. Is social life radically continous, only broken by the periodicity of text?' (Thornton 1988: 298–9).

Thornton's critique of ethnography presents a challenge to those who attempt to describe and interpret units as existing in the context of everyday life. Are socio-cultural units (such as clans, descent groups, villages) simply an artefact of textual distinctions and taxonomic classifications (economy, politics, etc.)? Do they have some independent reality beyond that of the text? Strathern (1991) for one registers the challenge and explores the extent to which ethnographies exhibit the rhetorical tendencies ascribed to them by Thornton. She acknowledges that the observer, through perceptual and recording strategies, imposes an organizational character onto anthropo-logical materials (through collation and systemization). At the same time, though, she suggests that this collation and systemization may 'already appear accomplished in the way the actors present their lives' (Strathern 1991: xiii). I read Strathern as saying that discretely bounded entities (units) are ordered and arranged in particular performative contexts. This can be illustrated through a consideration of material drawn from the Fuyuge of Papua New Guinea. It will be used to highlight a contrast with the western example, to which I will return in due course.

MAKING UNITIES VISIBLE

The Fuyuge make their 'homes' (see Hirsch 1994: 693) in the Papuan highlands about 100 kilometres north-west of Port Moresby, the national capital. In a number of previous publications (Hirsch 1990, 1994, 1995) I have described how Fuyuge social life is structured around the periodic performance of a multistage ritual known as *gab*. A *gab* is initiated through the coercive strategies deployed by one collective of persons in relation to one or more others. The host collective in effect challenges the others to come to their ritual village and perform in various ways: as dancers, as exchange partners and as witnesses or an audience. The coercion to perform, to accept the challenge and make evident their capacities to do so, is a process that occurs over many months. The coercion is a reciprocal process: the challenge of the hosts to the others is, in effect, also an internally directed challenge to demonstate their capacities as hosts. Through these processes of reciprocal coercion, Fuyuge men and women constitute themselves into units of particular kinds: the hosts and supporters vis-à-vis the dancers, exchange partners, witnesses/audience define themselves as discrete, bounded entities, existing in space and time, for the duration of the ritual. They momentarily submerge their diverse origins of relationships and place in order to bound particular 'homogeneous' named unities.

It is not, however, a process that occurs at once. Rather, the units build themselves up into an increasing scale through movement across space and in time and by pulling people and objects together. The culmination of this process is ultimately revealed in the long-awaited performances of dances and pig killings in the plaza of the *gab* village. Each stage of the process of unit formation, a process of collation and systemization, is simultaneously made visually evident and scrutinized to ascertain whether or not it has been successfully accomplished. For example, when the hosts gather together to challenge the others (dancers, etc.) to come and perform in *gab* an event is staged whereby each person is named and a cordyline plant is placed on the ground (Figure 11.1). At the culmination of these challenges one or more lines of the cordylines stretch across the plaza: the hosts have in effect visually collated and systematized the units they have challenged to perform as

Figure 11.1 Hosts challenging others to perform in *gab*: each person is named and a cordyline plant is placed on the ground

dancers, exchange partners, etc. (Figure 11.2). At later points in time each of these units is able to increase its size and scale through the process of pulling in and concentrating other persons and things; and again their collation and systemization will be scrutinized in the form of lines of dancers performing (Figure 11.3), lines of pigs laid out after their slaughter and before their distribution (Figure 11.4), and so on. In each related instance the unit is simultaneously a product of coercion and productive of a visual display anticipating the unit as it is to be performed.

Meaning is engendered through this constitutive process of bringing bounded entities into existence. The meaning does not reside in the unit(s), but is created through the process of making them visible. When men and women enact and scrutinize these processes (for example, of dancers gathered together, or of pigs gathered together) they are evaluating and comparing the capacities of others to reveal particular forms of units. In effect, they are assessing whether the revelations are comparable and thus substitutable one for the other, and thus in Fuyuge perceptions whether analogies can properly be drawn between the bounded entities so assembled – for instance, pigs assembled in relation to dancers assembled.

Figure 11.2 Lines of cordylines stretching across the plaza

CULTURE OF THE EXHIBITION

The Fuyuge example I have briefly described highlights the manner in which discrete, bounded entities are engendered through processes of coercive performance. Units are thus recurrently brought into existence and are not in themselves repositories of meaning. Rather, meaning is created through the constitutive process of unit formation. This view of units and meaning is, I want to suggest, different from what we conventionally recognize as occurring in the Euro-American context. In this context, we are increasingly accustomed to the culture of the exhibition, a culture predicated on the separation of audiences, persons and objects (cf. Carey 1988: 221–2). More

Figures 11.3 Lines of dancers performing: they replicate in part the lines of cordylines (see Figure 11.2)

specifically, persons and objects produced for exhibition (such as, for a television programme) are viewed as relatively discrete and isolated, and the point of observation of the person/object is itself relatively fixed (such as the ideal spectator of television). Fixed persons/objects are seen in relation to fixed observers, just as the producers of persons/objects and the spectators or viewers of those persons/objects are conceptualized as separate. Produced persons/objects become sites for the interpretation of meaningful discourses: the person/object, then, becomes a unit of either implicit or explicit meaning. Television and its programmes are one of the devices that exemplify this separation in a particularly vivid manner.

The separations sustained by the culture of the exhibition enable one to imagine the quantification of the realms so separated: the object becomes a repository of meanings, just as the audience is subject to more or less meanings.[5] How, it can then be asked, are these two realms of (potentially quantifiable) meanings related? This is a question pursued by Silverstone's (1990: 179) enquiries:

Television is potentially meaningful and therefore open to the constructive work of the consumer–viewer, both in terms of how it is used, or placed,

Figure 11.4 Lines of pigs laid out after their slaughter and before their distribution (by the hosts)

in the household – in what rooms, where, associated with what furniture or machines, the subject of what kinds of discourses inside and outside the home – and in terms of how the meanings it makes available through the content of its programmes are in turn worked with by individuals and household groups who receive them.

The ethnographic perspective in media and cultural studies is an outgrowth, I would argue, of the recognition and need to transcend the separation between person/object and audience for an informed understanding of television and its social contextualization. Hence the move to the details of the domestic context and what Ang (1996: 69) refers to as the method of 'radical contextualism' (that is, formulations for methods of studying the pervasive embeddedness of television and related media in the everyday contexts of domestic and social life; see below).

PERFORMANCE IN RELATIONSHIP TO STANDARDIZATION[6]

I would suggest that the relationship between performance and standardization are thrown into much greater relief in the Fuyuge context than in the example of the Simons. This is hardly surprising given what I have said above about the emergence and growth of standardization in Euro-America and beyond since the early nineteenth century. At one level the Simon family conform to a standardized example of middle-class life which began to take shape at roughly the same historical period in England (see Strathern 1992). They epitomize in a clear way the emphasis on a responsible, autonomous family life with concerns for standards of education, work and self-provisioning (cf. Rose 1989). At the same time, though, the Simons attempt to perform what they envision as their own unique variant of this middle-class project, where television as technology and content finds its place, but associated with numerous ambiguous sentiments. They ascribe to what we might call a middle-class project of performative self-creation.

It is clear that we in Euro-America live in a society predicated, in many respects, on the culture of the exhibition, fostering certain presuppositions about the relations between persons, objects and audiences which have hindered cross-cultural understanding in areas such as the anthropology of aesthetics and ritual (see Hirsch 1995). But contrary, I think, to what Baudrillard suggests (see Poster 1995), people do not actually seek to live their lives according to the culture of the exhibition. Rather, they attempt to arrange and systematize bounded entities through local forms of performance in a world increasingly dominated by such standardized units. It would seem that the key question for media and cultural studies (and increasingly anthropology) is how the medium of television, as one of the central generators of the culture of the exhibition (that is, as a separator of audiences and persons/objects), can be understood in context, where people attempt to relate and in the process often unbound entities in a manner which does not correspond to that generated by the medium itself. My answer in brief, and as already suggested, lies in attending to the way in which television is systematized and collated within particular performative local contexts.

The Fuyuge provide an example of this process, involving colonization and missionization, to which I briefly turn, where the performative and an imposed form of standardization are not so closely calibrated. My intention is to highlight the manner in which systemization and collation are attained in the way the Fuyuge make evident their visibility, that is, create themselves into units in the context of an *imposed* standardization. The history of colonialism and missionization was implicitly present in the Fuyuge material presented above; it is only now that I foreground this presence. In a sense these forms of western incursion correspond to a more general western pattern evident since the nineteenth century, whereby 'society' needed to be remade in a standardized form before it could be the object of quantification and measurement (see Porter 1994: 201; cf. Ang 1996, regarding the complicated issue of television audience measurement in an age of multiple channels and time-shifting devices).

The Fuyuge were colonized and missionized at the same time, beginning in the early twentieth century.[7] The goal of the government was to bring what it perceived as order and civilization to peoples like the Fuyuge (through the suppression of revenge killings and warfare); the goals of the missionaries were to convert the people to Catholicism and encourage them to live according to Catholic beliefs and ideals.[8] Other changes were intended to coerce Fuyuge men and women to live their lives more in line with a model of how such people should live, according to western spatial and temporal patterns.

One such pattern was the notion of village and 'villageness' itself. Here the interests of both government and missionary were directed to the unit of Fuyuge settlement and residence: concern was continually expressed that the Fuyuge did not live in large, relatively permanent villages. By contrast, the Fuyuge pattern of settlement and residence is in a continual state of flux, dependent on the build-up and intensity of ritual activity in any particular locale. Residence in a large, clearly visible village – which occurs for limited periods of time during a *gab* – is desirable for government and mission interests for a number of reasons.[9]

A second area concerned the attempt to curtail the performance of *gab*, which increased in frequency and scale after the curtailing of revenge killings and warfare. This led to local legislation during the 1960s aimed at limiting the time span of any *gab* ritual.[10] What the government and to a lesser degree the missionaries failed to recognize in implementing this legislation was the manner in which Fuyuge social life, as focused around gardening, pig raising, etc., all tends to the next *gab*, to the next coercive context of building up and revealing the capacities of bounded entities. In other words, *gab* is not an isolated event but the *raison d'être* of Fuyuge existence; their social life is systematized and collated in relation to its performance. Fuyuge visibility is created in a spatial and temporal field of emerging and receding *gab* centres, increasingly framed since the 1950s by the growth and physical expansion of Port Moresby as a centre of money and commodities (see Hirsch 1994).

There is now a wider region in which to work towards the revealing and comparison of capacities; of being able to draw persons/objects together, such as coastal betelnut with mountain betelnut in the *gab* context (see Hirsch 1990). The attempt to impose forms of standardization on the Fuyuge has had the unintended consequence of creating an expanded spatio-temporal field in which the work of systematization and collation is now undertaken. In general, colonial and mission interests in coercing the Fuyuge to live according to a spatial and temporal pattern more recognizable to western perceptions recall the analysis made by Mitchell (1988): they aim to render Papuan village life as an appearance of order; an order, moreover, that works by appearance (Mitchell 1988: 32). Colonial and mission interests have been unsuccessful in their attempt to calibrate the performative of Fuyuge social existence with their concepts of standardization. They have been unable to create the sort of disjunction between audience and object/person, or the culture of the exhibition, by which such a calibration becomes imaginable; that is, the disjunction of creating among the Fuyuge an order that works by appearance, predicated on the division of the world into a realm of representation and a realm of 'the real', and to which such representations self-consciously refer (for example, how a 'real village' should appear as codified in a set of plans or material imagery).

REFLECTIONS ON 'RADICAL CONTEXTUALISM'

In many respects media and cultural studies have developed as disciplines around this very disjunction. As indicated above, they have attempted over the years to provide a compelling analysis of the media and their audience which transcends their fundamental separation, in terms of both programme content and the manner in which programmes are consumed. Ethnography, as I have suggested, has been taken up for this purpose. But as the practitioners themselves have argued (e.g. Radway 1988), this has not been a wholly successful enterprise. It has led to, among various problems, what Ang (1996: 69) refers to as 'radical contextualism'.

> It is precisely the idea of the profound embeddedness of television consumption (and of media consumption in general in everyday life, and therefore its irreducible heterogeneity and dynamic complexity) that has been a central emphasis within culturalist audience studies, although the epistemological bearings of this emphasis, which amount to a form of *radical contextualism*, are not always thoroughly understood.

Ang (1996: 73) proceeds to explicate the conjunction of 'radical' and 'contextualism' in this conception of ethnography and the problems inherent in its undertaking.

> To put it differently, imagining the radical, that is, eternally expanding contextuality of the particular meanings produced through media consumption would imply the taking up of an *impossible* position by the

researcher, namely that of being 'everywhere', ceaselessly trying to capture a relentlessly expanding field of contextually overdetermined, particular realities. Although such a position may be epistemologically logical, it is, in the end, untenable ontologically, let alone pragmatically.

(*ibid.*)

Ang's answer to this dilemma is to argue that in today's world system of global space it is no longer possible to study culture in context. It might once have been, 'as in the classic case of anthropology's remote and primitive, small exotic island in the middle of the vast ocean, inhabited by people whose daily practices were relatively untouched and uninfluenced by the inexorably transformative forces of capitalist modernity' (Ang 1996: 75). One only has to think of Sahlins's recent writings (e.g. Sahlins 1985) on the historical anthropology of the societies of the South Pacific to understand just how outdated this characterization is. Instead of studying culture in context (which is now deemed limitless and requiring the radical contextualism of being 'everywhere'), Ang suggests that we follow Geertz and attempt to tell stories about a cultural complexity in motion: that is, stories that are situated between the local (indigenous) and global (transnational).

But in all the talk of local and global relations it has to be remembered that one never actually leaves the local; the local can never be left for a larger entity known as the global. Rather, it is the system of local contexts, their distributions and linkages, that creates a global field (such as IBM or Hollywood). If anything, the global is 'the infinitely recurring *possibility* of measurement – not the scales but the capacity to imagine them' (Strathern 1995: 179). We cannot but live in local contexts and yet have the capacity (put in motion by the wide-ranging standardizing tendencies of the nineteenth century; see above) to imagine ourselves in a constantly expanding field that takes on global proportions. When all is said and done, then, it is still the local contexts in which we must situate our ethnography.

I would argue, in contrast to Ang, that radical contextualism might *in principle* imply the problem and impossibility of being everywhere. In practice, ethnography that engages with particular persons, in particular local contexts, does not necessarily lead to this problem. In a sense the position of radical contextualism only becomes thinkable when one does not attend to the local interests, motivations and projects in a particular cultural context. This attending to local interest has conventionally been the starting point of the ethnographic perspective in anthropology in the way it describes and interprets local contexts. It is, I would suggest, on the local contextualism of bounded entities (such as television programmes) that the ethnographic perspectives of media and cultural studies and anthropology converge; in other words, on how systemization and collation are accomplished in particular contexts, and to what extent television is subject to the systemization and collation evidenced more generally. This is not a process of ordering that can be read off from the screen (or from persons' reflections on the contents of the screen). Rather, attention needs to be given to the manner in which the screen and its contents are implicated in ongoing social relations which cohere together in specific ways.

ATTENDING TO CONTEXT, ATTENDING TO BOUNDED ENTITIES

I would like to illustrate this briefly by returning to the Simon family. As indicated above, the systemization and collation that the Simons attempt to accomplish in their family life unfold in two spatially separate but related contexts: the large city home, comprising two adjacent terrace properties, and the country cottage and boat. The former corresponds to the values of openness, temporal availability and an emphasis on social visibility. The latter corresponds to the values of remoteness, invisibility and a spatial and temporal achievement of the ideal of the nuclear family.

In the London home there is one television, a VCR (video recorder; see below), and numerous pieces of computer technology linked to Mr Simon's work, which the children also use. Radio 4 is on during the weekday morning and for the *Archers* at 7 o'clock in the evening. Little in the way of media technology is found at the cottage. Both the parents and each of the children through individual and group discussions indicated that television viewing was not valued as a key individual or family activity. This was also borne out by an examination of their individual time-use diaries and participant observation. At the same time they indicated that the family as a whole will watch nature and science programmes and comedies such as the *Two Ronnies* and *Fawlty Towers*. In addition the younger children enjoy the after-school programmes and the cartoons at the weekend. Other than this, television viewing is carefully regulated and only the eldest is allowed to watch television after supper.

To bring into focus the way in which television as a bound entity is in a sense 'unbound' by the Simons it is useful, I think, to imagine a time map (Gell 1992) divided up into (temporal) units. Some of these units are dictated by a more general and standardized calendar (school time, opening and closing hours of shops, etc.) while others are distinctly Simonesque (and analogous to those like the Simons), such as the recurrent periods at the cottage and on the boat, during the unit of 'holidays'. The Simons attempt to achieve as much control as possible over the range of temporal units that are structured between their city and country ideals of existence; one as an anticipation of the other. So, for example, three of the Simon children attend a local theatre company. They were encouraged to do so by their parents in order to build up their confidence and be able to present themselves in public. This has led in turn to theatre and television parts. Television viewing for the children and adults alike is slotted in between these periods of performative temporal control. The programme preferences of Mr and Mrs Simon are in many respects an analogue of these periods: they have a preference for programmes about boats, weather and skilled performance (such as Clive James, drama). By contrast, they would not watch *Question Time* because there are party politicians involved, which they find boring. Mr and Mrs Simon said they would use particular politicians to get things done and they know a wide spectrum of different ones, but would not talk politics.

It is also of note that, in the six months that separated the commencement of fieldwork with the Simons and its conclusion, a VCR made its way into their home. It had been purchased by Charles at Natalie's insistence:

CHARLES: It invalidates everything we said to you . . . Too many people in the family on the television so we thought we had to get one to record ourselves.

NATALIE: [later in the evening] It was my idea, always been against getting a video. Occurred to me that the whole family is on television and I said to [Charles] 'This is ridiculous, I don't suppose ever in the future that it may occur that one of us ever is on television ever again'. We have two children on television in separate things and the whole family on television. I said . . . 'I think this is a good idea to have a video so that we could record it because we may never see any of our children on TV again, or us'.

What seemed to trouble Charles, and to a lesser extent Natalie, was their potentially more passive relation to television than in the pre-video time (that is, the tendency to watch more television). It was not the technology as such which was the problem but the capacity to construct an active relation with it. And this in the end was what preoccupied the Simon parents (and children) in their relations with television and its programming: that by its nature it made evident the possibilities and problems of achieving the sort of middle-class self-creation they aspired to. Among the Simons, I would suggest, television and its content are systematized and collated in relation to the other sets of bounded entities they attempt to relate together (and in a sense unbound, 'personalize') in space and time. Their middle-class project of performative self-creation, at once submitting to and resisting in their own way the forces of standardization, leads to an explicit downplaying of television where, ironically, the medium is often centrally implicated in their lives.

CONCLUSION: BOUND AND UNBOUND ENTITIES – PERFORMED AND WRITTEN

In many respects the argument of this chapter has been more suggestive than substantive. My concluding remarks continue in this way and also attempt to draw the various strands of the argument together briefly.

We saw in the Melanesian context how 'unbound' entities (persons and objects) predicated on a matrix of relationships were in a sense bounded through the processes of coercive performance. In the western context, performance was evidenced in the way one could relate to a range of bounded entities (objects, media, etc.) and, in the process, potentially unbound them. Each sort of performance involved particular forms of systemization and collation (as in the organization of the Fuyuge *gab*, or in that of the Simons's city and country lifestyles). These are processes which can be observed as a participant and written up as ethnography. Crucial to both is the issue of systemisation and collation: how the actors present their lives, and the way one imposes an organizational character on ethnographic material. It might be suggested that the latter should in some way attempt to model the former (cf. Strathern 1988, 1992).

One of the reasons an ethnographic perspective has become more central in media and cultural studies in recent years is the attempt to capture just these processes around the media. But as I have argued, media and cultural studies are generally ill equipped for this task, because their conception of ethnography is too limited and their privileging of the media tends to reify the world around them. If anything, the relationship between media and cultural studies and anthropology will need to converge on recording and writing strategies that capture the way bounded or unbounded entities come to be arranged systematically in local contexts of performance.

ACKNOWLEDGEMENTS

For their helpful comments and criticisms on a draft of the argument presented here I want to thank Nicola Abel Hirsch, Allen Abramson, Gail Baker, Catherine Harvey and Felicia Hughes-Freeland. A version of the chapter was presented at the Department of Social Anthropology, the Queen's University of Belfast, where I benefited from very useful discussions.

NOTES

1 It is important from the outset to state that my intention is not to compare a north London family with a Papuan highland society, as the two are incommensurable. Rather, my intention is to compare certain outcomes of the performances in each context. The performances are realized in forms of visibility which are assessed by a variety of actors for evidence of their successful execution.

2 I am using 'units' and 'unities' as interchangeable: 'units' is a shortened version of 'unities', and both convey similar ideas.

3 In certain respects one can see family life in the cottage and boat as an attempt to resist the objectifying features of standardization with respect to technology, time, etc.

4 Indeed, Carey (1988: 223) refers to the USA up until the late nineteenth century as a series of 'island communities' with little intercourse, and with few practical problems caused by a myriad of local times. The notable exception here is the railroads and their related commercial interests. On 18 November 1883 a standard

railroad time was introduced and, as it has come to pass, westerners among others now take it almost as natural that time is divided by a grid of time zones encompassing the entire globe.

5 In the Fuyuge example, men and women attempt to magnify themselves through the quantitative concentration of persons and objects towards a particular qualitative effect, that is, to appear efficacious and powerful.

6 It is important at this stage of the argument to highlight the fact that standardization or pre-formed unitness is present, in some form, in both of the contexts I have been discussing. *Gab*, for example, is performed in relation to a pre-formed unit notion of how each specific *gab* should appear. But the relationship between the performed and pre-formed is part of ongoing social action; there is no reference to formalized rules or plans (cf. Strathern 1991: 116). This is quite different to an explicit emphasis on standardized forms in reference to which social action is either explicitly or implicitly directed, as we regularly find in the Euro-American context.

7 The material in the following paragraphs is expanded and elaborated more fully elsewhere (see Hirsch n.d.).

8 From the outset the goals of government and missionary overlapped significantly, and over time the Fuyuge came to see both as a combined force of encompassing power.

9 It facilitates the orderly and systematic recording of census and related administrative material; inspection and surveillance of village life is more straightforward than in numerous dispersed and isolated hamlets; finally, a large, orderly village with a cleared central space, latrines and well-kept houses is what such a place is supposed to look like according to certain western aesthetic assumptions about 'villageness'. Patrol reports over many decades express the inability of patrol officers and missionaries to coerce the Fuyuge into what they see as appropriate modes of settlement and residence.

10 The Fuyuge have devised various ways of avoiding the constraints of these temporal limits.

REFERENCES

Ang, I. (1996) *Living Room Wars: Rethinking Media Audiences for a Postmodern World*, London: Routledge.

Carey, J. (1988) *Communication as Culture. Essays on Media and Society*, Boston: Unwin-Hyman.

Gell, A. (1992) *The Anthropology of Time: Cultural Constructions of Temporal Maps and Images*, Oxford: Berg.

Hirsch, E. (1990) 'From bones to betelnut: processes of ritual transformation and the development of "national culture" in Papua New Guinea', *Man*, 25: 18–34.

—— (1992) 'The long term and the short term of domestic consumption: an ethnographic case study', in R. Silverstone and E. Hirsch (eds) *Consuming Technologies: Media and Information in Domestic Spaces*, London: Routledge.

—— (1994) 'From mission to market: events and images in a Melanesian society', *Man*, 29: 689–711.

—— (1995) 'The coercive strategies of aesthetics: reflections on wealth, ritual and landscape in Melanesia', *Social Analysis*, 38: 61–71.

—— (n.d.) 'Colonial units and ritual units: historical transformations of persons and horizons in highland Papua', unpublished ms.

Mitchell, T. (1988) *Colonising Egypt*, Cambridge: Cambridge University Press.

Morley, D. (1992) *Television, Audiences and Cultural Studies*, London: Routledge.

Porter, T. (1994) 'Objectivity as standardization: the rhetoric of impersonality in measurement, statistics and cost-benefit analysis', in A. Megill (ed.) *Rethinking Objectivity*, Durham N.C.: Duke University Press.

Poster, M. (1995) *The Second Media Age*, Oxford: Polity Press.

Radway, J. (1988) 'Reception study', *Cultural Studies*, 2(3): 259–76.

Rose, N. (1989) *Governing the Soul: The Shaping of the Private Self*, London: Routledge.

Sahlins, M. (1985) *Islands of History*, Chicago: University of Chicago Press.

Silverstone, R. (1990) 'Television and everyday life: towards an anthropology of the audience', in M. Ferguson (ed.) *Public Communication: The New Imperatives*, London: Sage.

Strathern, M. (1988) *The Gender of the Gift: Problems with Women and Problems with Society in Melanesia*, Berkeley CA: University of California Press.

—— (1991) *Partial Connections*, Savage MD: Rowman and Littlefield.

—— (1992) *After Nature: English Kinship in the Late Twentieth Century*, Cambridge: Cambridge University Press.

—— (1995) 'Afterword', in M. Strathern (ed.) *Shifting Contexts: Transformations in Anthropological Knowledge*, London: Routledge.

Thornton, R. (1988) 'The rhetoric of ethnographic holism', *Cultural Anthropology*, 3: 285–303.

Van Maanen, J. (1988) *Tales of the Field: On Writing Ethnography*, Chicago: University of Chicago Press.

Index